W9-AJP-227

Suffragan Bishop
5309 Mandell Avenue
Houston, Texas 77005

SPEAKING WITH THE DEVIL

SPEAKING WITH

A Dialogue With Evil

VIKING

THE DEVIL

Carl Goldberg

VIKING
Published by the Penguin Group
Penguin Books USA Inc., 375 Hudson Street, New York, New York 10014, U.S.A.
Penguin Books Ltd, 27 Wrights Lane, London W8 5TZ, England
Penguin Books Australia Ltd, Ringwood, Victoria, Australia
Penguin Books Canada Ltd, 10 Alcorn Avenue, Toronto, Ontario, Canada M4V 3B2
Penguin Books (N.Z.) Ltd, 182–190 Wairau Road, Auckland 10, New Zealand

Penguin Books Ltd, Registered Offices: Harmondsworth, Middlesex, England

First published in 1996 by Viking Penguin, a division of Penguin Books USA Inc.

10 9 8 7 6 5 4 3 2 1

PUBLISHER'S NOTE
The names and identifying details of the individuals discussed in this book have been changed to
protect anonymity.

Grateful acknowledgment is made for permission to use the following texts, which have been revised
for this book:
"Courage and Fanaticism: The Charismatic Leader and Modern Religious Cults" by Carl Goldberg
in *Psychodynamic Perspectives on Religion, Sect, and Cult* edited by David Halperin. By permission of
Mosby-Year Book, Inc.
"Shameful Secrets" and "The Therapeutic Use of Intersubjective Shame" from *Understanding
Shame* by David Goldberg. By permission of Jason Aronson, Inc.

LIBRARY OF CONGRESS CATALOGING IN PUBLICATION DATA
Goldberg, Carl.
    Speaking with the devil : a dialogue with evil / Carl Goldberg.
        p.   cm.
    Includes bibliographical references and index.
    ISBN 0–670–85557–X
    1. Antisocial personality disorder.   2. Insane, Criminal and dangerous.   3. Good and evil—
Psychological aspects.   4. Psychopaths.   5. Acting out (Psychology)   I. Title.
RC555.G65   1995
616.85'82—dc20   95–34239

This book is printed on acid-free paper. ∞

Printed in the United States of America
Set in Fairfield Light
Designed by Brian Mulligan

This book is dedicated with appreciation to my clinical supervisors during my apprenticeship as a psychologist and a psychoanalyst. With their flexible and compassionate approaches to clinical work, they have served me as inspiring role models for the past three decades.

Acknowledgments

The author wishes to express his appreciation to his literary agents, Kathleen Anderson and Susan Golomb, who encouraged this project; and to Charles Flowers for editorial assistance. He is grateful to Peter Mayer, his publisher, and Robert Dreesen, his editor, and to the following colleagues who were generous with their time and thoughtfulness in reviewing the manuscript: Daniel Claster, Ph.D.; Virginia Crespo, M.S.W.; Maurice Friedman, Ph.D.; Samuel Klagsbrun, M.D.; David Miller, Ph.D.; Peter Olsson, M.D.; Thomas Robischon, Ph.D.; Angela Spencer, Ph.D.; and Myron Weiner, M.D.

Contents

Author's Note

W E LOOK TO THE HUMAN SPIRIT FOR GUIDANCE. IF EVER THERE was a need to find constructive ways of dissuading the forces of hatred and misunderstanding from destructive pathways that may lead to a series of calamities capable of consuming the entire planet, it is in our day. In almost every region of our world, in fact, we are witness to the fierce battle between "good" and "malevolence." It may seem naive to point to the central struggle of our age in terms of a primordial concept of morality. Nonetheless, we cannot easily ignore the fact that hatred battles with compassion and caring not only between nations but also within every human breast.

In this book I explore the potentials for malevolence in the development of human personality. I use the term "evil" in my subtitle because "malevolence"—strictly speaking, more appropriate to my argument—is less likely to be recognized by most readers as a strong destructive force that causes serious social problems.

But malevolence is indeed my subject, for malevolence involves the cruelty, viciousness, and indifference that fuel the forces of hatred and misunderstanding which prevent so much of humankind from building an existence transcending brute survival—as we have seen in recent years in Serbia, Haiti, and Iraq.

I am primarily concerned with the everyday consequences of malevolence, not with metaphysical questions about evil. Consequently, I make a radical distinction between the concepts of malevolence and evil—terms that many writers have traditionally used interchangeably. (To avoid monotony, I sometimes use such analogous words for "malevolent" as "wicked" and "sinister.")

Historically, those who have addressed the questions surrounding evil have tried to ascertain whether or not a supernatural diabolic force actually exists or, alternatively, whether evil resides unalterably in our genetic makeup. These questions have never been satisfactorily answered. Indeed, a multitude of religious and philosophical tracts on the subject of evil has been written through the ages, to no avail.

I take a different direction in this book. I do not belabor the metaphysics of cruel and destructive acts (aside from a summary of the history of evil in Chapter 2), for it is not necessary to attribute the problems of morality to metaphysics. Although I use the word "devil" in the title, it is in the metaphorical sense only, referring to individuals who have transformed themselves into beings capable of extreme brutality and atrocity. Such people are involved in significant events in our world, but because we are frightened by them and cannot understand them, we try to distance ourselves, rationalizing our reaction by telling ourselves that their behavior is senseless.

Actually, many of these people can be safely reached, as is suggested by my use of "dialogue" in the subtitle. As I have learned in my professional experience with people involved in cruel and destructive behavior, we can discover that their behavior, however wrongful, is not at all senseless.

My avoidance of metaphysical questions in this book is less an indication of lack of religious belief than a wish to keep tightly focused on a specific aim. In short, it is more productive to pursue explanations of human cruelty and destructiveness without reference to the metaphysical. If we limited ourselves, for example, to explaining destructive behavior by supposing the existence of a pervasive supernatural force that takes possession of people, compelling them to commit horrendous acts, we would in effect be conceding that our intelligence and understanding are limited to the level of the primitive. But by exploring the potentials for malevolence as I do in this book, we do away with the need to view people as predestined for "good" or "bad" because of fate or genetics—or, for that matter, with the need to regard human beings as reactive pawns of an evil culture or society.

As I will demonstrate, I have discovered that six concepts are crucial for understanding the problem of malevolence: shame, contempt, rationalization, justification, inability or unwillingness to self-examine, and magical thinking. These social and psychological processes taken together account for much of the cruel, destructive behavior that I refer to as malevolence.

The several patient histories I reconstruct in the following chapters reveal that no supernatural force or inherently destructive human trait is required as part of my theory. Rather, they chronicle my journey as a psychoanalyst trying to reach individuals in the grip of sinister forces. Each case represents one of five steps of progressive development of the malevolent personality—that is to say, my patients' struggles are used to illustrate the theory of malevolence that I introduce in this book.

I have used a variety of clinical methods in developing dialogues with these afflicted people: psychoanalytic insights, personal and spiritual recognitions about myself, and knowledge of human behavior provided by people of wisdom through the millennia. I have particularly turned to the sages for help in working with patients who believed themselves to be possessed by evil.

Often, I have needed to use approaches different from those I learned as a traditionally trained psychologist and psychoanalyst. Otherwise I could not have influenced and persuaded—or when necessary cajoled—these painfully vulnerable patients into surrendering their magical realm for a world that, though realistically more limited, would allow them to gain at last an authentic sense of personal power and self-worth.

The clinical material I have provided is intended only to illustrate my theoretical concepts, not to validate them empirically. In my view, clinical data cannot legitimately "prove" a psychological theory until many patients of the type being discussed have been successfully treated. Only then can the common influences in the treatment of the cases be systematized and the psychological theory used to work with them be tested against competing theories of treatment.

In accord with my professional ethical mandate and my own scruples, I have disguised the identities of my patients by making changes in their case histories. In addition, I have altered the exact circumstances of some of the vignettes in order to accentuate the critical issues under discussion. Finally, some of the dialogue has been condensed from what was actually said by my patients and myself.

SPEAKING WITH THE DEVIL

CHAPTER ONE

The Problem of Malevolence

*There are thousands hacking at
the branches of evil to one
who is striking at its roots.*
— HENRY DAVID THOREAU

AFTER SEVENTEEN YEARS OF TRYING TO REFORM WESTLEY ALLEN
Dodd by conventional methods used to treat sex offenders, the State
of Washington executed him. When he was arrested for the last time, in
the fall of 1989, he confessed to stabbing to death an eleven-year-old boy
and his ten-year-old brother and to killing a four-year-old after repeatedly
raping him.

"I knew what I was doing," Dodd said, adding that he killed the children because he enjoyed doing so and because he thought he could get
away with it. "I knew I would get the death penalty if caught. I killed
them anyway."

One of the most important functions we expect of theories that explain
psychopathology is to make predictions about which people are most
likely to exhibit highly disturbed behavior. When we hear about the
horrors perpetrated by serial and mass murderers, we ask why these disturbed people couldn't have been detected and helped before they set out
on their heinous careers. Couldn't they have been reached as immature
children, before they became less accessible as adults?

But the usual childhood "explain-all" conditions that behavioral scientists use to account for adult psychopathology were absent in Dodd's case.

Referring to himself and his siblings, he said, "We were never molested or beaten. We had sufficient food and clothes."

Although he did admit that he had been raised in a loveless family, this in itself cannot adequately account for his heinous behavior. As noted by psychiatrist Samuel Yochelson and clinical psychologist Stanton E. Samenov, compilers of the most comprehensive history of criminal lives and personalities ever written, the world is replete with loveless families that do not produce killers.[1] What was different about Westley Dodd? It is this question, in a larger sense, that lies at the heart of our examination of malevolence.

Paradoxically, we are both fascinated and frightened by accounts of malevolence. Not only do we find it impossible to understand what causes such acts of atrocity as serial killing, torture, and genocide; we can scarcely imagine their being carried out. What was it like to be imprisoned in Dachau, hunted like quarry by a determined serial killer, or rounded up for slaughter by one's own neighbors in Bosnia and Rwanda? So apparently inexplicable is truly sinister behavior that Hollywood has produced a parade of highly profitable feature films and television docudramas on malevolent subjects, including the cult madness that culminated in the Branch Davidian fireball and the Jonestown massacre in Guyana (see Chapter 11).

In other words, the public tries to come to terms with malevolence through the media and popular books, perhaps because psychiatry and the behavioral sciences have failed to do so. In fact, my colleagues have largely ignored the prevalence and tyranny of malevolence, which is perhaps humankind's most important problem.[2] This is a tragic failure of traditional psychoanalysis and behavioral science, for as an ancient saying warns us, "Those who avert their eyes from evil commit the worst of sins."

Abraham Joshua Heschel, the eminent scholar of Jewish ethics, has elaborated the point: "Indifference to evil is more insidious than evil itself; it is more universal, more contagious, more dangerous. A silent justification, it makes possible an evil erupting as an exception, becoming the rule and being in turn accepted."[3]

The theme is also stressed in *The Jewish Bible*, as when Jehovah outlines human responsibilities for evil acts of others: "Son of man, I have appointed you a watchman . . . but you have not spoken to warn the wicked man against his ways. . . . I will demand a reckoning for his blood from you. But if you have warned the wicked man . . . he shall die for his own sins, but you will have saved your life." (Ezekiel 33:9)

MALEVOLENCE DEFINED

Most people would probably agree that malevolence, though it can be plausibly defined in numerous ways, involves acts that produce undeserved suffering.

On the other hand, the highly subjective nature of judging specific events as "good" or "bad" makes it difficult to find a consensus on the criteria for malevolence. The English philosopher Thomas Hobbes spoke to this point in *Human Nature* (1650): "Everyman, for his own part, calleth that which pleaseth and is delightful to himself, good; and that evil which displeaseth him."

Nevertheless, when one's actions cause others to suffer unnecessarily—that is to say, the conditions cause avoidable suffering—we have reason to consider them malevolent.

For example, several weeks before a New York City surgeon performed an operation that led to his patient's death, the State Health Department had informed him that his license was being revoked for dozens of counts of unprofessional conduct and patient neglect. At least one hospital had rescinded his operating room privileges because he was, in the words of a staff physician, "intellectually dishonest, surgically incompetent, and lacking in good medical judgment." Yet the surgeon continued operating on patients in an unsanitary home office.

Consider another example. Several days before the Nazi occupation of Paris in 1940, a few anxious French men and women sat around a table in a café on Boulevard Saint-Germain, debating whether to leave the country or join a resistance group. All were downcast, except for one pretty young woman, who said she would literally welcome the Germans with open arms and sleep with every handsome enemy soldier she could. Several people became enraged, and one man started to strangle her before he was pulled off by the others. Later, they learned that the woman, far from being a traitor, was planning to serve her country the best way she could—she was dying of syphilis.

Most of us, I suspect, would have no trouble regarding the surgeon as malevolent. But the young woman? To the Free French, she was a heroine of a rightful cause. The Germans, of course, would regard her as a lethal adversary. To observers trying to ignore the competing political allegiances in this situation, her intentions might seem justifiable in cases where the German soldiers were guilty of brutalizing civilians. But what about her involvement with those who were innocent of atrocity? Can she justify her effect on them?

Despite the inherent problems of subjectivity, we must try to set down a working definition of "malevolence."

In my view, malevolence always involves treating other people without respect or consideration for their humanity. The malevolent person's actions are based upon one or both of two beliefs:

1. The other person is so weak, stupid, and incompetent that he or she can be treated as an object rather than as someone who deserves decent interaction.
2. The other person is so threatening to the malevolent person's physical and psychological safety that any destructive action is justified.

My analysis, including these two considerations, presupposes that the malefactor is capable of understanding the consequences of his actions. It follows, therefore, that malevolence is the *deliberate* infliction of cruel, painful suffering on another living being. Traditional moral and legal codes exempt—partially or wholly—people who commit destructive acts but do not understand their consequences.[4]

Gustave Gilbert, the prison psychologist who spent hundreds of hours with the twenty Nazis on trial at Nuremberg after World War II, described in detail their varied reactions to films of the brutality of the concentration camps. Hermann Göring, second only to Hitler during most of the Third Reich, reluctantly admitted that some of what went on was extreme, but he grandiosely justified the abuses as necessary to carry out his government's long-term policies for solving serious social and political problems that had plagued Europe for centuries. Julius Streicher, the paranoid anti-Semite newspaper publisher who was an architect of Nazi racial policies, rationalized the filmed conditions as necessary to counter centuries of Jewish scheming to seize control of his nation's economy. But most of the other defendants, even those specifically accused of brutal crimes against humanity, were horrified by the images on the screen. There is further evidence that some crimes are regarded as unacceptable even to other criminals. Patients I have treated in forensic settings told me how prisoners convicted of serious crimes have brutally beaten or even killed prison mates accused of raping or murdering a young child.

Therefore, a complete definition of malevolence must include its effects on nonparticipants as well; indeed, seriously malevolent acts are unique among human experiences in the power of their impact upon people who are not directly involved or even present when they occur. For example, such acts invoke discomfort in those who try to understand what causes them. This tension results from the unsettling combination of our curious fascination with mysterious power and our apprehension about the danger of its unsanctioned exercise. Other acts we consider immoral do not produce this paradoxical response of both captivating excitement and enormous fear.

Finally, our definition must include the context of malevolent acts. That is to say, they lack justification because they can feasibly be replaced by more rational, decent, and humane behavior. For instance, most of us would agree that it is reasonable to protect ourselves from an attack, even if our defensive actions cause serious harm to our assailant. But if we unnecessarily continue assaulting someone who has been rendered helpless, justifiable self-defense has turned into malevolent behavior.

I have purposely not included in my definition those people who kill without an intent to commit the crime in a cruel and painful way. Otherwise we would not distinguish malevolence from serious criminality, and they are not the same. While it is valid in the legal sense to contend that all malevolent acts are criminal, malevolent wrongdoers are distinctive in that their actions are abhorrent even to other criminals, as I noted above.

OBSTACLES TO BEHAVIORAL STUDIES OF MALEVOLENCE

Not only have behavioral scientists so far been unable to explain cogently the wellsprings of malevolence; their clinical methods have failed to prevent a Dodd and others of his ilk from torturing and murdering.

Generally speaking, behavioral scientists have relied upon two assumptions about malevolence, both of them problematic:

1. It can be safely ignored by clinicians because it is a moral issue better left to theologians and philosophers.
2. There are no malevolent people, only victims of mental illness.

One problem with the first assumption is that a number of theologians, as well as many victims of atrocities, have what I call a "moral objection" to examining wickedness. Furthermore, they urge others not to examine malevolence either. Consequently, I have to disagree with theologians such as Jeffrey Russell, who claims that science and psychology cannot substantially respond to what he calls "the question of evil":

Science is by definition restricted to investigating the physical and can say nothing about the spiritual. Further, the question of evil is a question of moral value, and science again by definition cannot discover moral values. Finally, moral evil is a matter of free choice rather than of cause and effect, and science cannot investigate truly freewill decisions, which by definition have no causes.[5]

Scholars like Russell have confused the physical causations described by physical scientists with the behavioral view of human motivation that implies access to personal choice. For that reason, they fail to recognize the actual influences in the development of the malevolent personality. Those who have a moral objection to examining malevolence consider that any such study would be both futile and dangerous. For example, many Holocaust survivors fear that the analysis of malevolence could replace the rectitude of condemnatory moral judgment with the arguably exculpatory insights of psychological explanation. They do not want attempted genocide approached in the manner of the famous French aphorism *"Tout comprendre c'est tout pardonner"* (To understand all is to forgive all).

Indeed, the scarcely conceivable brutality and irrationality of atrocities perpetrated in Nazi Germany, the Ukraine, Serbia, Cambodia, Rwanda, and elsewhere in recent memory make a compelling argument against trying to understand them. Some people are afraid that studying atrocity will contaminate them with evil. They may also want to believe that a horror like the Holocaust was a social anomaly with no relationship to the rest of the world. But as the long list of other large-scale atrocities proves, they are seriously mistaken.

Moreover, I believe that events in Israel in recent years demonstrate that being the victim of malevolence does not necessarily provide insight into how to avoid becoming an agent of malevolence. That is to say, the suffering of one generation in the Holocaust has not prevented its children and grandchildren from involvement in systematic brutality toward Palestinians or from implicitly sanctioning the Arab Christians in their massacre of Arab Muslims in Lebanon. Too often, with individuals and nations alike, a pernicious consequence of having been wronged is the unwillingness to examine why these wrongs were committed.

The reality of both those who have participated in and those who have witnessed sinister events is experienced dramatically. Undergoing malevolence on a mass level, for most people, results in a passive, unwilling attitude toward taking action against subsequent sinister events. It leads to what contemporary philosophers refer to as a "deconstruction of reality." In other words, what has largely contributed to our contemporary inability to deal effectively with the problems of cruelty and destructiveness is our inability to understand a world that is rapidly becoming more unfamiliar to us.

A willingness to take an active and constructive role in an orderly society is based on an implicit *social contract,* with the expectation that others will act prudently in accordance with acceptable rules of behavior. Therefore, if we treat others decently, they should behave accordingly.

The philosopher Robert Nozick describes in *The Examined Life*[6] how the Holocaust changed everything for humankind by radically altering our sense of humanity. The Age of Enlightenment, with its hubristic concept of a superior Western culture, confident of its values and its future, ended with the onset of the Age of the Holocaust. In other words, Nazi Germany gave humanity a shattering moral blow by cynically divesting us of our naive belief that the world we live in is a just place, in which individuals are protected because human life is respected. As a result of the Holocaust, personal innocence that came from a trust in other people has been lost; the human species has been desanctified.

According to Robert Lifton,[7] the loss of trust in other people is a feature of *historical dislocation,* in which the roles and obligations that bind people together in cooperative relationships in society have lost their traditional meaning. Historical dislocation results from natural disasters such as floods, earthquakes, and epidemics, or from war and any other type of cruelty people inflict upon one another. Lifton depicts our age as one in which by taking on the use of nuclear weapons we have assumed an "Identity of the Doomed." In other words, our age of violence and mistrust can be said to be an aftermath of our use of nuclear weapons.

In fact, the only way to address malevolence intelligently and effectively is to confront it. The moral inquiry must include a willingness to take action to resolve the problems caused by malevolence, recognize ways in which we may have contributed to those problems, and then explore our own motivations. How Jews and Christians differ on how to address this concern is discussed in Chapter 12.

The second assumption calls forth the "psychological objection" to studying malevolence, which follows the conviction that the character structure of the perpetrator of a heinous action can be reduced to known, well-understood concepts and psychiatric diagnoses. But this is no less troublesome to frank inquiry than the "moral objection" of the first assumption.

Because unsanctioned power is so terrifying, succeeding generations have tried to find logical, comforting explanations for malevolent deeds. In our culture, psychiatry—our preferred decoder of the unacceptable—has explained sinister behavior in terms of childhood abuse, the influence of deviant peers, inadequate parental role modeling, chemical or neurological imbalances, and the unrecognized encouragement parents often provide their child for acting in socially undesirable ways.

These theories remove ominous spiritual and animistic implications of malevolent actions by, in psychoanalyst Otto Rank's phrase, "rationalizing the irrational."[8] The word "evil" itself frightens people. As a consequence, there is a widespread reluctance to speak seriously about the problem of malevolence, as if ignoring it would diminish its power and presence. By changing the language used to discuss the problem, Rank objects, we have merely discarded the traditional words for moralistic and metaphysical concepts while retrieving the concepts under new terms. Worst of all, he warns, such "psychological sanitation" becomes a dismal failure of understanding. Rank's reasoning can be applied to such cases as when

Hitler is given diagnostic labels like "paranoid schizophrenic," "manic depressive," "borderline personality," and "criminal psychopath." To speak of the Hitlers, Stalins, Idi Amins, and Pol Pots of the world so glibly is to assume that their heinous crimes are readily explicable by standard, well-understood diagnostic concepts. They are not.

In sum, we like to believe that today's scientific knowledge, drawing upon empirical studies as well as logic, has freed us from the need to explain heinous crimes as demonically caused. Put another way, the behavioral sciences have produced psychological theories that quiet our primitive apprehensions about strange, frightening events.

The same kind of thought process that prevents behavioral scientists from studying malevolence is behind the arguments for using insanity as a legal defense. The aim is to show that the defendant has a diminished capacity for moral reasoning but at the same time to avoid discussion of the cause of the crime committed. In fact, declaring an accused person "insane" is an implicit admission of inability to understand his or her reasoning and motivation.

In other words, the use of insanity as a legal defense relieves vicious behavior of its immoral status, while at the same time straddling the fence as to whether to hold the accused responsible for his actions. Therefore, to interpret someone's malevolence by conventional clinical and legal concepts, such as psychosis and insanity, does not meaningfully explain the cause of the behavior. It acts only as a temporary means of reducing malevolence's awe and terror. Once that malevolence is reenacted by someone else, however, we are not in any better position to deal with the particular behavior than before it was given a clinical or legal label. Thus, our uneasiness about malevolence is driven underground, to take insidious shapes and influences on our psyches.

TRADITIONAL VIEWS OF EVIL AND MALEVOLENCE

Basically, four positions have been established to account for the presence of evil in the world:

1. Powerful external malevolent forces either seduce, conjure, corrupt, or overpower the individual, driving him to evil acts. This is one of the oldest religious explanations of evil.

2. People have free will. Their corrupt appetites lead them into sin.

3. As Saint Augustine was the first to suggest, evil is not an active principle but an absence of virtue. Just as cold is the absence of heat and dark is the absence of illumination, evil is an insufficiency of good.

4. In contemporary psychology, childhood trauma is generally thought to be the cause of malevolent behavior.

Taken individually, each of these positions is, to some extent, more persuasive than the others. Therefore, none of them is a reliably comprehensive insight into the problem of malevolence.

I offer a fifth approach, a new theory of the origins of malevolent behavior, which aims at once to combine aspects of the four traditional views and to illuminate aspects of malevolence they do not address. Many of my patients have struggled with debilitating emotional injuries that have thwarted their lives and in some cases led them to cause pain to others. Drawing upon their varied reactions to shame and humiliation, I have been able to develop a new theory of the malevolent personality. To my knowledge, the ideas discussed in this book represent the first consistent, serious attempt to explain the psychological basis of malevolent behavior. My theory is based upon a consideration of moral choice.

We learn by doing. Opportunities to choose between good and bad occur continually in our daily lives, even in the smallest matters. How we have responded to earlier choices shapes our moral decisions now and in the future.[9] In sum, such extreme behaviors as serial killing and genocide are usually the last of many steps along a continuum of unkind, indecent acts. And the rationalizations used early on facilitate more extravagant rationalizations, which are progressively less subject to rational and moral scrutiny.

Questions of good and malevolence should profoundly and personally concern each one of us. Throughout my twenty-five-year psychoanalytic career, I have experienced and come to understand better the presence of malevolence from events in my patients' lives as well as in my own. But I have actually been grappling with this issue since I was a child: why do people do such awful things to each other and to themselves, and thereby cause unnecessary suffering?

When I was nine or ten years old, a loud, foulmouthed great-uncle who showed up for a family gathering asked me to bring out my collection of a dozen foreign coins. Their cash value was negligible, but I loved these coins more than any other possession. The lettering, symbols, and sometimes unusual shapes sparked daydreams of faraway lands that someday I would visit. When I handed my treasure to my uncle, he put half of them in his pants pocket, grinned at my dismay, and refused to return them. In other words, this boorish older man had found a way of ruining my good feelings about my hobby and replacing them with pain.

I ran to tell my mother what had happened. For a puzzling long moment she was silent, then she snapped, "You should be ashamed of yourself for being so selfish. After all," she pointed out sternly, "he didn't take them *all* . . . and he *is* your uncle."

I dropped the matter. Even so, I continued to feel miserable for months, though I was too young and psychologically unsophisticated to associate my unhappiness with the incident and my mother's scolding.

Now I can see that the most damaging thing about the whole affair was not my uncle's behavior but my mother's: her reproach undermined my trust. Suddenly, the external world was no longer safe. It was a place where people did not always deal fairly with one another. By taking my uncle's part, as in earlier incidents in which she had undermined my trust and belief in fairness, protectiveness, and reasonableness, my mother invalidated my values and judgments. Worse, I was accused of being selfish so that she could avoid admitting her shame at the behavior of her aunt's husband and her inability to handle the problem.

As this apparently minor incident in my own life and similar or more dramatic events in the lives of my patients will show, the role of shame and reproach in child-adult relationships provides important insights into understanding how a person develops the potential for committing malevolent acts. The media have given considerable attention to physical and sexual abuse in families. But no less important is the devastating effect of the shameful, humiliating ways many parents, who would be horrified to be called abusive, speak to their children, undermining their youngsters' sense of competence and self-esteem.

Because we are all vulnerable to shame of some sort, we can all be psychologically manipulated or "blackmailed" into acting as others want. In childhood, shaming can be used to "shut us up" and force us to bear our hurts alone. I was vulnerable to the shame of being called "selfish." As a result, I felt unable to have fair exchanges with significant others based on mutual respect and compassion. I began to hide my feelings from everyone, including myself.

Happily, a wise schoolteacher detected my shame-imbued behavior. With caring and understanding, she drew out the story that I had "forgotten" and explained that I was in no way to blame for how my great-uncle and my mother had treated me. Most important, she was able to help me recognize the separation between others' actions and my own responsibility. Put another way, she helped in enabling me to redefine my identity in a positive way. Not everyone is so fortunate.

Consider how the famous French writer Jean Genet felt at age sixteen, when he was incarcerated in a children's penal colony: "I was suffering. I underwent the cruel and shameful ordeal of being shave-headed, dressed in a loathsome costume and detained in that vile place; I experienced the contempt of other inmates who were stronger or nastier than I. . . . Within myself I could feel the urge to become what I had become accused of being . . . a coward, a thief, and a queer."[10]

By the time he escaped, Genet was fully transformed into a criminal. He lived a miserable life, begging and stealing, betraying his friends, and prostituting himself to anyone who would pay. But nothing could stop him, he recalled later, because he had decided to behave as badly as possible. Not until he was serving time as an adult did he realize that his worst crime was not committing evil acts but boasting about them. Within prison walls, he wrote "Apologies for Evil," which became famous overnight and rescued him from a cycle of shame and malevolence.[11]

Genet's private *shame*—the first crucial concept in understanding how the malevolent personality is formed—filled him with contempt, both for himself and for anyone who had either participated in his brutal life, witnessed it, or stood by without offering help. I need to point out that shame and the other essential defenses I describe in this chapter are used to some extent by everyone. It is, however, their particular development that is crucial in the development of the malevolent personality.

Contempt is the second concept. It provides insight into the common observation that malevolent people are often cowards. Having been habitually shamed themselves, they try to project the defects they sense in themselves—or even fail to detect in themselves—onto other people, hoping to deflate them. Then they boast about their ability to humiliate, thus attempting to reverse the humiliating status that they have suffered in their own eyes and in the image other people have of them.

In Genet's case, as he admits, even worldwide literary success did not mute his self-contempt. Over the years, he used desperate rationalizations to forge a way of seeing himself as justified in disdaining the feelings and concerns of other people, including his closest friends.

Rationalization, then, is the third important concept in the development of the malevolent personality. Each decision to rationalize a contemptuous act makes it easier to perform subsequent contemptuous acts; inevitably, the result is an addiction to rationalizing cruel, insensitive behavior. This addiction is pernicious for malevolent people, because it enables them to justify as superior the very behaviors that others regard as indecent. Indeed, some boast that they live by a higher morality than conventional people.

This *justification* of malevolent actions, the fourth concept we must understand in the development of the malevolent personality, is so resistant to reasonable discussion that it becomes the reason for failure to discontinue the malevolent life.

The shame that fuels contempt and compels the need to rationalize in order to justify wickedness as a higher form of morality is the most complex, least understood of human emotions.[12] In Charles Darwin's view, shame is the parent emotion in a cluster of closely related responses that preserves the human species by energizing the autonomic nervous system with strong, rapid reactions to external threat.[13] Therefore, to understand malevolence, we must determine how shame becomes sidetracked from its evolutionary function as a response to external peril and derails itself by promoting dangerous behavior. Shame, as I will show in Chapter 3, is the monitor of our personal identity, crucially influencing how we feel about ourselves and the world we live in. Indeed, awareness of shame enables some people to examine their place in the world, but those who feel self-contemptuous are unwilling to do so.

And so we come to the fifth concept essential to our understanding of malevolence: the *inability or unwillingness to self-examine* one's dark side.

A second incident early in my life is a good illustration of this. I was twelve years old, attending a summer camp in rural Western New Jersey. One starless night, during the break between dinner and the scheduled evening activities, I was standing inside my group's unlit cabin, staring out a window into the still, pitch-black sky. Carleton, a tall, attractive boy admired by girls and boys alike for his natural athletic grace, was looking out another window. A couple of years older than I, he was typically reticent and aloof.

Suddenly, an eerie blue-white light blazed across the sky, pulsating and cascading like a luminescent waterfall. I shot a glance at Carleton, who looked back at me, and although neither of us said a word, our eyes acknowledged that we were sharing something uncanny.

Quickly turning back to stare at the phenomenon, I was transfixed by its sheer beauty, which lasted for several minutes. Then, just as suddenly, the sky faded to black once more. I looked over to Carleton again, eager to discuss this event, but he was no longer there.

A few days later, on an overnight hike with our group, I started to talk about what we had seen and turned to Carleton for confirmation. A look of fear distorted his features.

"I don't know what you're talking about," he said softly. "Besides, there are some things I just don't want to know about. I already know what I need to know." He walked away from the rest of us.

Years later, when I was home from college for a vacation, there was a front-page story about the arrest of a young man for the kidnapping and strangling of a girl. The accused was Carleton.

I remember few details, except that he had dropped out of college, couldn't hold a job, and had difficulty establishing relationships with women. He admitted his guilt but refused to discuss what had happened or why. A detective surmised that the victim had unwittingly touched on some dark secret that threw Carleton into a violent frenzy. This supposed secret was not explained.

Having shared a bizarre experience with Carleton, who later committed a horrible crime, has had a lasting effect on me. I have often wondered exactly what differentiated us so that he became a murderer and I a psychotherapist, concentrating on trying to understand and help people like him. One clue might lie in the experience of the blue-white light. Certain aspects of my personality encouraged me to gaze raptly at the display with open curiosity and wonder. Carleton, on the other hand, seemed to quake in horror of its presence. I cannot be certain, but I assume he was convinced that some sinister force might be revealing aspects of his hidden psyche that he did not want to recognize.

And because malevolent personalities are too fearful to examine un-known aspects of themselves, he relied upon *magical thinking*, the sixth important concept in understanding malevolence. Magically, he con-vinced himself that he knew everything that needed to be known. His only problem, he may have thought, was to convince the rest of us that he was superior.

To repeat, six concepts are essential to understanding my theory of the development of the malevolent personality: shame, contempt, rationaliza-tion, justification, the inability or unwillingness to self-examine, and mag-ical thinking. Throughout this book, we will see how these factors have shaped the tormented lives of my patients.

Some may claim that a theory trying to account for behaviors as com-plex as cruelty, viciousness, and indifference requires more than six cru-cial factors in its explanation. Such a claim misses the essence of sound scientific theorizing.

What is a theory, after all? It is a model of behavior that tries to ap-proximate what is operative in the actual behavior. But no theory at the present time can comprehensively explain all instances of a complex be-havior. Realistically, all contemporary theories are compromises of one sort or another.

A theory judiciously based on a very few crucial factors can be consis-tent with more cases than one with a large number of significant factors; it is also more likely to lack the capacity to describe any of the cases in depth. For example, a psychologist who explains violent behavior on the basis that all perpetrators of outrage are angry during their aberrant act can accurately find his crucial variable in virtually every case of violence. At the same time, relying on this factor alone leaves out a great deal of in-formation we need to know in understanding the etiology of violence. On the other hand, if we pooled every significant factor we could conceptual-ize as operative in cases of violence, we would be able to find all of these factors in a few cases, but we might have a considerable amount of infor-mation about those few cases. In other words, both the theories that have an overabundance of supposed significant factors (some of which are not found in a large number of cases) and those that have too few factors to provide adequate information are not the most useful.

The best present theory of human behavior would have the least num-ber of factors, but each of them would be found in all the cases; at the same time, each factor selected would provide a high degree of significant information and explanation in each case.

In developing my theory, I sought to provide a small number of irreducible factors to account for what is operative in all the cases I discuss; together with these crucial factors, I provide a discussion of the particular variables that make each individual case study I explore in this book different from other cases.

WHY STUDY EVIL?

The menacing reach of wickedness—what has been traditionally regarded as "the work of the devil"—can affect virtually any of us. Malevolence as a destructive force and so-called senseless acts of cruelty seem so ubiquitous that few people feel safe, even in their own homes. Many of our children face wickedness daily, as their classmates die from drug use or gunfire or gang beatings, or as a consequence of deprivation or emotional abuse. A central message of this book is that while we must condemn the vices of hatred, violence, and other destructive acts, we must also decipher the subliminal clues about human desires gone astray when behavior becomes aberrant. As a society, we can ill afford merely to rail against vicious behavior, blithely assuming that malevolence will just magically disappear on its own. Neither the recent surge in prison construction in the United States nor the growing number of jurisdictions that impose the death penalty has stemmed the rising tide of violent and cruel crimes. There seems to be an inexhaustible supply of offenders.

Whether random or systematic, the insensitivity, cruelty, and abuse of malevolence demoralize us, leaving us depressed, pessimistic, and alienated from what is good, hopeful, and worthy in our lives. Eventually, we may fall victim to a chronic sense of overwhelming oppression, losing our ability to strive in support of those things we respect and cherish.

To examine malevolence in contemporary society, however, is not necessarily to adopt a pessimistic perspective. Such an investigation, which originates from our curiosity about what we do not understand in ourselves, can become a healthy exploration offering inspiration and rewards. Indeed, we can inquire in the most profound ways about the human condition itself, assessing which conditions make life meaningful or at least tolerable. We can learn, consequently, how we can concentrate on constructive, creative, and compassionate human pursuits and, just as important, what we can do to ward off the apprehensions, limitations, and weaknesses that force us to live fearful, cloistered lives.

We all try to find constructive purpose and importance in our lives, but we will not succeed unless we realistically accept our human limitations. By exploring the dark side of our personal and interpersonal worlds, we can become actively involved in determining whether our shared experience in American society becomes more optimistic, compassionate, and caring or instead increasingly subject to pessimism and despair. In other words, unless we successfully address sources of conflict and ignorance both in ourselves and in our dealings with others, the cruelty and destructiveness in our daily lives will remain perpetually beyond our control.

Of course, serious obstacles lie in the way of self-acceptance. As will become clear in the vignettes I present later, the toxic experiences of shame impair the self-esteem that smooths the way to self-examination. And yet the emblematic tales I will tell in this book are intended not to frighten or amaze but to help make a difference in our struggle with malevolence by relating those encounters to issues that touch the lives of us all.

The next chapter begins with a survey of the history of evil that is necessarily cursory, for no one book, let alone a brief chapter, can do justice to the complexity of the debate waged so vigorously over time by theologians, philosophers, and others as Western culture has worked to define itself. To find enlightenment in the past, we must search through our legacy of myth, scripture, and popular beliefs to find a motif that will help guide us—in this case, an overarching moral.

CHAPTER TWO

The History of Evil and
Its Psychological Theories

Evil is but the shadow that, in this world,
always accompanies good. You may have
a world without shadow, but it is a world
without light—a mere dim, twilight world.
If you deepen the intensity of the light,
you must be content to bring into deeper
blackness, and more distinct and definite
outline, the shadow that accompanies it.
— F. W. ROBERTSON

IN EXPLORING THE HISTORY OF EVIL, I CONFINE MYSELF TO THE Western tradition, in which monotheism is a relatively recent concept. Indeed, as we learn from Richard Cavendish, a historian of myth, magic, and demonology, most humans throughout history have viewed the world as populated by a multitude of spirits.[1] What is the basis for this widespread, enduring belief?

The human mind is a relentless hunter. Its psychic eye casts upon the world the projection of every fear and every delight fashioned within its imagination. As with us today, our ancestors were unable to observe their lives with detachment and objectivity. As the mind evolved through the various stages of emerging consciousness, it scripted the heavens and the underworld in ways that seemed plausibly to explain frightening experiences which defied empirical investigation.

19

In other words, humans first understood the universe in terms of themselves. They believed that there were intentions behind natural events, just as there were in their own actions. Consequently, every object, whether animate or apparently inanimate, must have its own spirit. A certain specific class of these spirits—some of them benevolent, others malevolent or indifferent—played a role in human experience: from bountiful harvests to victorious battles to healthy births, from famine to plague to sterility.

Sigmund Freud suggested that preliterate people created demons from projections of their own hostilities; subsequently, these malevolent forces evolved into benevolent spirits. Originally, the demons derived from a highly significant relationship of the living to the dead: "Nothing testifies so much to the influence of mourning on the origins of the belief in demons as the fact that demons were always taken to be spirits of persons not long dead."[2]

After being psychically reconstructed, these spirits of deceased relatives became deities and were called upon to intercede with the powers of the universe to bring prosperity and ward off misfortune.

This reverence for dead ancestors was the basis for early practices of *magic,* which was usually "white" or "black." The rituals of white magic were designed to procure benefits from the departed spirits without causing harm to anyone else. Black magic called down injury or even death upon one's enemies.

Appearing in virtually every era of the human species, magical practices are essentially wishful attempts to deny human impotence against nature and gain apparent control over universal forces. The rituals incorporate specific formulas for entreating spirits in service of these aims.

Our earliest notions of *sin,* as the eminent French philosopher Paul Ricoeur tells us, are related to magic: "sin" was conceptualized as a defilement of the *sacred*[3]—those objects and human actions that were valued by the spirit world and, consequently, considered inviolable: any contamination would bring down upon humankind the wrath of the supernatural. Special rituals were devoted to removing human stain from the sacred; these rites would later evolve into formal religious worship. Once purity was ritually restored, the spirits would again look favorably upon human welfare.

How did the concept of a devil, a particularly powerful unitary personification of the evil forces that plague human life, emerge from this universe of good and bad spirits? For a likely explanation, we need to examine the role that myths about society and the universe played in prehistoric attempts to try to simplify the mystery of human experience.

First, certain spirits evolved in the popular imagination into the contrasting personalities of the gods and goddesses of polytheism. The stories to account for the attitudes and behavior of these sharply delineated deities toward humans are known as *myths*. Derived from a number of sources, many myths evidently originated in preliterate times, or so ancient cave drawings and recovered artifacts imply. The most important myths were created to explain human *pain* and *suffering* and are often "universal"—that is, found in variant forms in different cultures in virtually every part of the world. On the other hand, the interpretations provided to explain the meanings of these myths appear to vary from culture to culture, indicating that the variety of options available for human development is multifold.

Humans are meaning-oriented beings. In every era, in every culture, people recognize their personal identities—who they are—by telling stories that explain whatever happens in their lives and in the lives of their forefathers. These stories reflect and affirm how people feel about the world, its resources, its opportunities, and its impediments to the achievement of their desires.

Humans experience pain, but pain does not become suffering until it is translated into a category of meaning. This interpretation of our experiences is derived from assumptions and expectations conveyed to us from others. Often, we do not know what to make of our experiences without trying to see ourselves as others do. Suffering, therefore, is an interpersonal and learned process. Socioemotionally, our state of being is intolerable when it contradicts the way we have been led to believe our lives should be experienced. In other words, societal myths create the scenarios for suffering.

In many myths, pain and death are regarded as primary evidence of human limitation. The ultimate outcome of limitation is nonexistence, but our imagination cannot tolerate the thought of a state of nonexistence, the image of total negation and extinction of our consciousness. Therefore, stories have been invented since earliest times to overcome this curse in our imagination.

One strategy was to conceive pain and death as retribution for actions that offended powerful spirits rather than as natural consequences of the human experience. In the opinion of many theologians, Christianity and

Islam similarly invented the devil as a systematic way to explain human suffering.[4] In both religions, Satan has become the leader of an "evil empire," an army of hostile spirits that makes war on humankind and God as well.

Actually, the origins of the concept of a devil are lost in prehistory but probably, according to anthropologists, predate the concept of a single God. In the paleolithic period, a horned god, presumably an early pagan version of the devil, was depicted in frescoes on the walls of the Caverne des Trois Frères at Ariège, in what is now France, and in caves in present-day northern Spain.[5] The horned god was to survive the theological vicissitudes and revisions of subsequent ages, enduring as the dominant religious figure in many regions of Europe until at least the fifteenth century. Even today, the pagan horned god is celebrated by people from all walks of life nearly everywhere in the world.

Most scholars of demonology, such as Dennis Wheatley, agree that the Christian priesthood did not systematically or forcefully oppose the ancient pagan gods, including the devil, until the thirteenth century, essentially because pagan beliefs had been too firmly entrenched to be rooted out effectively.[6] If forced to choose between a monotheistic God and their pagan pantheon, the common people would have turned away from Christianity. Indeed, many Christian priests, as the Church hierarchy well knew, conducted pagan rites in addition to celebrating the mass.[7]

By the fifteenth century, however, the Church believed its authority sufficiently established for it to launch an effective campaign against all competing beliefs and practices, from paganism to Judaism and Islam. The most infamous result, of course, was the five-hundred-year reign of the Holy Inquisition. But this religious war against the accused worshipers of the devil, fed by deep-seated fears and cowardly false testimony, was largely unsuccessful.

Today, fascination with satanism is still alive and well. For some reason, it is considerably stronger in the United States than in Western Europe. A Gallup poll taken in 1988 revealed that 66 percent of American respondents claimed to believe in the devil, compared with only 30 percent or fewer in France, Great Britain, Italy, Norway, and Sweden.[8]

Despite his ancient lineage, the horned god generally known as Satan, though he has many other names, has remained a puzzle in the history of

Western religion. Only rarely mentioned in *The Jewish Bible*, he remains relatively unimportant in Jewish theology, in contrast with the powerful role he plays in Christianity and Islam, where he is seen as the former archangel Lucifer. (In Hebrew, the name Lucifer means "bringer of the morning light" or "truth before conformity.")

The Jewish Bible describes him as God's favorite son and adjutant, charged with the task of prosecuting human beings for their sins against his father. In other words, in his original capacity he is neither God's adversary nor a contaminator of the good.

His transformation is memorably narrated in Isaiah 14:12:

How art thou fallen from Heaven, O Lucifer,
Son of the morning!
Cut down to the ground!
And once you dominated the people!
Didn't you say to yourself, I will be as high as Heaven!
I will be more exalted than the stars of God!
I will indeed be the supreme leader!
In the privileged place!
I will be the same as the most high God!
But you shall be brought down to Hell,
To the bottom of the pit.
And all who will see you, will despise you.

John Milton elaborates this account in his epic poem *Paradise Lost*, which depicts Lucifer being cast out of heaven for leading troops of other dissatisfied angels in open revolt against God. The renegade had previously been his maker's favorite, by far the wisest, the most beautiful and powerful, of the angels. Once he rebelled, however, he was given the name Satan, meaning "enemy" or "adversary," and banished to earth and hell for eternal suffering.

Milton's Lucifer is a personified spirit who combines the highest virtues with the basest motives. In contemporary psychology, anyone with such serious conflictual contradictions might be described as having a *paradoxical* personality.

Thus conceived, Lucifer is a projection of humanity's uneasy feelings about its conflictual nature. On the one hand, we are flesh-and-blood

beings doomed to a lustful animal body; on the other, we have the capacity to envision a spiritual paradise in which we can reign sovereign,
just as Lucifer dreamed. And like this fallen angel, we suffer for these
ambitions.[9]

In an important sense, suffering springs from humankind's passionate
desire to live forever. We long for unlimited, unending paradise. We create symbols and abstractions to illustrate our conceptualization of this
world without end. But we pay a terrible price for our supreme dream.
The unending bliss of paradise sought eludes us. Our frustration with our
shameful inability to transcend human limitation interprets the earth for
us as a seething, threatening, and destructive place.[10] In other words, our
ability to be vibrantly alive and to thrive is undermined by the belief we
should and must operate at full capacity at all times. We suffer because
we can neither obtain nor deny all our wants. Consequently, when we become disabled by illness or dire circumstances, we assume that our suffering is meant to be. Buttressing this belief is the myth that there is a
rational force that controls the universe. The advent of illness or despair
indicates that this force has decided our fate and no effort on our part can
change our destiny.

THE PARADOX OF GOD

Like humanity and the devil, the Old Testament God Yahweh is presented as a highly paradoxical figure. The Swiss psychologist C. G. Jung
advanced an intriguing if controversial psychotheological view of this
paradox.[11] By the time the Book of Job was written, Jung argues, Yahweh
had been portrayed contradictorily throughout the earliest scriptures. A
deity immoderate in His passions, He often suffered for His fiery temper.
He frequently admits to being eaten up with instinctual rage and jealousy
that have no understandable origin—an awareness that disturbs Him. He
recognizes that owing to His lack of self-examination, He occasionally
presents his "chosen people," the Israelites, with insoluble conflicts.[12]

The famously troubling Book of Job ("he who repents") is the story of a
man who was not an Israelite. It may have its origin in a myth told by a
Semitic people who lived in Canaan and were defeated in battle by the
invading Israelites between 600 and 300 B.C.E. In the version told in the
Old Testament, Job was "upright and perfect" in God's eyes, for he feared

the Lord, kept His commandments, and was "happy in the midst of his family and goods."[13]

God boasted of this man's perfection to Satan, His chief prosecutor in ferreting out impiety against Himself. The devil countered that Job's virtue was in fact directly proportional to Yahweh's generosity. If God relieved him of his earthly joys and plentiful goods, Job would turn against Him. Yahweh permitted Satan to cause great suffering for this upright man and his family. Job's flocks of sheep and goats were slaughtered, his cropland razed, his body afflicted with disease and disfigurement. Worst of all, his ten children were slain by fierce winds.

In Jung's view, God could have permitted such cruel satanic mischief only because He at times forgot to use His omniscience. In this instance, He did not recognize how much He actually favored his dark son, Satan, over the welfare of humanity.

As Jung also points out, the Yahweh so often seen raging and seeking vengeance in the Old Testament is no less frequently shown demonstrating loving-kindness and charity toward His chosen people. Jung contends that this paradoxical portrait of the deity manifests a psychological condition conceivable only when one does not consciously reflect upon one's actions and intentions or lacks a highly developed capacity for reflection. Jung persuasively shows that Job has a more well-developed consciousness and sense of morality than does God. Job uses these assets to cleverly encourage God to separate His loving goodness from His terrible, irrational rage and to become an advocate for Job in protecting him from Yahweh's own madness.

HISTORY OF EVIL: THE CORE CONCEPT

According to anthropologists, our sense of what is "bad" is rooted in our perception of "bad death" as opposed to "natural death."[14] The former includes a child dying before its parents or the painful, premature death of someone who is unusually virtuous.

Job's children, not only young but nearly as virtuous as their father, died unfairly on both counts. As I've noted, Jung argues that they perished because Yahweh "forgot" to use His wisdom and was unaccustomed to self-examination. Jung's insight also relates to the first crime depicted in *The Jewish Bible*: Cain's murder of his brother, Abel, which is

symbolic of the crux of malevolence. For it was not merely the murder itself that was evil. Rather, the act was a symptom of a more fundamental
problem, the refusal to examine one's feelings and motives. An inability
to self-examine, as I will show in the cases discussed in this book, provides the crucible in which the malevolent personality is crystallized.

This interpretation is evident in the account of the fratricide in Gene-
sis 4:3–9:

> The Lord looked with favor on Abel and his offerings, but on
> Cain and his offerings he did not look with favor. So Cain was very
> angry, and his face was downcast.
>
> Then the Lord said, "Why are you angry? Why is your face down-
> cast? If you do what is right, will you not be accepted? But if you do
> not do what is right, sin is crouching at your door; it desires to have
> you, but you must master it."
>
> Now Cain said to his brother Abel, "Let's go out to the field."
> And while they were in the field, Cain attacked his brother and
> killed him.
>
> Then the Lord said to Cain, "Where is your brother Abel?"
>
> "I don't know," he replied. "Am I my brother's keeper?"

Yes, Cain, you *are* your brother's keeper, as are we all our brothers'
keepers—which Cain might have recognized for himself if he had been
able to self-examine. Our greatest virtue and our highest development as
human beings come not from avoiding temptation but from trying to understand what the temptations of our dark side can reveal to us about
which aspects of our humanity we have neglected and need to master.

The fundamental paradox in human history is this: healthy human development requires that we take responsibility for ourselves and not remain overly dependent upon others; at the same time, we must be the
keepers of our brothers and sisters, and vice versa. As the poet John
Donne warned, no one of us is an island. We all belong to one solidarity.
Therefore, an act involving any one person inevitably has spiritual impact
upon us all. Horrible, otherwise unthinkable actions are unleashed when
we, like Cain, ignore or deny this central moral truth.

Once we understand the paradox—we must be responsible for ourselves, but we are also the responsibility of others—metaphysical myster-

ies can be set aside in examining the problem of evil. Rather, it becomes a *practical problem,* whose psychological and social causes can be traced empirically. Consequently, many possibilities for taking constructive actions to address malevolence become readily available.

PSYCHOLOGICAL THEORIES TO EXPLAIN MALEVOLENCE

Two considerations are useful to keep in mind when reviewing psychological theories about malevolence. First, most are only partial explanations. Only two of them, in fact, are comprehensive enough to be called theories. Second, few of the remaining near-theories were formulated in the context of clinical work. Rather, most theorists have been attempting after the fact to explain the behavior of historical figures or other people they did not know personally.

If we expect psychoanalysis to be the most articulate psychology on momentous social issues, we will be disappointed in the case of malevolence. With considerable reluctance and great difficulty, psychoanalysts have struggled unsuccessfully with humankind's continuing predilection for cruelty and atrocity.

Not long before World War I, Sigmund Freud explained all acts of psychopathology as manifestations of "drive conflict" theory, which supposes that sexual and aggressive urges dominate all other emotional needs. Thus, he believed that destructive adult behavior was caused by traumatic, unresolved sexual and aggressive experiences in childhood. But he was shocked by the enormity of the destructiveness of the war. Drive conflict, he recognized, could not adequately account for such extreme brutality or for the social impact of aggression on civilization. Previously, he had agreed with the ethnocultural theory that early humans lived harmoniously with their neighbors until the rise of cities.[15] Now he needed a new theory to encompass the unexpected abuses of the war as well as the history of political animosity.

So he added a third factor to his drive conflict theory: the *death instinct,* conceptualized as the converse of Eros. If the aim of Eros is to join people, objects, and ideas in sexual, creative ways, that of the death instinct is to free the individual from active participation in the world.[16]

In formulating this new theory, Freud returned to his original goal of trying to integrate his psychological insights with a generally accepted biological theory. Late in his career, he recalled the thinking that inspired his hypothesis:

> Starting from speculation on the beginning of life and from biological parallels, I drew the conclusion that, besides the instinct to preserve living substance, there must exist another, contrary instinct seeking to dissolve these units and to bring them back to their primeval, inorganic state. That is to say, as well as Eros there was an instinct of death.[17]

Could the massive human destructiveness of war somehow be averted? In his responses to Albert Einstein's letters asking this question in the late 1930s and in his book *Civilization and Its Discontents,* Freud answered in the negative.[18] Since the death instinct is a drive, it cannot be denied, and the destruction it causes cannot be prevented.

As a destructive force, Freud's theorized death instinct has only two avenues of discharge: toward the self, or toward other people. Therefore, its harmful effects can be blunted in only a limited way. Society can do little more than advocate whether the individual's destructive drives are to be forced inward into masochistic psychic conflict or allowed freedom of action, perhaps most innocuously when subdued by creative expression in the form of aggressive and sadistic themes in the arts.

Even though Freud translated human destructiveness from a metaphysical concept (evil) into psychological terminology (sadism, masochism), the pervasive destructive force he describes as an innate universal urge may be viewed as an inherent human evil. Of course, the implication that in part we are all naturally evil is a disturbing, distasteful reading of human nature.

Not surprisingly, then, Freud's theory has not been widely embraced by behavioral scientists or intellectuals in other fields. To believe in universal malevolence is to interpret horrifying events as the result of forces beyond our ability to understand and control. Preferring to include the possibility of at least some control over our propensity for destructiveness, most contemporary psychologists explain acts of malevolence as expressions of hate, vengeance, and fear precipitated by early childhood conflicts. In other words, when a malevolent act is attributed to personal action, these psychologists believe that ideally it can be controlled either by imposing constraints on the individual or by intervening therapeutically.

Carl Rogers is one expert who has taken the humanistic view that human nature is inherently good until warped by painful, abusive life experience.[19] Disagreeing, psychoanalyst Rollo May has staked out an interesting position that accepts evil as inherent in human nature but, in contrast with Freud, portrays human destructiveness as an innate component of the dialectics of personality. Following the tradition of Greek philosophy, he considers the life energy of personality to be a daimonic force that is the source of both our constructive and our destructive impulses. When the daimonic is effectively integrated with the positive values of personality, it serves constructive actions. If not, destructive behavior results.[20]

Michael Eigen is another analyst who has not shied away from writing of evil as inherent, arguing that it cannot be validly dismissed as an illusion:

> My years of clinical experience teach me that the devil is very much alive as a *psychic reality* in the self-feelings of our age. He emerges with predictable regularity in sensitive depth analysis of individual patients, and his face may be plainly seen in events throughout the world.
>
> When I speak of a devil, I can feel myself being both apologetic and provocative, but also true to phenomenological events that arise in the course of depth-oriented therapy. Given half the chance, patients sooner or later may well report having at some point in life made a pact with the devil. They are somehow nagged by a sense of selling out for survival or power, to get by or to triumph.[21]

Alice Miller has worked clinically with many of the same types of patients as has Eigen. She has made important contributions to our understanding of how a child's early relationships with parents and authority figures shape its sense of self, and agrees more closely with Rogers than with Freud and May. When the child's relationships are supportive and caring, she points out, it develops a healthy sense of self and a benevolent attitude toward others. Conversely, childhood mistreatment and abuse directly cause criminal and destructive behavior.[22]

Miller's clinical studies are especially useful because they document the specific types of relationships and early life experiences that influenced her patients' adult conflicts. But her work fails to explain why people who experience painful childhoods often manage nonetheless to live decent, harmonious adult lives. Just as puzzling from her perspective, why do children who ostensibly seem to be treated favorably later exhibit malevolent behavior? The answer to this apparent contradiction is that children suffer shame and humiliation not only from physical abuse; indeed, they can experience painful "borrowed shame" from their close identification with others who are shamed and dishonored. (See Chapter 3 for a description of the dynamics of "borrowed shame.")

Another child analyst, Melanie Klein, describes her psychotic patients as being unable to feel good about themselves no matter how hard they try.[23] In their tortured experiences, they feel caught in a struggle between their primary megalomaniac self (god-aspiring self) and their extremely megalomaniac other self (demon self), both filled with hatred. In search of salvation, the primary self splits off its "bad" feelings, attributing them to the demon self. When this strategy fails, as eventually it does, the primary self casts its badness into the external world, using the psychological mechanisms of externalization and projection to attribute it to other people, social and political causes, even fate.

We get some idea of fate's connection to malevolence from Jung, who argued that each of us can encounter a devil within, because we all have a dark side or "shadow." He warned that it is extremely dangerous to deny this dark side, for that which we do not bring into consciousness will appear in our lives as destiny. He meant that the past clings to us forever, and if some past event is too terrifying to examine, its tenacious shadow becomes our eventual fate.[24]

Less than a decade ago, in *The Nazi Doctors*, Robert Lifton presented an in-depth sociopolitical-psychiatric investigation of the Nazi concentration camp physicians. He sought to demonstrate that many of them, though involved in mass torture and murder, were for the most part gentle, decent men. Much as they were caring and sympathetic to family and friends, he argued, they justified their participation in atrocities as integral to their roles as physicians charged with protecting the state, metaphorically viewing their victims as "gangrenous limbs" who imperiled the corporal well-being of the Aryan race.

In addition, Lifton found, they were able to continue leading their normal family and social lives because of the psychological mechanisms "psychic numbing" and "doubling."

Psychic numbing, as defined by Lifton, was essential:

[It is] a general category of diminished capacity or inclination to feel. Psychic numbing involves an interruption in psychic action—in the continuous creation and re-creation of images and forms that constitute the symbolizing or formative processes characteristic of mental life. Psychic numbing varies greatly in degree . . . But it is probably impossible to kill another human being without numbing oneself toward the victim.

He borrowed the concept of doubling from Otto Rank and applied it specifically to the Nazi physicians:

[It] is the division of the self into two functioning wholes, so that a part-self acts as the entire self. An Auschwitz doctor could, through doubling, not only kill and contribute to killing, but organize silently, on behalf of the evil project . . . virtually all aspects of his behavior.[25]

Reviewing *The Nazi Doctors*, Bruno Bettelheim, a renowned expert on destructive behavior who had himself survived the concentration camps, wrote that he could neither understand nor forgive such torturers and killers. Further, he argued that no useful purpose would be served by trying to do so. I hope that my book refutes his position, in regard not only to the Nazis but to other evildoers as well. Forgiveness is one thing; understanding is another.

Serial killers have an accentuated need for control over the lives of their victims—a desire to intimidate and terrify—because the psychological and physical abuse that they suffered as children has left them feeling impotent and less worthy than other people.

In fact, they are quite distinct from other malefactors. They have usually been subjected to severe sexual mistreatment. They have not been able to form lasting bonds with any person who could provide them with the compassion and caring necessary to enable them to perceive others as worthy of being treated decently. Almost always male, they are sexually dysfunctional and unable to work or live successfully with others. And they are preoccupied with their lifelong trauma, which fills them with periods of intense resentment and rage.

Unlike most killers, they are subject to a regular pattern of lust for stalking, seducing, sexually intimidating, and then torturing and killing their victims. They are searching for an apocalyptic sexual orgasm that will compensate—by giving them a sense of power, importance, and superiority—for all the abuse they have suffered, but the fulfillment of this fantasy continually eludes them. Disappointed yet again, they direct their fury outward, as if their victims were responsible not only for their immediate lack of sexual release but also for all the hurt they have ever suffered. And they often choose victims who possess similar vulnerabilities as they or someone who has hurt them in the past.

Much as Lifton discovered psychic numbing among his Nazi physicians, prison psychologist Joel Norris found that the incarcerated serial killers he examined were indifferent to the ordeals of their victims.[26] His work, based upon clinical experiences with several murderers, is important because it provides systematic, detailed descriptions of the rituals and cycles that controlled their chaotic lives.

Also from clinical experiences, M. Scott Peck has developed his own theologically focused ideas about evil. Essentially, he echoes Jung: "It is not their sins *per se* that characterize evil people, rather it is the subtlety and persistence and consistency of their sins. This is because the central defect of the evil is not the sin, but the refusal to acknowledge it."[27]

In Peck's view, this refusal is a manifestation of a malignant narcissistic personality, a concept first used by the psychoanalyst and psychologist Erich Fromm to account for evil actions characterized by an unsubmitting will.[28] Fromm theorized that there are three psychological orientations that provide the basis of the most vicious and dangerous forms of malevolent personalities. These disturbed conditions—"love of death," "malignant narcissism," and "symbolic fixation"—when combined, form what Fromm called "the syndrome of decay," which he claims prompts people to destroy for the sake of destruction, and to hate for the sake of hate.

Also influenced by Fromm on this issue, the social psychologist Ervin Staub, after reviewing the literature on mass murder and genocide, theorized that perpetrators change both as individuals and as a group as they become involved in a series of destructive acts that eventuate in mass murder or genocide.[29,30,31] His ideas are more helpful in understanding the behavior of the "foot soldiers" of malevolence—the German soldiers involved in the atrocities, for example, or the followers of Charles Manson—than the motivation of the solitary malevolent individual.

Hannah Arendt argued that malevolence most frequently emanates from the banal mentality of ordinary people, a view that seems most accurately descriptive of the "middle management" of fanatic nationalistic groups like the Nazis, Serbs, and Rwandans. In fact, her theory grew from her observations of Adolf Eichmann during his trial in Israel in the 1970s.[32]

But many theorists have attacked Arendt's basic concept, famously encapsulated in her phrase "the banality of evil." Ernest Becker agrees with her in part about the banality of Eichmann's personal ambition "to be admired and rewarded for a job efficiently done and who wielded his rubber stamp on the death of millions of people with the nonchalance of a postal clerk."[33]

On the other hand, he faults Arendt for failing to recognize that malevolence rests on the passionate motive of perpetuating oneself at all costs, so long as someone else is sacrificed. Becker believes, in other words, that she ignores the rage and contempt that fuel a malevolence which rests like a heated coil just below the surface of the persona, waiting for just the right conditions to trigger acts of cruelty that are firmly rationalized on the basis of the malefactor's previous acts of insensitivity and disregard for others.

Becker's ideas are predicated upon Otto Rank's notion that humans cannot come to terms with the idea of their own death: "All our human problems, with their intolerable suffering, arise from man's ceaseless attempts to make this material world into a man-made reality . . . aiming to achieve on earth a 'perfection' which is only found in the beyond."[34]

In Becker's terms, destructive aggression is fostered by a desire for the kind of power that can erase this very fear of mortality. For today's killer, gaining the power of life and death over others may produce a magical feeling of invincibility against death, much as human sacrifices did in some ancient cultures. But Becker's theories, too, are not without serious shortcomings. Most important, he does not explain why—if humankind fears death—some people deal with their fears with decency and courage, others self-destruct, and still others commit cruel, murderous acts.

Finally, we turn to Erich Fromm, the psychoanalytic theorist whose ideas about malevolence have most strongly guided me in developing my concepts. Fromm was a highly regarded best-selling author in the 1940s and 1950s, whose fame had faded by the middle of the 1960s despite his publishing important work until his death, in 1980. However, even at the crest of his popularity among the general public, who enjoyed the clarity and common sense of his writing, and among academics, who appreciated the intellectual vigor of his work, Fromm was either dismissed or ignored by most of the psychoanalytic establishment.

Undoubtedly, there were many reasons for this lack of appreciation by other psychoanalytic clinicians. However, one stands out most clearly: Fromm not only spoke with an analytic voice that described the causes of neurosis, conflict, and human unhappiness with lucidity and considerable insight, but also spoke with a messianic voice that described the desirable spiritual and moral principles of the ideal society he envisioned. Typically, psychoanalysts have veered away from clinicians who speak baldly about morality, fearing that their efforts to establish psychoanalysis as a scientific enterprise will be compromised by philosophical speculation.

To understand the reasons for Fromm's attention to moral and spiritual values, it is necessary to recognize his theoretical point of departure from Sigmund Freud's ideas. In brief, Freud saw the basic human drives as rooted in our primitive past. Fromm, on the other hand, didn't disregard the importance of our biological nature but emphasized that some of our strongest drives are unique to the human condition. In particular, he indicated that interpersonal relatedness is a cardinal human motivation that cannot be reduced to Freud's pleasure/pain principle. Believing that the satisfaction of specific psychological motives is just as important, often even more crucial, than is satisfying physiological needs, Fromm chose not to focus on what we have in common with our early ancestors, but rather to accentuate the novel characteristics of the human being. His concern with humankind's evolutionary existential condition in the 1940s and 1950s was a completely new approach in psychoanalysis to studying human nature. He began with an examination of the following contradictions in human nature:

1. Although we are animals, our instinctual equipment in comparison with other mammals is incomplete. Unlike them, we are not born with essential survival skills—in our species, speech and manual dexterity—but have to develop them.

2. We share with other animals the capacity to attain practical, immediate aims, but we alone have an awareness of ourselves and our past and a sense of our influence on the future. While this existential sense offers us opportunities to plan ahead and create, it also casts the disturbing shadows of diminution, powerlessness, and termination across our path. As Fromm wrote in *The Heart of Man*, "Human self-awareness has made man a stranger in the world, separate, lonely and frightened."[35]

3. We are subject to nature. But because of our awareness of history and our understanding of how we influence others' actions toward us, we have the intellectual capacity to override our instinctual natures. To do so, however, we must recognize that the contradictions in our nature demand continual choices and decisions, many of which cause angst.

Based upon these three basic contradictions, Fromm maintains that human character prior to experience is neither good nor bad, caring nor antagonistic, compassionate nor indifferent. Rather, our character is shaped by the choices we make throughout our lives:

There is no such thing as the choice between "good" and "evil"— there are concrete and specific actions that are means toward what is good, and others that are means towards what is evil, provided good and evil are properly defined. Our moral conflict on the question of choice arises when we have to make a concrete decision rather than when we choose good or evil in general.[36]

In other words, Fromm did not regard human choices in absolute terms; he conceptualized them as either more progressive or more regressive in the development and realization of our humanity. These choices continually forge our character. He also believed that some people lack the freedom to choose the more virtuous options:

> Their character structure has lost the capacity to act in accordance with the good. Some people have lost the capacity of choosing evil, precisely because their character structure has lost the craving for evil. In these two extreme cases we may say that both are determined to act as they do because the balance of forces in their character leaves them no choice. In the majority of people, however, we deal with contradictory inclinations within the person's character.[37]

If in most cases people actually do have freedom of choice, why have so many philosophers argued that it does not exist?

> The argument for the view that man has no freedom to choose the better as against the worse is to some considerable degree based on the fact that one usually looks at the *last* decision in a chain of events, and not at the first or second ones. Indeed, at the point of final decision the freedom to choose has usually vanished.[38]

Fromm's ideas are based on his readings about malevolent people he never met, rather than on the cases of patients he treated. Consequently, his intuitive theory is not supported by a discussion of the specific psychological and social forces that influence the choices and decisions he recognized as leading to malevolence.

But now, as outlined in Chapter 1, the key concepts that account for malevolent personality development are available to us. In the following chapter, I discuss various obstacles that have prevented our recognizing these factors and applying them constructively to the problem of malevolence. I also suggest how we can circumvent these obstacles so that we can deal effectively with the most serious social problem humankind has ever faced.

CHAPTER THREE

Shame and
Malevolence

I regard as lost the man who
has lost his sense of shame.
— PLAUTUS

DEFINING THE MALEVOLENT PERSONALITY AS BEST WE CAN, COM-ing to grips with the concepts essential to understanding malevolence itself—this was our aim in Chapter One.

But to grasp how the individual actually develops a malevolent personality, we need to look at an interplay of forces and events in a journey toward malevolence that typically progresses through five stages. My terms for these stages are intended to underscore the profound emotional stakes at issue here:

Stage I—Child of scorn: the shaming of the vulnerable child
Stage II—Child of the devil: the inculcation of the "bad" self
Stage III—Transition from victim to perpetrator of malevolence
Stage IV—Experimental malevolence: the proliferation of contempt
Stage V—Forging the malevolent personality: the devil's representative in atrocity

Before we look more closely at each of these phases, let me make clear that they are not rigorously separate from one another. On the contrary, there is usually an overlap between one stage and the next to follow.

The concept of separate stages is nonetheless valuable, however, because each stage can be seen as a distinctive crucible for a specific type of healing approach. The therapist working with a child experiencing Stage I, for example, can work most effectively in transforming her supposedly "wicked" or "immoral" behavior by dealing with the issue of negative personal identity.

STAGE I—CHILD OF SCORN

Shame and pride are the monitors of our personal identity. When a child can feel pride in his competence and knows that he has won the esteem of others, he forms a sense of positive personal identity. But if he is instead disregarded and mistreated, and indeed subjected to a pattern of humiliation and shame, he will acquire a negative personal identity. This depleted sense of self-worth is not passive. It will continually inform him in painful, destructive ways that he is incompetent, inadequate, unwanted. In thus diminishing one's sense of self-regard, chronic shame prevents the individual from positively defining himself to others and also leaves him vulnerable to their further abuse and neglect. In sum, shame undermines both the child's sense of well-being and his interpersonal relationships.

If she is unable to express clearly her feelings of hurt and anguish, she develops a disparaging inner "narrative voice" that constantly warns her away from situations in which she might again be hurt or painfully exposed. Her dilemma is especially cruel because the situations that test or reveal vulnerability are likely also to be the most opportune occasions for receiving attention and affection. In other words, the child afflicted with a negative personal identity is always at risk when she asks for what she craves most.

STAGE II—CHILD OF THE DEVIL

Children begin to imagine the ideal intimate encounter during the "age of belief"—between the ages of four and eight. An ideal person, embellished with details borrowed from actual people the child encounters, is sought over the years, until the age when objects of desire actually become accessible.

If a child's early experiences of lust and desire are treated in healthy ways by his caretakers, he will have good feelings about these yearnings. But if he is treated with shame and betrayal by his caretakers during his first awakenings of strong desire, they will impose a sense of badness upon his personal identity—that is, they will inculcate a "bad" self in the child. This conviction that he is somehow "bad" will be strengthened when others continually inform him, either verbally or through their actions, that he is flawed and unwanted.

In order to try to hide from his painful badness, a child in this second stage of malevolence will lie and practice deceit—with himself as well as with others. Such deceit, of course, makes effective self-examination very difficult.

In other words, since the sense of badness cannot readily be recognized and understood, it cannot easily be uprooted and replaced with reasonable expectations for oneself. On the contrary, the inculcated, hidden feelings of self-contempt gradually stabilize the child's negative personal identity. He becomes convinced that he is helpless and all alone in the world.

STAGE III—TRANSITION FROM VICTIM TO PERPETRATOR OF MALEVOLENCE

Unrelieved, unremitting self-contempt is virtually unbearable. To survive both psychologically and physically, the sufferer must somehow cast off the terrible feelings of self-hate. Some sufferers try *bravado,* performing risky or heroic deeds in order to restore self-esteem. If this course fails, *shamelessness* is likely to follow, demonstrating indifference toward society's approval or disapproval of one's behavior.

In the two previous stages, the sufferer passively tolerated shame and humiliation inflicted by others; now she will lash out, becoming the perpetrator of malevolence. Using rationalizations and other forms of justification for insensitive behavior, she convinces herself that any indecencies she is about to commit have already been, or will soon be, directed at her. Indeed, the perpetrator comes to believe that everyone in the world should be held responsible for committing or permitting mistreatment of her.

Deprived of the benefit of self-examination, the self-hating individual is prone to *magical thinking,* a suspension of any critical assessment of her personality or behavior. She does not need to improve her character when magically convinced that she is already special; obviously, only the flawed perceptions of others prevent her superiority from being recognized. As perpetrator now, she will use whatever means are available to convince others of her special status.

STAGE IV—EXPERIMENTAL MALEVOLENCE

In order to continue behaving contemptuously toward others over the years, the self-hating individual must rationalize ever more desperately, thereby perceiving himself and other people ever more inaccurately. Each rationalized choice to behave insensitively chips away at his freedom of choice until, inevitably, cruel behavior is always and unarguably justified. At one extreme, the malevolent criminal may rationalize that he is providing a social benefit—that is, he explains that he does what others would like to do if they were not too "gutless" or dishonest to admit it. He is a role model for the fearful, inspiring them to stand up for their authentic aspirations.

At this fourth stage, other people can be seriously harmed as a result of the perpetrator's indifference to their well-being. He has not yet, however, begun to inflict cruelty or cause destruction intentionally.

STAGE V—FORGING THE MALEVOLENT PERSONALITY

At this stage, the perpetrator is accustomed to using magical thinking instead of self-knowledge to deal with his disquieting doubts about the possible absence of meaning in his life. When reality threatens his magical notions, he is likely to erupt in the cruel, destructive behaviors of atrocity.

Basically, three types of people practice actrocity—foot soldiers, leaders, and lone wolves.

Under normal circumstances, such heinous criminals as Adolph Eichmann, the paramilitary killers in Serbia, and the terrorist followers of fanatical religious leaders will appear as innocuous and absurd as Dickens's Uriah Heep[1]—perhaps annoying because of petty displays of self-importance but easily dismissed and forgotten. Fearful and unreflective, they are emotionally trapped in barren lives. But during stressful periods of great social unrest, these people find themselves magnetically drawn to malevolent leaders and become the *foot soldiers* of atrocity. They make a terrible bargain: in exchange for their services, the forces of malevolence grant them a role in a powerful movement that gives to their lives at last some semblance of meaning, however vicious.

The *leaders* of such movements have, like their foot soldiers, progressed into the fifth stage of malevolence. People are drawn to them because of some outstanding physical, social, or psychological attribute and because they are skillful in articulately justifying their advocacy of brutality. To accept their message is to participate in a magical triumph over one's own weakness by joining in attacking others: the malevolent leader is seen to be living an enviably higher "good" than are the "weak" and "cowardly" upon whom he imposes his will.

Lone wolf perpetrators are most often involved in serial or mass murder and are more likely than the other two types to be diagnosed as "mentally ill." Their psychological disabilities prevent them from interacting easily with other people; even other perpetrators regard them as "odd." Typically, they commit their crimes either alone or with only one other, similarly disturbed lone wolf.

The frightening consequences of Stage V may cause it to seem far removed from Stage I, but the progression can be like a boulder rolling down a hill, gradually and terrifyingly accelerating. It all begins simply enough with shame, the crucial concept in Stage I.

The stories that follow—of adults unaware of the psychological factors that motivate their behavior toward each other—reveal the roles played by shame in fostering malevolence.

Near 6:00 P.M. on a weekday in December 1993, Colin Ferguson walked through the third car of the rush-hour commuter train to Long Island as it approached Garden City. Nearly one hundred passengers were seated or standing in the car, most lost in thought or engrossed in their newspapers. When the impassive Ferguson reached the end of the car, he drew a 9-mm Ruger semiautomatic from a carrying case, took careful aim, and shot three men dead. As he began shooting randomly, panicked commuters rushed to the exits, which were locked, pounding and screaming for help.

Ferguson was heard yelling over the tumult: "I'm going to get you."

He calmly reloaded his weapon and shot still more passengers. By the time he was subdued by courageous, unarmed men in the car, Ferguson had killed or fatally wounded six commuters and seriously hurt many more.

What triggered this apparently senseless rampage?

We may never know for certain, but some commonly predictable factors are missing. For instance, there are no reports of abuse or serious trauma in Ferguson's upbringing. He was born into the advantages and securities of an upper-middle-class household; he was able to attend an exclusive private high school. In sum, it would appear that the usual explanations of behavioral scientists to account for a brutal attack upon a group of strangers do not apply in this case.

The problem in accurately assessing Ferguson's behavior stems from the overarching psychology we accept in contemporary life. Derived originally from the guilt morality of the Judeo-Christian tradition, this shared psychology insists that stories like the Hicksville shootings require us to specify first a victim, second the guilty perpetrator. But this approach, though psychologically satisfying and legally necessary, does not enable us to understand the motivation behind Colin Ferguson's actions on the commuter train.

On the other hand, understanding how shame can explain malevolent acts will provide us with a view of human behavior quite different from the Judeo-Christian model. In most conflicts of daily life, we learn, all of those involved are victims.

Previous to Ferguson's rampage, there had been numerous occasions when he became angry and abusive with others for failing, in his view, to meet his needs adequately. For example, he accused bewildered administrative personnel of racial prejudice after he failed his college courses, refusing to recognize that his poor class attendance was responsible. In turn, other people apparently felt helpless to respond adequately to his behavior and certainly did not provide the guidance he required. In these angry interactions with others, the important dynamic in Ferguson's behavior seems to have been the phenomenon of *intersubjective shame* (a concept examined in this chapter). During experiences that involve intersubjective shame, victim and perpetrator are mutually influenced by each other's inarticulate inner hurt.

To explore this serious problem in a less incendiary case than Ferguson's, we will analyze the ordinary-seeming story of Richard and Jennifer. Neither is a criminal or even has cruel and hurtful tendencies; on the contrary, both are intelligent, decent, and compassionate. Yet in a moment of stress, contempt aroused in one of them by the unrecognized shame in the other brought out uncharacteristically cruel behavior. In anyone's life, such unrecognized shame can produce disasters. Whether in the decent person or in the violent perpetrator like Ferguson, the same acerbic emotional syndrome of shame is key to developing the character structure of malevolence.

Just after eight o'clock on a Tuesday morning, there was a soft knock at the door of Richard's high-rise apartment in Manhattan. He assumed that his fiancée, Jennifer, a book editor who had stayed the night and left for work only fifteen minutes earlier, must have forgotten something. Perhaps trying too hard to get to her office on time, she had left a manuscript behind.

Indeed, when he opened the door, there stood Jennifer, a small, slim woman with dark, alluring Mediterranean features, her soft hair worn long. Richard felt a sudden rush of uneasiness, for she seemed frozen in place, with her eyes downcast and her slight shoulders rounded. Himself a man of imposing height and presence, an aggressive advertising executive, he knew this posture very well. Obviously, something terrible had happened.

"What is it, honey?" he asked. "What happened?"

"Someone took my money," she replied bitterly, "stole my whole wallet." She broke down in sobs.

Rather than immediately comforting her, Richard felt his emotions reel. His thoughts raced back over the five years they had been together, recalling incidents that had exasperated him. As he found himself growing angrier, he managed to keep his thoughts to himself by drawing a deep breath. *Jennifer, when will you ever learn to take care of yourself!* he wanted to say. *Why don't you just hand over your hard-earned money to anyone you find in the street! That way, at least, you won't have to worry about being robbed!*

This scornful inner diatribe uncorked his contemptuous feelings. Glaring at Jennifer with unmistakable disgust, disregarding the consequences, he baldly told her that he felt nothing but pity for her.

"If I ever loved you, it was a sick love," he added. "It doesn't mean anything any longer."

Without a word of protest, Jennifer turned and fled down the corridor, blindly making her way down several flights of stairs to the lobby. Sobbing aloud, she bolted into the street, running wildly until the stares of passersby embarrassed her into slowing down and trying to conceal her agitation. Torn between self-contempt and self-pity, she collapsed in her lonely studio apartment.

Why does Richard hate me so much that he could be so cruel? she asked herself. She pictured the angry words of the man she had hoped to marry as her epitaph. This was the end of her dream of sharing a happy, meaningful life with another person. She was doomed forever to solitude and intense loneliness.

Her reaction, of course, is extreme, and illuminatingly so. For most of us, shame seems to be an occasional and not very devastating emotion: shyness in a new situation, feelings of foolishness after committing a social faux pas, keeping secret some minor moral transgression. But shame as a force in our emotional lives extends far beyond these recognizable situations. In fact, I would estimate that more than 90 percent of our everyday experiences of shame remain buried beneath the surface of conscious awareness. There is a mechanism of denial: during moments of serious shame, both our painful hurt and our ability to identify what we are experiencing can be "bypassed." Instead of a conscious image of what is happening to us, the hurt is registered on the psyche as a sharp but momentary "wince" or "jolt."[2]

But like an invisible electric current, the cloaked emotion of shame can cause serious harm. Jennifer's humiliating moment with Richard is not an isolated event in her life. Therefore, even if he were to apologize for his wretched behavior and try to renew their relationship, she cannot quickly get past her intense pain. Her self-condemnation is part and parcel of a pervasive, persistent, destructive set of emotions that cripples her existence with terror and pessimism. The results, a lifetime of cover-ups about feelings of inadequacy and an inability to share them with anyone else, has intensified her misery.

We can understand her situation only by learning exactly how shame plays such a crucial role in establishing our sense of who we are.

SHAME AND PERSONAL IDENTITY

Personal identity is a highly complex affair. Not only does it consist of the sense of who one is currently; it also includes beliefs and desires about who one should be and can become. As a result, every interaction and action on one's part might possibly be judged in terms of the information they provide for either substantiating or denying the self one desires to be.

When there is a harmonious fit between the experiences of the *tested self* (the conclusions drawn from our sense of the circumstances of our lives) and the images, fantasies, and intentions of our *desired identity,* we feel competent. In this instance, as defined by the psychologist Robert White, *competence* is an expression of the ability, fitness, and capacity to wage life effectively.[3]

In contrast, the experience of being shamed instills a conviction of incompetence. Consequently, the potential for *shame anxiety* appears when there is disparity between the tested self and the desired self.[4] Shame, in other words, is the powerful and unquestioned conviction that in some important way one is flawed and incompetent as a person.

It would be unrealistic, of course, to believe that we could always be the self we want to be. Even with the kindest of parents, the cream of life experiences, and the gift of conveying a sense of competence and self-confidence, we are all vulnerable to a critical assault on our self-worth by people who are significant to us.[5]

Certainly, worldly success is no reliable shield from the insecurities that invoke shame. Agatha Christie, the internationally beloved and best-selling mystery novelist, could only once in her long life bring herself to attend a party given to celebrate the usual rave reviews and financial success of one of her books. According to her grandson, she was painfully shy and terrified of making a fool of herself. Sadly, Dame Christie's shyness was in effect a shrinking away from the potential of her full presence in the world. This depleted sense of personal identity, for both the famous and the obscure, is an essential characteristic of shame.

Recently, a very successful corporate executive confessed his sense of humiliation to a *New York Times* reporter: "I'm responsible for overseeing about one billion dollars a year and sometimes I think maybe the fact that

I am ruled by this one thing—cigarettes—means that the wrong person is sitting in this chair. Sometimes I think the kid in the stockroom who doesn't smoke is brighter than I am."

The manager of a health care system, this executive goes to great lengths to avoid being seen smoking by his employees. Appropriately, our word "shame" comes from the Indo-European root *schame,* meaning "to hide" or "to cover up."

Many of us create masks to hide our hurts and humiliation—masks that convincingly smile or laugh, as if we harbored absolutely no psychic pain inside. But the truth is that no one is effectively immune to feelings of shame. At different moments of our lives, some aspect or other of the self will appear shameful.

Nor do we have to be humiliated in a direct, verbal way. If a friend or an acquaintance passes in the street without speaking, we might suddenly feel uninteresting or unattractive to other people. In such cases, it may do little good to reason that the acquaintance was probably preoccupied. Shamed, we are convinced that the disregard was an intentional slight.

For most of us, fortunately, such reactions are only occasional, but for others, being ashamed has become their continuous sense of being-in-the-world. When, for example, someone feels habitually taken advantage of in his significant relationships or on the job, but also feels powerless to change these situations because of fear of losing his livelihood or his role in a dependent relationship, he is the victim of *debilitating shame.* In the throes of this condition, he will feel that life is happening to him, that he is helpless.[6]

Such painful shame threatens the integrity of personal identity, instilling doubts about one's competence and self-worth. The eventual result is what psychoanalyst Erik Erikson has called *negative personal identity,* a contemptuous sense of self in which one feels scornful and hostile "towards roles of responsibilities provided by family and society for the achievement of esteem."[7]

Being regarded as "incompetent" is Jennifer's primary vulnerability to shame. Sadly, her lifelong mistrust of her own common sense renders her dependent upon the opinions of others; thus, she values Richard's opinion of her worth as a human being more than her own. To her, this clear-thinking, knowledgeable man of the world mirrors reality. His criticism becomes an ordaining message, validating her fearful innermost beliefs about herself. When he perceived her to be inadequate, incomplete, and inferior, he finally confirmed her own continuing nightmare of being helpless to protect herself from the abuses of living.

Jennifer, like other easily humiliated people, is likely to become upset by interactions and events that most people either do not notice or regard as too inconsequential to warrant any emotional involvement. For example, Jennifer is often deeply upset when a store clerk doesn't smile or thank her for making a purchase. In reaction, she has usually felt compelled to show the item to Richard and ask if he thinks she really needs it.

Not only does this dependency cause her to be ashamed of herself; it also persuades her that she can never be part of a relationship characterized by mutual respect, dignity, and pride. Too embarrassed by her displays of incompetence to ask Richard or anyone else for help with her feelings of shame, she experiences a hopelessness so absolute that she wants only to flee.

But she cannot break free, because she is unable to believe that any moment in the future will be different from the present pain, too entrenched in her way of being to imagine a way out. She is not even aware that the root of her suffering is this devastating, self-blaming sense of shame.

Can she be written off as hopelessly high-strung and unstable? Perhaps surprisingly, the emotional cripple we've seen so far would be unrecognizable to her professional colleagues. Highly regarded as an editor, Jennifer never hesitates to offer her informed opinions on literature or publishing practices.

Why is someone capable of such superior intellectual functioning so clearly incapable of using her intelligence effectively to discover what is actually bothering her . . . and then take constructive action to alleviate her disturbed feelings about herself? This apparent absurdity is not so unusual as it might seem at first glance. Let's look for a moment at how easily most of us accept the familiar psychological explanations that social scientists have provided for explaining neurotic behavior.

Influenced by Sigmund Freud, theories of psychiatry have commonly accounted for human misery by resorting to the guilty-conscience rationale.

By this reasoning, a Hedda Nussbaum sets herself up for being brutalized by a Joel Steinberg; she feels that she deserves such punishment for morally unacceptable thoughts and/or deeds in her past. Moreover, she unconsciously believes that the mistreatment will cleanse her of these sins. Even though common sense may suggest that it is hardly compassionate to blame the victim for her suffering, clinical theory nonetheless goes even farther today: many psychotherapists promote the outrageous belief that Nussbaums perversely seek out abuse because the pain itself has become a pleasure.

In fact, my work as a psychoanalyst strongly suggests that the Freudians' emphasis on the guilty-conscience theory ignores the existence of much more constructive avenues for understanding human unhappiness and doing something about it. The very concepts "masochism," "sadism," and "guilty conscience" are only rarely verifiable with evidence.

In Jennifer's situation, for example, Freudian thinking might encourage us to read her hysterical flight from Richard's apartment as an admission of her guilt. But guilty of what? Certainly, her fiancé thinks she is "guilty" of incompetence, but guilt is derived from a violation of the moral code, such as intentionally acting to harm or violate someone else.

Yet Jennifer was the victim, not the perpetrator, of the wrongful act of robbery. Shame and guilt have been confused by Richard's reaction, and the confusion causes Jennifer to be punished for her victimization. For people suffering her affliction, the pattern can result in continued punishment, over and over again.

It would be a mistake—and quite a common one—to attribute Jennifer's unhappiness to guilt over some unknown wrongful act. All too frequently, we unthinkingly make the same misjudgment about friends who are actually harboring a feeling of shame that causes them to feel like the helpless victim or powerless observer of some grievous event.

For example, many people feel helpless at being unable to avert illness in themselves or to save others from disease and death. Indeed, a powerful barrier to responding to the needs of victims of AIDS is the anger that potential caretakers among family and friends may feel toward the patient. This anger, seeded by a feeling of helplessness, blames the victim for rendering the caretaker unable to affect the inevitable downward course of the illness. Such reactions are often misread as stemming from guilt rather than from shame, perhaps because guilt has an articulate voice but shame is generally experienced as an unfathomable uneasiness, expressible, as in Jennifer's case, only as a muffled cry.

For this reason, I would go so far as to describe shame as an *ironic* emotion: often, the stronger the experience of shame, the less the sufferer is aware of her true feelings. As Jennifer's hurt intensified under Richard's disapproving glare, she became increasingly unable to do anything constructive about her unhappiness. At the same time, this heightened shaming made it increasingly difficult for her to understand and express what she was actually feeling at that moment.

But if she had been guilty of wrongful behavior, she might well have felt less pain, misery, and confusion. Suppose that Richard accused her of encouraging a coworker's flirtations during a party they both attended, and she admitted that she had done so. In this instance, the solution for Richard's jealousy is readily available. There are conventional words and agreed-upon actions for admitting guilt, which enable the wrongdoer not only to confess but also to redeem herself. Jennifer might acknowledge that she enjoys feeling attractive to other men and then promise that she will never again encourage their attentions. She can ask Richard for forgiveness, affirming that he is the only man she really loves.

After the robbery, however, Jennifer has nothing to confess. She simply has no idea what happens within her psyche to prevent her from taking proper care of herself. But to the outside observer, her agitation is not necessarily so mystifying.

The helpless despair felt by victims of shame is continually fueled by a feeling of "lack of legitimate entitlement" to those aspects of life that create a happy, fulfilling existence. The term "legitimate entitlement" is best understood by looking at how we react to the innumerable everyday situations that suggest potentially exciting interpersonal opportunities. What do you do when your eyes encounter someone you find very appealing walking down the street or sitting across the aisle in a train? Smile in order to encourage the attention of this attractive person? Or nonchalantly pretend to be unaware of her? Or, even more sadly, quickly avert your glance in embarrassment?

When Jennifer responds to an attractive stranger, she almost always averts her eyes, a common sign of shame. She never feels that she deserves

the best. By contrast, people who feel a healthy sense of legitimate entitlement are confident that those they find attractive will respond in kind.
They believe that they "deserve" to find and gain friendship or intimacy
with the most appealing, interesting, and worthwhile people available.

Not surprisingly, feelings of lack of legitimate entitlement replay the
shameful, humiliating events of one's past. To a child, his mother's face is
a window on the external world through which he forms a sense of who
he is. Children depend almost entirely upon maintaining an exact correspondence between their voracious needs and the attentiveness of a
warm, approving caretaker. If an infant is feeling happy, then sees an expression of anger, depression, or hurt in his mother's face, his confidence
in his own perceptions falters momentarily. He assumes that his mother's
face is reflecting *his* inner state. If such experiences occur on a regular
basis, he learns to distrust his ability to make judgments. The younger
children are and the more often they are shamed, the more pliant they
become to unfair and abusive treatment.

Shame represents a special fear. It operates similarly to animal instincts for self-preservation. The actions evoking shame in children are
experienced as threatening to their survival at a period of development in
which they are incapable of an accurate assessment of reality. The adult
who is shamed returns to the feelings of fear of abandonment by his caretakers that he experienced as a child. At that excruciatingly painful moment—whether in childhood or in adulthood—the ashamed feels small,
helpless, and worthless. Time seems large and endless. He experiences
no way to escape, because he senses no time in the future when he expects to be beyond the present painful moment.

Obviously, any parent's ability to be emotionally, physically, and spiri-
tually available to a child at all times is subject to reasonable strains and
limitations. In preparing to discipline a child, parents are often unable to
perceive a distinction between a wrongful act they disapprove of and the
child's entire personality as flawed and worthless. Consequently, in these
instances, they are unable to convey clearly to their child that they love
and value him but are displeased by a specific deed he has committed. In
other words, many parents are unable to make the separation between
their child's improper behavior and the child's being a "bad" child—either
in their own thinking or in statements to the child. The operating belief is
that only inherently bad children can do bad things. Consequently, when

the child is punished and the focus of the punishment is the child's character rather than his specific behaviors, shame rather than constructive guilt is fostered. Such faults in the early caretaking relationship are not alone responsible for creating the debilitating shame that produces the malevolent personality. Rather, it is the result, as stories in the next few chapters will illustrate, of shame-sensitive people acting in collusion with those who humiliate them on an ongoing basis.

Initially, under the aegis of others, the person embarked upon a life of malevolence will act as if magically imbued with special hateful qualities that set her apart from everyone else. Actually, she is ashamed of her limitations. Because she does not harbor an essential sense of her own goodness, she is put in harm's way as a potential victim of the cycle of malevolence. She has come to believe that she is destined for wickedness; consequently, all of the adversities and miseries of those around her, as well as her own, are her fault.

A variety of sources, in addition to childhood abuse or neglect, can produce this feeling of predilection for malevolence. For example, it is high among those who have been subjected to expectations they are not equipped to meet. In the cases of Jason (Chapter 10) and the Reverend Jim Jones (Chapter 11), the humiliation, duplicity, and coercion they inflicted on their victims sprang from the unreasonable demands of their families, who expected to be saved from the ills and offenses of the world. The Jasons and Jim Joneses have been repeatedly inculcated with shame by the message that being less than perfect is equivalent to being wicked; rendering one undeserving of human company.

Still another type of shaming, betrayal, can be found in malevolent people who commit atrocities, like the serial killer and cannibal Jeffrey Dahmer. He had been adamant that his parents never mistreated him or were unreasonably demanding. But his recollections were steeped in other kinds of humiliation, such as the shame and betrayal he experienced in regard to his bedridden, emotionally unstable mother and his remote, inattentive father; who, as he said, "just didn't seem to like each other very much,"[8] and were unaware of the loneliness and self-hatred he suffered through childhood and adolescence.

Dahmer's recollections show that he also felt betrayed by classmates and authority figures with whom he tried to make emotional contact. As a preadolescent, he tried to show his fondness for a favorite teacher by giving her a jar filled with tadpoles he had caught. She thanked him, apparently appreciating this gift. Some days later, when he went to visit a classmate at home, he happened upon the same jar of tadpoles in a corner of the garage. This was just one of many times, according to Dahmer, that he felt betrayed in his childhood years.

So far, I've discussed only clinical and anecdotal evidence to support my conviction that a malevolent personality develops when severe shame and humiliation are experienced as a regular component of one's life. Recently, research published by a group of psychologists at George Mason University made a related discovery: people prone to feeling shame about their behavior tend to exhibit unconstructive responses when they become angry in a relationship significantly more often than people who are more susceptible to guilt. Specifically, the shame-sensitive participants in the study either reacted passively by withdrawing from the relationship or took the extreme of expressing vehement retaliation.[9]

Why should this be?

To begin with, in the response of another to our overtures for friendship and intimacy we tend to see reflections of how we have been led to regard ourselves from early in life. If we were permitted to be useful and attractive only in limited ways in our own families or in countless other significant growing-up experiences, we may be emotionally crippled by feelings of shame and pessimism.

In many families, one or two members become targets of blame for whatever problems the whole family is experiencing. Jennifer served this role. Throughout her growing years, various relatives repeatedly said or did hurtful things to her, all the while ignoring her emotional needs. Because her immigrant parents had trouble making ends meet for their large family, she was made to feel a burden, an unwanted younger child.

Although Jennifer still longed for the privileges her more affluent classmates regarded as their birthright—ballet and piano lessons, higher education—her hardworking mother was unsympathetic. "You ask too much," she said often. "Sometimes I wish you'd never been born." Jennifer did make it to college, but when she bought some expensive clothes, her father exploded in anger: "The more education you get, the dumber you are."

Jennifer, and many of the rest of us, may have moved away physically from our families yet continue to perpetuate the limited ways of expressing ourselves that they have imposed upon us. If we dislike our appearance, the way we speak or walk, or the fact that we are less intelligent, skilled, or admired than someone else, then we are victims of our own shame and self-contempt, which were taught to us in the bowels of our families.

And yet Jennifer was not the only victim on the morning of Richard's callous treatment. There was Richard himself. Unless we appreciate the precise way in which Richard is also a victim of shame, we cannot grasp the complexity of this debilitating factor in our emotional lives.

Let's examine the very important consideration that much of the hurtful shame we are usually involved in—as either the shamer or the ashamed—arises from our inability to protect those whom we love. In other words, the shaming that is normally a part of our daily lives is not the result of intentional meanness or even ill wishes.

Richard's side of the story will show that shaming events leave few participants unscarred, but first we need the groundwork for understanding this cruel reciprocity.

INTERSUBJECTIVE SHAME

According to the German philosopher Georg Hegel, shame is an anger about "what ought not to be."[10] His definition proves to be exceedingly accurate in everyday life. Take the allegorical case of a father who slaps his young daughter when she runs home crying, her knees badly bruised from falling out of a tree. Viewed from the outside, he is punishing her for wrongdoing, acting as society's representative in trying to discipline her into taking proper care of herself. His anger and her guilt seem to be the major emotions at play here.

But the view from within the father's psyche is quite different. Caretaker of the child, he loves her deeply. Seeing how vulnerable she is to injury upsets and frightens him. Moreover, he is ashamed that he has failed as her protector. This forced recognition of his inability to shelter his daughter from all harm stirs anger and resentment against "what ought not to be." In other words, he feels self-recrimination that he is not an adequate father. To expunge this painful impotence that he neither understands nor knows how to deal with, he strikes out at his daughter.

In addition, by blaming her for his uncomfortable feelings, he unconsciously transforms his daughter from victim of injury to perpetrator of a wrongful act: she was irresponsible to climb the tree. By so doing, his anger serves to protect him by separating him from his vulnerable identification with the girl and by diminishing his own vulnerability to feeling impotent as her protector.

But a dangerous precedent is now established in the father's repertoire of moral judgments. In punishing his daughter for behavior that makes him aware of his own impotence, he will find it all the more difficult in the future to respond empathically to her pain and confusion. For that matter, if he repeats this pattern, he will find it increasingly difficult to respond to anyone else with care and concern.

He is not alone. Most of us have not learned to identify the feelings of shame caused by a despairing sense of helplessness, much less express them directly. We, too, are more likely to respond with annoyance and anger in the face of events that assault our sense of self-worth.

Unfortunately, such secondary reactions to shame as anger are powerful, surging emotions. They can cause explosions that capture the attention of others, temporarily overthrowing our feelings of impotence and isolation. But anger—especially when it leads to violence and abuse of other people—produces painful embarrassment, making a further assault on our sense of being in control and evoking still more shame. In sum, the combination of fierce reactions to being shamed with the inability to recognize what is at work can cause a vicious cycle of uncontrollable emotion.

Given this background, let's consider Richard's point of view. Standing in the doorway that morning, he had flashbacks to several other experiences with his fiancée.

One wintry evening just six months before, for example, Jennifer had also arrived on his doorstep visibly upset. She had been mugged and robbed a couple of hours earlier in a subway station. She had not called the police.

"It's too humiliating," she said, "to have to tell them that this has happened several times already." She had simply walked back up out of the station and wandered aimlessly through the snowy streets for more than an hour.

Richard responded very differently then. Gently drawing Jennifer into his apartment, he took her briefcase and helped her take off her heavy winter coat and boots. He put his arms around her reassuringly and guided her to the sofa. He held her close, and they sat there for a long time without speaking.

When at last she began to stir, he told her with tears in his eyes how susceptible he was to her feelings. He said that her hurts, fears, and sorrows made him feel as if he were being jabbed by something sharp. In a split second, he went on, he could sense when something was wrong with her, even if they were talking on the telephone. This attunement with her feelings was spontaneous, he explained, not the result of any effort to be empathic and understanding.

But Richard decided that evening that his emotional responsiveness was not enough. He felt bound to teach his fiancée how to protect herself and her valuables. To his surprise and dismay, however, Jennifer rapidly became bored and annoyed when he tried to explain a few effective, practical strategies for taking care of herself on the city streets. What he could not recognize, understandably, was that Jennifer is like most shame-vulnerable people in that she specializes only in those activities at which she excels, avoiding those that make her anxious and uncomfortable. In this case, she airily dismissed Richard's concern for her safety, maintaining that thinking constantly about such things is not worth the trouble. As a matter of fact, she said, it angered her that she had to concern herself with the "psychopaths" who preyed on her. Richard let the matter drop.

There was yet another incident, only a month previous to his blowup, when the two of them took a taxi home one night. Jennifer paid the fare, setting her purse on the seat as she reached forward to hand the money to the driver. Only after he was pulling around the corner did she realize that she had left her purse in the cab. She began yelling, but it was too late.

"I am worthless!" she sobbed, as they entered Richard's apartment. "I am a loser! I can't do anything right!"

This time, Richard was surprised to find himself feeling uncharacteristically cool to her suffering. He perceived that he was not only annoyed by her carelessness but also angry that she had not listened to his advice about protecting her valuables. If she had, she would still have her purse. He realized that he was very uneasy, too, about Jennifer's vulnerability and her inability to protect herself.

But his fiancée's desperately self-punitive mood gradually overcame his irritation. He saw that the most important thing for him to be concerned about at the moment was neither the lost money nor her carelessness but the depth of her dejection. He urgently wanted her to know and believe that she was a valuable person in her own right and he truly loved her. Putting his anger and uneasiness aside, he hugged her and spoke softly of her many admirable attributes.

Although the earlier incidents ended tenderly, they nonetheless paved the way for Richard's final outburst, for he realized with dismay that his close identification with Jennifer portended continual hurt and rage for himself. He found the precariousness of her life upsetting, her despair intolerable. Their sanctuary of intimacy had become a crucible of self-hatred.

Moreover, because Richard realized that she would continually depend upon him for reassurance that her life was worth continuing, he saw that he was no longer willing, or able, to assuage her misery. The only way he could escape his unbearable feelings of helplessness in taking care of her was to tell her with heavy irony that he felt sorry for her—even though he intuited that this would drive her away. For self-protection, he suppressed his tender feelings and acted as if he no longer cared about her.

Why was the seemingly self-confident and highly competent Richard so vulnerable to Jennifer's shame? The answer lies in his own childhood. Because his mother was highly critical and made incessant demands on him for attention, he felt safer with his father, who always seemed to understand and love him.

But just a few months before Richard's fifth birthday, his father mysteriously disappeared. Although the boy peppered his mother and other relatives for an explanation, he got only the vague (and, he would later realize, embarrassed) reassurance that his father was away working and would be home "soon." Finally, a few weeks before his birthday, a letter from his father arrived. Richard remembers to this day what his mother read to him: that his father would be home in time for his birthday, that he would be bringing a wonderful gift for his son.

The waiting seemed endless. But his father did not show up. At his birthday party, the other boys asked, "Where is your father? Don't you have a father?" In Richard's eyes, this was the first time his father had ever lied to him. Confused, he assumed that he must have done something awful to make his father so angry. Every night, he bolted awake from nightmares with scenarios in which he was responsible for his father's disappearance.

Then, a week after Richard's birthday, his father suddenly reappeared. He did not tell Richard where he'd been or why he'd missed the party. He just smiled, said "Happy birthday, son!" and handed Richard the promised gift.

In that instant, and from then on, Richard considered the man he had known as his father to be a stranger—someone he neither recognized nor trusted. Even though this man acted as if he knew Richard well, the boy would realize in retrospect that no gift could erase his bitter disappointment at being deserted and left alone to endure his mother's bitterness.

Today, Richard does not remember what the gift was, but he distinctly recalls how he hurled it to the floor and how his father reacted. Surprised, the man turned quickly away, as if he was furiously trying to compose himself. From that day forward, Richard felt his father's displeasure in virtually all matters, except for the boy's achievements in academics and athletics.

Nevertheless, Richard continued to view his father as a man of strong character and high moral values. He lived in fear that if he ever did anything wrong, his father would somehow know and would again desert him. Consequently, he was dumbfounded to learn from his mother when he was an adult that his father had left home because she had banished him. She had caught him in an affair with one of her friends.

As it happens, I knew Richard's father well. The rancor and disapproval the five-year-old boy saw in his father's eyes was actually the man's own diminished self-regard. Until his son's angry rejection of the gift, the man had considered himself a reliable father and assumed that his son would never question his love. The boy's rejection revealed the hard truth.

Indeed, our feelings of shame come not only from revealing our frailties to others but also, and perhaps more important, from being forced to face in ourselves some aspect of our vulnerabilities that has gone unrecognized. In this case, shame arises from realizing that one has lived a lie and is closely associated with animosity directed toward oneself. For people like Richard's father, this kind of shameful experience is impossible to communicate to another human being. And since the moments or revelations we cannot share are our most terrifying, they frighten us into flight and secrecy, leaving us isolated.

As disturbing as his father's shame might have been for him, it had a no less devastating effect on Richard. His father's continual sense of inadequacy about how his life had been lived fostered a destructive bond between him and his son.

Indeed, shame is highly contagious. It can be broadcast, as it were, in such subtle, indirect ways that the recipient, though sensitive and vulnerable, is unaware of the painful feelings of humiliation that are being communicated. This process is called *borrowing shame,* and very few of us go through life without at some time or other acquiring this unfair burden. We are especially susceptible when a person we care about or closely identify with is harboring self-punitive feelings.

Although Richard cared deeply for his father, he was too young to recognize what had happened to the man or help with his pain. On the contrary, the boy interpreted his own bad feelings to suggest that he was the one who had done something wrong. Understandably, he could not recognize that he was "borrowing" his father's sense of failure and wrongdoing. When a child tries to love a parent but is unable to do so because of unrecognized borrowed shame, he is apt to explain this inability by deciding that something deficient, wrong, or even wicked in him is preventing him from doing the right thing.

Richard's story shows how a child's borrowed shame, resulting from close identification with a beloved parent, is just as effective in causing toxic shame as physical or emotional abuse. Moreover, this particular source of shame is more difficult to recognize than direct abuse, and therefore more difficult to deal with constructively.

My task in this chapter is not complete. We should not leave this story without asking ourselves what any of us could have done differently had we been in Richard's or Jennifer's situation. For shame, I believe, *can* be healed other ways than through prolonged recourse to an analyst's couch. Indeed, there is much all of us can do in our everyday lives to address shame effectively.

First, we must replace the outmoded view that focuses on the remote shadows of our childhood as the major causes of our present unhappiness. Of course, each of us is influenced by the mishandling and the misfortunes of our early days as well as by the good things that transpired in our lives. However, as we should be able to see from her story, Jennifer had opportunities to change the course of events in ways that would have enriched not only her encounters with Richard but also her relationship with herself. Hiding from shame means hiding from ourselves. For most of us, as for Jennifer, what causes us to feel unhappy and dissatisfied with our lives is not what happened to us in our childhood as much as how we tolerate shaming and humiliation in our adult relationships. Therefore, it is important to recognize that we continue to allow the kinds of humiliating experiences that happened early in the shaping of our personalities to repeat themselves in our adult interactions because we do not recognize their presence. In other words, it is quite erroneous to assume that the basis of human unhappiness is unconscious guilt because of things we have felt or done wrong in the past. We must look instead to the everyday causes of dissatisfaction in our lives. In doing so, we need to become more aware of precisely how we shame ourselves and others and the ways in which we allow others to humiliate us.

Second, we need to consider shame from a multivariant perspective. Shame is normally part of life. As a complex emotion, it comes in a variety of shapes and has a multitude of different functions. Not all experiences of shame are deleterious. Quite the contrary! In small doses, shame can be a prod to self-improvement, spurring freedom by providing a means for penetrating self-discovery. Positive shame comes from the recognition that we do not know ourselves and the significant people in our life sufficiently well to live fully and with pride. Healthy responses to feeling shame derive from our willingness to examine openly and do something constructive about distressing aspects of ourselves that we can reasonably change.

Being negatively shamed is an occurrence of daily life. It cannot be entirely avoided. Consequently, we must recognize and learn how to differentiate clearly those qualities of our personalities that we can reasonably improve from personal conditions over which we have no control.

Self-recrimination over aspects of our situation or person that we cannot change has no functional use. Therefore, we need to be less self-condemning. For example, as destructive as our anger may be, we need to realize that our distancing mechanisms toward others may be indicative of our deep susceptibility and caring about the pain and misery of others—as it was for Richard. Judging ourselves with self-contempt for our vulnerability to others only exacerbates the problems that breed noxious shame.

Above all, to remove the hazardous minefields of debilitating shame, each of us needs to find specific ways to demonstrate our caring to others. To remove the ready opportunities for painful shame and humiliation, we need to influence our interpersonal world, making it a better place for ourselves and others to express caring and concern.

I will discuss in Chapter Fourteen specific ways in which Jennifer and Richard might constructively deal with their shame and guilt.

We turn next to Julius, a "child of scorn," at the first stage in the development of the malevolent personality.

CHAPTER FOUR

Child of Scorn

Imaginary evils soon become real by indulging our reflections on them.
— JONATHAN SWIFT

IN THE PRELITERATE OR SO-CALLED PRIMITIVE WORLD, THE HUMAN psyche is believed to be dual—divided into person and shadow. This idea has been reflected in the self-images of several of the more disturbed patients I have treated. Each had a restless nature and only a tentative sense of the boundaries of personhood. In other words, they often could not tell where their own bodies and personal space ended and those of others began. Occasionally, they consider the bodies and personal concerns of others to be extensions of themselves. During particularly stressful times, they became frightened by the awareness of the presence of a mysterious second self. Often, but not always, this self was identical to them in such superficial ways as physical appearance but strangely dissimilar in, for example, degrees of self-confidence and even ruthlessness toward other people.

Soon after completing my doctorate, I became a staff psychologist at a federally run psychiatric hospital. One of my first patients was Julius Loschild, a talented jazz musician in his late twenties, dark-haired, and short but compact in build. In each session, Julius obsessively bemoaned his fate. In his view, he had been destined from his youth for great musical success but had been derailed by unfortunate personal events. Because of his drug abuse, alcoholism, and assaults on hospital staff and fellow patients, Julius had been in and out of psychiatric hospitals, maximum-security installations, and self-help groups for a decade. In addition, numerous serious suicide attempts, combined with his substance abuse, had caused a severe deterioration in his health and the ability to concentrate on his craft.

Julius's propensity for unreasoning anger and violence was a continual threat to our clinical work. One morning, he began the session by slumping down across from my gray metal government-issue desk and complaining bitterly that he had been unfairly restricted to the hospital grounds for the next two weeks. Even though he admitted that he had returned high on drugs and alcohol after a visit to the city—a violation of hospital rules as well as a contradiction of the treatment goals he had set for himself in our sessions—he ranted about the psychiatrist–administrator who had grounded him. It was as if Julius would not have been high if someone else had not decided that he was high. This totality of denial of his own participation in how others treated him, a pervasive theme in his life, never ceased to amaze me.

On this occasion, I tried to point out reasonably that he was, as so often in the past, acting as if he felt sorry for himself. Once again, in other words, he was refusing to take responsibility for his own actions.

Suddenly, Julius jumped to his feet, tears in his eyes, and loomed over my desk, threatening to slug me.

"Are you trying to tell me I'm not a man?" he shouted, with a mixture of arrogance and self-pity.

I told him to take his seat or leave. He glared at me for a tense moment, then scooped an ashtray off the desk and flung it against the wall across the room.

My observation had been perfectly appropriate from my professional point of view, since I was trying to help him recognize his own responsibility in the unfortunate things that "just happened" to him throughout his life. Unwittingly, however, I had humiliated Julius, because of his tenuous sense of personal identity. His was a vivid example of the painful shame we examined in the last chapter, the unbearable and unrecognized feeling that leaves its victim feeling vulnerable and utterly helpless.

Debilitating shame is an alienating feeling. It conveys an anxiety that all is not right with one's life, that one's existence is not safe and harmonious. It carries the opprobrium that the sufferer is unlovable and should be cast out of human company. The shame-bound person has learned from others and now accuses himself of the "crime" of being surplus, unwanted, and worthless.

People who are highly prone to pathological shame have grown up believing that they are not fully human. They have been treated by significant people in their lives as if their "true" self, and their judgment of what is right and wrong, were defective and flawed. This deprives them of the entitlement to proper treatment from others. Each shame experience depletes our sense of self-worth. An inability to secure proper treatment and respect from others renders us vulnerable to feelings of self-blame and self-loathing, the emotive forces that fuel a negative personal identity. In other words, shameful experiences seriously and continually prevent us from facing life courageously, honestly, and with full confidence in our ability to deal competently with its problems and opportunities. For Julius, the way to repair his flimsy self-esteem was to commit acts of arrogance, self-glorification, aggressiveness, and pseudomasculinity.

"You're not a child anymore," I said levelly. "What you do affects not only you but other people as well." Julius paused, looking toward the door. "I am going to have to set some rules against your violence in my office. You've injured other people in the past. It's not going to happen in here."

Julius wheeled back toward me, face flushed and chin thrust out.

"Fuck you! I really thought you were going to help me. But you don't give a shit about anyone but yourself. You're just another 'cop' trying to bust my chops, because you enjoy giving people a hard time."

From clinical studies, we know that someone who regards aspects of himself as unacceptable because they contradict how he likes to be seen will often attribute these characteristics to others. Rather than analyzing his own character, Julius was dumping his worst attributes in my direction. The greater the need for such shame-driven people to transfer their unacceptable characteristics onto someone else, the more likely they will express their self-hatred in "uncontrollable" behavior toward others, such as forceful dominance, aggression, and violence.

Not surprisingly, then, Julius swore obscenely and slammed my door, shouting that he didn't need help from anyone.

When he got back to his small room on the ward, he sat and listened to an all-jazz radio station for hours. Consumed with envy of the successful recording artists, he talked aloud to them and the disc jockeys. He asked, rhetorically, whether there was anything he could do to escape the misery and futility of the way he lived his life.

This went on for about two weeks, until the night when a voice on the radio spoke back to Julius and demanded to know why he was bothering the musicians. Startled enough at hearing his name called by an unseen person, Julius became absolutely terrified when he recognized this voice. It had the accent and vigor of a certain man who had grown up on and fearlessly walked the mean streets of Manhattan's Lower East Side at the turn of the century—it was the voice of Julius's father, now deceased.

Too frightened even to imagine what the old man had in store for him, Julius was not entirely surprised by his "appearance." Childless, the man and his wife had adopted Julius as an infant. Early in childhood, the boy sensed that in some mysterious, destructive way he was psychically joined to this man, old enough to be his grandfather. In fact, the quiet, powerful man had an unsettling effect on others too. He had a trick of looking at people on first meeting as if he knew them better than they knew themselves. It was rumored that he had worked as a hit man for organized crime in his younger years.

Julius ached to win his father's admiration throughout his childhood, but he believed himself too weak to be respected by anyone. On the other hand, he fantasized that his father was a kind of superman, never needing to question his own behavior. Specifically, the boy developed the idea, based upon fragments of overheard conversation between the old man and his longtime friends, that his father was capable of something called "the first power"—the gift of being able to restore his mortal being after death. Laughing and affectionately slapping his father on the back, the old-timers recounted the many times he had escaped dangerous situations and miraculously recovered from serious wounds. Julius took the love and admiration of these old men to mean that the stories were literally true.

At the same time, he believed that his father's uncanny influence over others was based on the "evil eye," a concept thought to be virtually synonymous with evil throughout the ages. Of all forms of superstition, this belief is among the oldest, most widespread and still tenaciously held.

The psychoanalyst H. H. Hart has described its appeal: "No science, religion or law has been able to eradicate it. Incantations and references to it go back to early records of Egyptian, Assyrian and Chaldean civilizations. The Persians believed that most diseases were due to it, and the Athenians and Etruscans were both susceptible to it."[1]

According to this superstition, certain individuals have the power of causing injury or harm to other people, animals, and even inanimate objects with an intentional stare or even an unwitting glance. A nineteenth-century pope was reputed to have the latter power. Early in his reign, the common folk enthusiastically lined the streets of Rome to cheer his procession, and children shinnied up into trees to get a clear view. As the pontiff turned, smiling and waving, strange mishaps occurred to those who caught his eye: children fell from the trees, adults became seriously ill. In subsequent years, people were warned whenever he approached, so that they could hide from his indiscriminate glances.[2]

The notion of the evil eye is an intriguing conception of vision, because it metaphorically portrays the eye as both searchlight and mirror. In other words, the eye is viewed as both actively knowing and passively disclosing.

The tendency of many people to describe the eye as a mysterious organ, according to Otto Fenichel, is inspired by the eye's paradoxical qualities. Fenichel, author of the most widely read textbook on psychoanalytic theory, characterized the eye in two essential ways: as the sensory organ that represents our search "for the inner nature of others, and as that bodily part that is most vulnerable to the exposure of those aspects of our character that we want to hide."[3]

Fascination with the eye has a venerable tradition in literature. From the earliest known writings to the present, eyes have been regarded as crucial indicators of the true natures of literary characters and of the power they might hold over others. Several clear examples occur in Shakespeare. In Act I, Scene 2, of *Julius Caesar*, Caesar turns to his friend Marc Antony and whispers about a political rival standing nearby:

Yond Cassius has a lean and hungry look.
He thinks too much; such men are dangerous.

In *The Merchant of Venice*, Bassanio describes Portia, the woman he loves, as having eyes that command such power and magic that an artist daring to paint her portrait would be in serious danger of losing his own vision if he but looked into her eyes.

Unlike normal eyes, the evil eye is not content with the surface persona; it plunges, unbidden, into the dark secrets of the soul. In other words, it has no respect for the image a person wants to present to the world. It is threatening because it might possibly replace one's internal "objective" reality with base motives.

Before the advent of the X-ray machine, the microscope, and other diagnostic instruments, it is likely that people with especially sensitive eyes developed an ability to detect disease in others. By extension, if someone's eye could diagnose physical illness unrecognized by normal vision, perhaps it could also uncover maladies of the soul. Or so many people came to believe.

Fear of the evil eye, then, is the anticipation of being found out, of having one's malevolent rage, resentment, and envy discovered. After all, what we fear in others is often decisively shaped by what we refuse to acknowledge in ourselves.

Parenthetically, it is interesting that people have always feared physicians who probe into their bodies. Perhaps they suspect that not only physical maladies but also conflictual hidden urges will be uncovered. Small wonder, then, that by projective mechanisms—that is, by attributing to others the qualities one tries to deny knowing in oneself—physicians have traditionally been suspected of systematic evil and depicted as such dangerously malevolent figures as Dr. Frankenstein, Dr. Jekyll, Dr. Moreau, Dr. Caligari, and other mad scientists.

Young Julius was profoundly influenced by his belief in his adoptive father's evil eye. He found himself running errands and doing chores around the house with no conscious intent of his own. When he completed one of these tasks, it seemed that the old man smiled knowingly, as if he had actually willed the boy to do the work through one of his cold, deeply set dark eyes.

Meanwhile, Julius endeavored arduously to please others, because he was uncertain what was expected of him. He wrestled alone with the feeling that no one really cared about him, a fear that wore at him around the clock, preoccupying his days and causing frequent nightmares. He had no one to whom he felt sufficiently close or trusted enough to discuss these anxieties. Only when he played his saxophone or listened to jazz did his fears subside.

In a very real sense, Julius became like the protagonists of novels by Franz Kafka, terrified of being in the world with no one else to share their concerns. A fable of Kafka's concerns a young man—a petty bureaucrat in some insignificant governmental office in Prague—who was disturbed by the insignificance of his life. One day, he awoke and realized that his life was scheduled by his attention to a series of meaningless activities. He decided to free some of his time from trivial tasks so that he could attend to more worthwhile pursuits. First, he quit shaving in the morning. Next, he totally stopped grooming himself. After a few days, because of his self-consciousness about his unkempt appearance, he remained in his apartment. After a while, he would not leave his couch. He just lay there idly until he died.

When I first read this story, in college, I interpreted Kafka as implying that the young man died of prolonged boredom. Youth is prone to regard boredom as life's most serious malady. Even my father in middle age spoke of the need to "kill time" during his brief respites from the years of difficult physical toil on the jobs he held, as if time were life's archenemy.

Looking back at Julius's case, I recognize that I had completely misconstrued Kafka's message. Many people go through life with little or no awareness and interest in what is happening *inside* themselves until they are physically or psychically disturbed. With all the trivial activities of his life removed, Kafka's young man had no means of distracting himself from what was happening inside him. He must have died rather quickly of sheer fright from what he was discovering about himself.

Julius, too, had been going through life with little interest in or awareness of what was happening inside himself. He disregarded his own feelings because he wanted to absolve himself of all responsibility for his failures. He hid behind the claim that no one else had to bear as much pain as he—anyone who did would have to spend the rest of his life institutionalized and on painkillers. Julius himself, unwilling to deal directly or consistently with his fears, used drugs and alcohol to mask his shame and self-contempt for being cowardly and inadequate.

When the voice of his father emerged into his hospital room that night, Julius, deprived of drugs, had no means of distracting himself from what was happening inside his psyche. He hastily wrote me a letter, pleading for help. Now, he claimed, he was ready to really get to work on his problems.

Meanwhile, I had begun to realize that conventional psychological theories and treatment methodologies were inadequate for reaching Julius. On the contrary, after we began working together again, his condition worsened over the next several months. He sensed that his father's presence was intensifying, the hostile voice ever more viciously accusing him of moral depravity and homosexuality.

The indirect psychoanalytic methods in which I was training then in a postdoctoral institute could not address Julius's fears, which were too immediate and pressing. According to therapeutic standard practice, we were to talk about his past and I was to suggest that his feelings about the apparition were actually feelings about himself. This approach made no sense to Julius, and he withdrew. The "talking cure" could not help him deal with his demon. Worse, I worried that Julius was a prime candidate during this stressful period for yet another serious suicide attempt.

The seeking of meaning is a common dimension of human experience—one that summarizes the way in which we relate to our personal world and to the shared world of others. It is from an ability to use language intelligently that we acquire a facility in seeking personal meaning for ourselves in relationship with others. In other words, it is language that enables us to be human rather than brute and solitary beasts.

Children who at an early age were made to feel ashamed for having "unacceptable" feelings don't have access to their vulnerable feelings. Accordingly, they frequently don't have the words and linguistic concepts that would enable them to share a caring identification with other people.

Language disorders are commonly found in those who have been charged with crimes of violence. But it is important to recognize that it is a facility with the language of *felt emotion,* rather than language per se, that serves to ward off violence as a means of addressing conflict. This point of view is found in the words of Herman Melville's character Billy Budd, who explains after he was compelled to strike and kill an abusive officer, "Could I have used my tongue, I would not have struck him."

In consultation with a more experienced psychotherapist on the hospital staff, I decided to try a new tack. As it happened, my fiancée was an accomplished psychodramatist, having worked directly with J. L. Moreno, the founder of psychodrama, at his institute in Beacon, New York. From working alongside her and participating in numerous psychodrama training sessions, sometimes role-playing as a "patient," I believed that I had learned enough about the technique to take the gamble of trying to reach Julius in this way. There was the danger, of course, that I might push him toward an even more desperate withdrawal from the world.

Allowed by the hospital to add to our regular thrice-weekly sessions as necessary, now, for several meetings, I set up a psychodrama in which Julius "brought" his father to my office. First, I taught my patient how to self-induce states of consciousness similar to his experiences on drugs. Next, I encouraged him to allow his father's "evil eye" to make contact and then invite the old man to join us.

Our structure was the so-called empty chair situation. I sat in one chair, Julius in another, and a third was left vacant for his father. Julius would speak in his own person, then go over and sit in the third chair to speak for his father, back and forth.

When Julius and I had originally begun working together,[4] he said that he knew nothing about his biological parents. In some deep sense, he felt "illegitimate." Now, however, Julius in the role of his father reported some new information. Occasionally, as the boy Julius played with friends in the park or schoolyard, he would become aware of a shadowy figure, a poorly dressed, unpleasant-looking woman who seemed to follow him about only when his adoptive parents or other caretakers were not around. He sensed that she wanted him to know that she was there but did not want any actual encounter. With a child's intuition, Julius guessed that she was his real mother.

The mysterious woman's appearances made him anxious and upset. He could not decide which he felt more strongly—happiness that he had escaped having to live with her, or anger that she had abandoned him. All he actually knew about his parents was that his biological father, who disappeared before Julius's birth, had long been a friend of his adoptive father. About his mother he knew nothing. He suspected that she had not married his father.

But it was not so much this circumstance that made him feel illegitimate; it was his adoptive mother's treating him like a burden as he grew older. At the beginning, delighted to have a child at last, she had been kind. When Julius grew past the toddling age, however, she seemed annoyed at his need for continual reassurance that he was wanted and loved.

As we have seen, malevolence is fostered by the cruel, shaming messages about one's personal identity that caretakers can convey during the developmental years; the immediate result is that one is rendered vulnerable to further disregard by other people. To understand Julius and others like him, we should not look for a bad seed sown into the genetic inheritance. Instead, we have to understand that they act in a way that makes sense in terms of what they perceive as their available choices. Julius's sense of identity came from trying to make his experiences, whether the annoyance of an adoptive mother or the rejection of a biological mother, meaningful to himself.

Remember: we get our self-esteem, our sense of living well, from feeling desired, understood, and appreciated by others. Moreover, our sense of trust and security is bolstered when we know that there are people who care about us, to whom we can turn. Repeated rejections and failure to receive caring from others, on the other hand, lead directly to feelings of inadequacy, loneliness and intense depression.

Historians designate certain historical periods as eras that exhibit a particular orientation to human experience. So it is in individual development. For the child, ages four to eight is the *age of belief*. In this era of development, we trust innocently in the sincerity and benevolent intentions of those with whom we are significantly involved. Naturally, because of the considerable number of opportunities for deceit and betrayal in the daily round, this period is for many of us the most emotionally vulnerable in our entire life. So it was for Julius.

In one psychodrama session, he recalled a wrenching scene from his own age of belief. Trustfully, he asked his adoptive father to protect him from the ugly woman who was always spying on him. When the old man understood what he was talking about, he angrily told the boy to stop acting like a sissy and sent him out of the room. Julius, deeply hurt that his father considered him a coward, resolved never again to ask him for help. It was too upsetting for him to be regarded as inadequate.

As with this patient, the sense of "badness" comes initially from being continually informed, whether verbally or through the behavior of others, that we are flawed, surplus, unwanted. The emotional means for conveying this message is humiliation. Over the years, the shame-sensitive person's negative personal identity becomes stabilized, and his "inner voice" reminds him to become, as Jean Genet wrote, whatever he is treated as already being.

In a later psychodrama session, Julius remembered another significant moment. Walking home from high school one afternoon, he was attacked by two older boys, just as his father happened to drive by. The old man stopped the car, jumped out, and drove off the attackers in a rain of jabs and punches. Julius was mortified. He had been trying diligently for years to gain his father's respect by not asking for his help. Now the boy felt intense rage at the old man for humiliating him by rescuing him. He wanted to strike out violently at both of his adoptive parents.

Julius thought he must be an unusual child to have this horrible feeling, but in fact he was not. Most of the people who come to see me for intensive analysis have been suffused with a similar sense of wickedness for the greater part of their lives. Virtually all have admitted feeling self-recrimination for having at some time steamed with murderous rage or even obsessively plotted the details of a cruel and painful revenge upon someone they believed had treated them unjustly. Often the imagined victim was a parent. Most of these patients believed that cowardice alone prevented them from acting on these malevolent thoughts and feelings.

Immediately after his father's intervention in the fistfight, Julius felt that something had happened to undermine permanently his confidence and self-respect. As he became preoccupied with his own needs and his dependency upon others, he also became increasingly more demanding of them. He was unwilling to acknowledge that since other people also have needs, personal relationships must be nurtured.

Some people are blessed, growing up in essentially loving families that intuitively recognize how crucial caring about other people's concerns is to living a harmonious life. Others learn this lesson after they leave their families. Being a psychotherapist has brought out qualities in me that I had been aware of in myself but had not given priority earlier in my life. Altruism, for instance, I had not held in high esteem when I was growing up. Nevertheless, the seeds of recognition were sown from events I witnessed in my family.

When I was in high school, for example, my mother and I visited my grandmother in a city-operated hospital during the dinner hour. All of the patients on her ward had visitors, except for a frightened, blind old woman. The nurses' aide had simply put her food on a tray and left her to her own resources. The old woman seemed unable to feed herself. She fumbled with the food, spilling it all over herself and the bedcovers. We heard the nurses' aide in the hallway, laughing with another aide, apparently unconcerned about the blind patient. My mother said in Yiddish that it was a pity to be treated that way. She went over to the old woman and fed her, speaking comfortingly to her all the while.

The whole appalling process of being guided toward feelings of worthlessness is, of course, patently unjust. I cannot avoid feeling considerable compassion for my seriously disturbed patients like Julius who have had growing experiences different than mine. That we call them "mad" indicates the fury of their reactions to the shameful injustices called to our attention by their disturbed behavior.

It follows that, in an important sense, the goal of psychoanalysis (or any other form of genuine psychological healing) is to exorcise the patient's sense of badness. In the relational exchange known as *psychological exorcism,* a perceived "bad object"—the patient's internal representation of a significant, condemning authority figure from the past—is replaced with a "good object": a caring, concerned, emotionally reflective person in the present. At first, the good object is the psychological healer; gradually, the patient himself becomes the good object.

During our last few psychodrama sessions, therefore, I first taught Julius how to tell the sinister evil eye that enough was enough: he would not tolerate any more punishment, because he had become a person determined to treat himself with more compassion. This approach was useful to some extent, because it enabled Julius to relate with less fear to the threatening "bad object," his father, to become more direct and appropriate in his behavior with other people, and to define his own personal identity more clearly to himself, gaining greater understanding of where his personal boundaries ended and those of others began.

But more was needed. As a second step, I showed Julius how to observe his own thoughts and feelings without immediately judging his internal processes. Thus, he became able to complete his thoughts and look at them objectively. It was not until then that I encouraged him to evaluate what he was experiencing. To do so, though it is a psychological exercise that has been used by shamans and students of Eastern arts for centuries, is initially a rather difficult task. It takes considerable practice and patience. Our minds seem naturally to evaluate continually whatever we observe, both within and outside ourselves. From these premature judgments, our momentary, unstable feelings of self-worth or self-denigration, as well as a sense of security or pending danger, are formed. To stabilize his sense of self, Julius needed to avoid premature judgments of himself.

In short, for Julius it was essential to develop some skill in avoiding constant self-judgment. Over the months of treatment, I had come to recognize that it was his inner critical voice, whether accusing him of cowardice or incompetence or homosexuality, that was keeping the apparition of his father on the scene and also fueling his self-contempt. By suggesting the analogy that he was like a fictional character whose personality could not accurately be evaluated until several chapters into the story, I was able to help Julius begin to develop competence in reacting in a measured way to his own urges.

Third, I told Julius that the despairing assumptions behind his self-recriminations were false. For example, he did not recognize that he had obviously achieved an important development in his personality—that is, he had a moral sense of right and wrong, and it was this sense that prevented him from behaving malevolently. In fact, I argued that it was probably his moral sense, not cowardice, that prevented him from becoming as brutal as his father was reported to have been.

At the same time, it was true that although Julius had often behaved destructively toward himself and others, he felt immediate remorse after each violent act. Hurting someone never made him feel good about himself. I took this to mean that he actually wanted to be a good person, wanted to learn how to participate cooperatively with other people. The problem: he just didn't know what to do to become more thoughtful and competent as a person.

Using the imagery of Pandora's box from Greek mythology, I suggested that Julius might actually discover more good than bad about himself if he pursued a thorough self-examination. I discussed with him my belief that most of us avoid self-examination because self-discovery forces us to recognize what we do not know about ourselves and, as such, imposes a threat to our wish to transcend the limitations of the human condition. Only by giving up our magical hopes (as I explore more fully in Chapter Seven) can we expect realistically to have access to the deepest strata of our actual human capacities, as well as to authentic interpersonal relationships made possible by our courageous imagination and compassionate interactions.

Before long, I took a new post as director of a community mental health center and could no longer work with Julius. Soon he left the hospital, feeling some hope about his prospects and with concrete plans to support that hope. I cannot say that the last time I saw him he was an ably functioning person. He wasn't. Yet he was involved in a vocational rehabilitation training program and had been drug-free for a couple of months. I continued to get letters from Julius every few months after I left the hospital. He had come a long way.

The years when I worked with deeply suffering but fascinating patients like Julius were for me a time of insight and important self-discovery. Because I was still a beginning practitioner, I could not reach these patients using clinical and psychological knowledge alone. I also had to seek within myself, struggling to find out who I was as a human being. To meet this challenge, I was forced to recognize aspects of my own character that I saw in my seriously disturbed patients—hurt, helplessness, rage.

I soon came to realize that the "mentally ill" have and act upon moods and instincts that are shared by all men and women, if in less exaggerated form. Indeed, these characteristics are unavoidable when one is in touch with the frailties, paradoxes, and absurdities of the human condition. With my patients, the availability of this shared human bond enabled me to reach and help free them from the rage, hurt, and malevolence they had been unfairly shamed into believing was their inevitable fate. Their journey of self-discovery would be fearsome, no matter how caring and supportive a guide I became, but our mutuality made the endeavor possible.

Even so, because of the formidable rationalizations erected by those in the formative stages of malevolence to justify their behavior, it is often true that I could help my patients make only small gains. But as a wise, forbearing supervisor taught me during my apprenticeship, it is better to light even one candle in the journey toward self-understanding than to give up and forever curse the darkness. In that spirit, I continue to explore the possibilities of treating the malevolent personality.

I have not attempted in this chapter to account for the manifestation of Julius's stepfather. An adequate explanation would require some knowledge of both neuropsychology and of the literary and philosophical concept of the "second self." I explore the latter in the next chapter, working from sources not only in literature and philosophy but also from neuropsychology and clinical studies of seriously disturbed patients.

CHAPTER FIVE

The Role of the Double in Malevolence

Any of us could be the man who
encounters his double.
— FRIEDRICH DÜRRENMATT

B EFORE THE ADVENT OF THE PRESENT RACE OF HUMANKIND, AC-cording to a myth retold by Plato in the *Symposium,*[1] the earth was inhabited by a more noble group of beings. Marvelous in countless ways, they had four arms, four legs, and two heads, which faced away from each other. Indeed, they looked like two beings perfectly combined into one, and they moved by executing cartwheels. Arrogant in the extreme, they were so audacious that they scaled Mount Olympus and tried to put their hands on the gods. Zeus, in a terrible rage, wanted to destroy them all, but the more prudent Apollo pointed out that gods need beings to worship them. Cleave them in half, he suggested; they would lose their beauty and strength, and the number of worshipers would be doubled. Zeus agreed.

Now, though long vanished from the earth, the tortured souls of these sundered beings wander the spiritual realm, forever longing to find their other halves, their *soul mates.* Plato describes this spiritual quest for harmonious reuniting as fearsome: "For the intense yearning which each has toward the other does not appear to be the desire of lover's intercourse, but of something else which the soul of either desires and cannot tell, and of which she has only a dark and doubtful presentiment."[2]

In addition to Julius's evil eye in the last chapter, we will encounter apparitions in Chapters 7 and 10. Who or what are they? How is the identity of each related to the problem of malevolence?

Plato's myth of the severed twin souls provides an intriguing lead, although it contrasts sharply with mainstream thinking in contemporary psychology, which argues that personality is a solitary definite self. To explain why we seem to behave very differently in diverse social situations, today's psychologist theorizes that this single self perceives its role differently in each situation. Generally speaking, then, most psychologists believe that any theory involving more than one personality in an individual human being probably falls outside the province of serious scientific inquiry.

Down through the ages, however, myth and popular belief have suggested not only that we all have several distinct selves but that they conflict with each other. Only by recognizing the nature of such conflicts, according to folk wisdom, can we understand why our dark side is on board.

A BRIEF LITERARY HISTORY OF THE SECOND SELF

A hallmark of modern literature is the use of split characters or double selves to dramatize psychological conflict. From at least as early as Shakespeare, dramatists and novelists have tended to depict a major character's internal struggle by creating minor characters who act out the contending sides.[3] In this way, Otto Rank, according to his translator David Winter, analyzed the enduring legend of the lascivious Don Juan: "It would be impossible to create the Don Juan figure, the frivolous knight without a conscience and without fear of death or the devil, if a part of that Don Juan were not split off in Leporello [Don Juan's servant and reluctant accomplice in his clever schemes], who represents the inner criticism and the conscience of the hero."[4]

The most concentrated intellectual attention to the phenomenon of the double probably occurred in Europe in the latter part of the nineteenth century, when there was considerable speculation about the divergent makeup of the soul in terms of personality. Literary works that portrayed two opposing sides within a character were generally accepted by the reading public, perhaps because both psychoanalysis and the Romantic movement in literature, which emphasized spontaneity of feeling and imagination and spiritual exploration, made the concept of the inner life fashionable.

Freud, by unveiling the nature of the human mind, made irrationality a topic of great popular interest. Experimental psychology also was having an impact upon the intellectual climate, as writers produced a spate of short stories and novels dealing with the possibility that each person incorporates a shadowy second self.[5]

We should also recognize that these works of fiction served as "psychological experiments," even if unwittingly. Psychology, in the throes of breaking away from philosophy and theology, required some form of demonstration of the new ideas. Novels like Robert Louis Stevenson's *The Strange Case of Dr. Jekyll and Mr. Hyde* or Oscar Wilde's *The Picture of Dorian Gray* and short stories like Edgar Allan Poe's "William Wilson," therefore, can quite usefully be seen as literary psychological experiments in the spirit of the new psychology. It is Dr. Jekyll, after all, who proposes the thesis that "man is not truly one but truly two."

Hermann Hesse elaborates on this theme in his novel *Steppenwolf*:

There is not a single human being . . . who is so conveniently simple that his being can be explained as the sum of two or three principal elements . . . It appears to be an inborn need of all men to regard the self as a unit. However often and however grievously this illusion is shattered, it always mends again. . . . The delusion rests upon a false analogy. As a body everyone is single, as a soul never.[6]

Typically, the nineteenth-century writers of double-self tales focused on the disquieting psychological conflict that prevents separate selves from functioning together harmoniously. These literary works, particularly those of Wilde, Poe, Maupassant, Dostoyevsky, and E.T.A. Hoffmann, dramatically depicted the suffering that emanated from the conflict of attempting to integrate the "different" selves within the personality. Each of the authors examining a double or second self in his literary works, according to a literary study by psychiatrist S. M. Coleman,[7] was himself a tormented person. Maupassant was a cold, impersonal, and extremely detached man, who would in the morning write of his sexual exploits of the night before as if he were describing someone else. He was not very introspective, attending more to his exterior image than to the conflicts within himself. According to Coleman, Maupassant had been warned repeatedly by his friend the novelist Flaubert, by medical advisers, and by others to curb his drinking and sexual activities. Maupassant wrote about occasional terrifying experiences of entering his study at night and encountering his own double sitting in his chair.

The introspective Dostoyevsky, in contrast, was, according to Coleman, neurotic, hypochondriacal, and epileptic, his mind seething with incompatible, contradictory urges. His novel *The Double* was supposedly largely autobiographical. It is not surprising, then, that its most impressive virtue was the author's ability to see, so to speak, everything that was happening under the skin of the hero.

This novel describes the onset of emotional disturbance in a petty government official who is unable to recognize his symptoms because he is afraid of candid introspection. He paranoiacally views all his painful experiences as caused by his enemy, who resembles the protagonist down to the smallest detail, as if he stole his appearance from a mirror. The double represents the psychological principle that a person with deeply harbored hate for his own unacceptable behavior cannot free himself from fear—the preoccupation that other people are aware of his vulnerabilities, along with his wrongful deeds, and are relentlessly seeking to destroy him.

What might Maupassant, Dostoyevsky, and the other writers who used the double theme have been trying unwittingly to achieve in their literary efforts? In my view, the literary double serves as a graphic mirror for aspects of the author's self that he seems compelled to present—but only in literary form, since he does not wish to acknowledge these attributes as his own. In the double-self stories, the heroes are given the opportunity to reconcile themselves with the fearful and despised qualities of their hidden personality. In each of the stories, they refuse, and their original personality is destroyed, the second taking over the original's life. In other words, a consistent theme in the legend of the double self is the notion that our doubles reside in the mirror, likely at any moment to step out of the frame and into our lives. This imagery reflects the Platonic concept of the soul as duality; we are linked to our shadow. And it also represents, according to Rank,[8] our eternal conflicts with ourselves and with others, the puzzling contradiction and agonizing inner struggle between fear of life and fear of death, as well as the paradoxical contradiction between love of self and love of others. The doubles in the nineteenth-century works, unsure of their identity, represent elements of morbid self-love which prevents the formation of an effectively integrated personality.

From Rank's perspective, Dorian Gray is a universal archetype.[9] He is Everyman, and his foibles reverberate in each one of us; as with Narcissus, his famous portrait of himself is a reflecting pool that shows the truth below the surface. Because other people distract him from his search for his inner identity, he discards them.

Is he not the self we wish to be? We envy his eternal youth, his unchanging beauty. We would also like to have such self-confidence and be so deeply admired by others. Yet at the same time, he is the corrupt self we fear we can become. Certainly, we do not want to suffer as he did for our indulgences.

Legends of a second self might be considered nothing more than metaphorical representations of the considerable contradictions and paradoxes of typical human behavior. But a startling, controversial theory advanced by Julian Jaynes in 1976 suggests that these legends may have a factual basis.

Few questions have puzzled ethnoculturalists and psychologists more than the problem of understanding how human consciousness evolved. For example, many of these scientists believed that the conceptualization of a complex community—one that binds people together in a social unit for mutual interest and for protection from each other, as well as from strangers—exceeded our early ancestors' mentality at the time these social communities developed.

Jaynes uses the generally agreed upon observation that people seem to possess a *sixth sense,* which relays information to the brain without relying on the sense of sight, hearing, touch, taste, or smell. He suggests that our extrasensory perception, which we all possess to a greater or lesser extent, is a throwback to a crucial form of communication of preliterate humankind.

In *The Origin of Consciousness in the Breakdown of the Bicameral Mind,* the Princeton University professor of psychology claims that the authors

of *The Jewish Bible,* the *Epic of Gilgamesh,* the *Iliad,* and the *Odyssey*
lacked entirely what we call "self-consciousness." Since their awareness
was directed outward, toward the external world, these ancient writers
were unable to examine their own motivations and intentions. They could
not be subjective: "We cannot approach these heroes by inventing mind
spaces behind their fierce eyes. . . . Iliadic man did not have subjectivity
as we do; he had no awareness of his awareness of the world, no internal
mind-space to introspect upon."[10]

To people of the twentieth century so accustomed to "looking inside of
ourselves" before choosing a course of action, this is a baffling, even non-
sensical statement, and Jaynes was answered by a flood of negative reviews from psychologists, ethnologists, theologians, and philosophers. For
one thing, on even the simplest level it is difficult to conceive how a person can make any complex decision without some sort of introspection.
When deciding to take a trip, we might ask, "How far away is my destina-
tion? Would it be better to fly, drive, or take the train?" And so forth.
Could the fictional Odysseus of Homer and the actual Canaanites in biblical times have made up their minds without going through the same
process?[11]

Jaynes answers that they heard voices telling them what to do, voices
they regarded as divine. He directs us to passages in Homer's *Iliad* in which
Hector, the stubborn Trojan superwarrior; Ajax, one of the mighty Greek
fighters, and other characters claim to be responding to the voices of the
gods commanding their actions or chastising them for their egocentric
behavior. He argues that an auditory hallucination, a major symptom of
schizophrenia, considered evidence of serious emotional disturbance today, is in fact a throwback to the neurological commands of an ancient
era of human development. This "bicameral" period, as Jaynes terms it,
began before 10,000 B.C.E., when auditory hallucinations served to orient
and direct a humankind not yet intellectually evolved enough to exercise
deliberate personal self-control. In his view, when an ancient hero thought
he heard the voice of a god telling him what to do, the voice actually originated in the man's right brain and was heard by the left, as if through a
transmitter. Jaynes believes that this mechanism operated as late as the
composition of the *Iliad* and the *Odyssey,* or only a few centuries before
the flowering of reason in fifth-century Athens.

The theory of an ancient "bicameral" mind not only contradicts the concept of the unitary self prevalent among contemporary psychologists; it also conflicts with ethnological theories of human evolution. Still, there are many recent clinical and experimental studies that call into question the portrayal of the self as a solitary, integrated, irreducible component of human nature. These experiments involve sophisticated analyses of the human brain.

Let's take a moment to review some general information about the physical brain. Scientists have long known that it is composed of two hemispheres that seem to mirror each other. They are connected by a thick bridge of nerves, the corpus callosum, which passes information between them. Although identical in surface appearance, the two hemispheres have separate neurological functions, and they are regarded as having separate ways of comprehending reality.

According to neuropsychologists, "each half of the brain has developed its own strategy for perceiving, processing, and expressing information, as well as specialized neuroanatomical interconnections that assist in mediating these functions."[12] In this view, the left hemisphere is analytic, capable of reasoning and literate communication. The right speaks in the languages of movement, imagery, metaphor, and design, understanding only a few spoken commands. The hemispheres seem to have entirely distinct memories of experience.[13] These two apparently distinct realities recall the traditional Eastern belief that no single reality exists.

R. Joseph, a leading neuropsychologist, believes that the two halves of the physical brain were originally similar in function as well as appearance. About forty thousand years ago, he contends, they gradually began to reorganize in response to dramatic developments in the essential tasks of human survival: increasingly sophisticated weapons and tools, agricultural skills, and speech, and, about ten thousand years ago, written language.[14]

According to Joseph, the left hemisphere of the modern brain has evolved to handle those newly acquired functions, such as language and manual dexterity. It is also the seat of conscious memory, which is dependent upon the ability to put experience into words. The right brain specializes in experiences that do not require conscious processing, such as intuition and emotional responsiveness; it cannot talk, read, write, or spell. It is therefore regarded as the place where the unconscious resides.

Even though the two halves of the modern brain have different mental systems—indeed, "think" differently—they usually work cooperatively to exchange information. Joseph notes, however, that there are exceptions:

> It is not at all unusual for each to have its own likes and dislikes, hopes for the future, goals and aspirations, social values, and politi- cal affiliations, as well as its own unique attitudes regarding their personal life.[15]

> Further, lack of communication can be intentional: The left brain just does not want to know what is really going on emotionally as the information may be too painful or upsetting to consider con- sciously. Indeed, the left hemisphere may deny the significance of an intuitive conclusion drawn by the right half of the brain, even when someone is pointing it out.[16]

The question to be asked here is whether or not there is sufficient empirical evidence that the right brain—what Joseph calls "the other mind"—is *actually* a separate personality from the psyche in the left brain. Split-brain research, a relatively recent field, based upon the work of Nobelist Robert Sperry, suggests that we now have the relevant infor- mation to answer this question. Sperry himself made the remarkable dis- covery that when the connecting corpus callosum is severed, injured, or even just anesthetized, the affected individual becomes two different per- sonalities: "Some patients began to complain that the left half of the body sometimes did unusual and cruel things that they . . . did not understand and could not control. . . . [One] patient's left hand attempted to choke his own throat and had to be wrestled away."[17]

Such evidence implies that our sense of personal identity inhabits the left hemisphere, while the right brain harbors the "stranger within." Colin Wilson[18] argues that information from split-brain research, though rare, tells us much about dual personality in most people. Indeed, do we not all operate as if our brains were surgically split in two? Consider: When we have an intuitive hunch, it occurs in the right brain; in order to decipher its meaning, the conscious, literate left brain takes over. We all sense this transferral from insight to analysis. It is not surprising, therefore, that the right brain seems to be the gateway to consciousness, a different way of experiencing the world than the rationalizing of the left brain.

Other recent evidence affirms the theory that more than one personality can exist within a single brain and body. Using a battery of neurological and psychometric tests, Frank W. Putnam and his team of psychiatric investigators at the National Institute of Mental Health found distinctive brain waves and personality styles linked to each of the selves in patients with multiple-self syndrome.[19] Moreover, reviews of one hundred independent cases of the syndrome revealed that more than three quarters of the clinicians have found personality-specific physiological differences among their patients' alternative personalities. These contrasts occurred as dramatic changes in voice, posture, motor behavior, and left- or right-handedness.[20, 21] Frequently, the alternative personalities differ in age or gender. They claim to have a continuous existence, even when they do not manifest their presence.[22] Astonishingly, Putnam and his associates discovered that approximately half the multiple-personality patients they studied had differing reactions to medication, depending upon which personality was manifested at the time. Furthermore, about a quarter of these patients had personality-specific allergies.[23]

Obviously, one has to consider the possibility of playacting with such patients, and Putnam did, setting up a control group of people with no history of dissociative personality patterns and asking them to act during personality assessment as if they had multiple personalities. The results suggested that control subjects were unable to fake a multiple-personality condition.[24]

CLINICAL MANIFESTATIONS OF THE SECOND SELF

Dr. Hans Frank, a defendant in the Nuremberg war crimes trial, told a prison psychologist[25] that during his trial he felt he was two distinct selves, facing each other.[26] One was the war criminal accused of butchering the Jews of Poland, the other the highly respected jurist he had been prior to the Third Reich.

How does the disturbing second self come into being? The evidence suggests that it develops in the right brain, unheeded by the rational left, until a moment of particular vulnerability and stress, when it precipitously erupts into full-blown life. This phenomenon is often, but of course not always, seen following drug inhalation. Angrily and frighteningly confrontational, the second self demands that the reality-oriented conscious left self meet its considerable needs.

But there is a problem with this scenario. Remember: the right brain supposedly has no verbal skills or ability to reason. But, certainly, Julius's "evil eye" cannot be described as nonverbal or totally irrational. Therefore, we need to picture the second self, which I will refer to as a *doppelgänger*,[27] emerging from the right brain but not consisting solely of right-brain experiences. Both the child of scorn, like Julius, and the child of the devil, whom we discuss in the next chapter, tend to avoid conscious awareness of the shame and humiliation inflicted by others and of the self-contempt they feel for not achieving the fulfillment of their personal identities. In trying to avert pain, they cast their disavowed experiences into their right brain, relegating the shaming experience to emotional processing rather than to cognitive awareness.

In other words, they have stored their hurtful experiences in the right brain, along with a negative narrative voice. Over time, this doppelgänger, continuously fed the psychologically powerful diet of contempt and rage, gains ascendancy over the unexamined vulnerable conscious self. Without the mediation of reason, the afflicted person becomes more prone to primitive rages, as well as to irritation and annoyance. He is also perilously susceptible to the external influence and persuasion of people who encourage dangerous and destructive behavior.

A second fact about the right brain is critically important: originally, the right hemisphere of the brain was dominant, then it was gradually surpassed in important ways by the left half, because it lacked literacy and other skills needed in the modern world. The older right half is imaginative, physical, and volatile, craving excitement and challenges, but it requires the left brain to articulate and justify its demands.

For one personality to operate, however, the other has to be disregarded, because we usually behave as a whole being. We do not have dual hearts, stomachs, and so forth. It is as if each brain had its own separate videocassette, but only one VCR is available. In other words, when one mind dominates, its personality has access to the physiological functions of the entire body, which becomes the mechanism for expressing the cassette that the dominant mind is programmed to play.

THE DOPPELGÄNGER IS NOT A DIABOLIC SURROGATE

We should not make the nineteenth-century Romantic mistake of believing that each of us has dual personalities—one good, one bad. This literary notion, though often dramatically compelling, is not to be confused with empirical evidence, particularly since it implies that the wicked self can overpower the good self and force us to act malevolently. My clinical experience discussed in the chapters to follow indicates that this doesn't happen.

Believing that we are powerless before a malevolent self absolves us of responsibility. A similar conviction must operate with those who are able to perform horrifying acts. To repeat, on the basis of his study of Nazi physicians, Robert Lifton concluded that it is virtually impossible to kill another human being without initially becoming *psychically numb.*[28]

Seen in light of the theory of dual minds, this means that the socialized left brain is gradually "put out of the way," anesthetized by rationalization and denial. In its place, the emotional, violence-prone right brain is given authority. Over time, continual rationalizations and denial erode the sense of positive personal identity. The idealized values that are vital for self-esteem are compromised and finally cast off, a surrender that is experienced as shameful. Hurt, resentment, and self-contempt accompany this shame; in the end, the combination of contempt and increasing rage produces a malevolence that lashes out at the world.

Yet, what distinguishes the more benevolent person is not the absence of hostility and contempt toward oneself and others. Most of us harbor such feelings—certainly, everyone I have ever known. What makes the difference is willingness to struggle against our troublesome urges, to work to understand them, and to deal courageously, compassionately, with the hurt that has provoked them.

Please note that my account of the doppelgänger, though related to some established scientific knowledge, is speculative.[29] Others have explained the phenomenon of apparitions in different ways. Some religious people believe that it is a personification of Satan or some other demon. Traditional psychologists believe it to be a delusion or hallucination caused by trauma, toxic stimulants, or abnormal brain physiology and chemistry.

Whatever the explanation, my theory of the five stages in the development of the malevolent personality does not necessarily stand or fall on the validity of my commentary about the doppelgänger.

Let us continue with cases that exemplify those stages: Christopher, in the second stage, also encountered a doppelgänger that seriously disturbed him.

CHAPTER SIX

Child of the Devil

It is some compensation for great evils,
that they enforce great lessons.
— CHRISTIAN NESTELL BOVEE

WE CAN MOST PROFOUNDLY UNDERSTAND THE WORLD OF MADNESS as a self-imposed excommunication from human company. Psychotics have repudiated what you and I regard as reality because, tragically, the satisfactions and securities available to us are off-limits to them. They have been led to believe, by people powerful in their lives, that they are guilty of unpardonable sins.

In this sense, madness is a declaration of moral requirement: for their wrongs, the mad must forfeit the interpersonal relations that give the rest of us a sense of living fully and well. But this separation is unbearably lonely. Deprived of other humans, the madman is compelled to create his own world and animate it with beings that reflect what he believes to be his own flawed moral character.

Prior to my first consultation with Christopher, I received a psychiatric report showing that he had considerable difficulty living with other people. It failed to warn me that he lived in a special world of his own.

Chris proved to be lean and muscular, but his well-tanned facial features were surprisingly delicate, setting off darkly mysterious eyes, and despite his short beard he seemed younger than his actual age of twenty-five. During our first meeting, after bouncing about with staccato movements in a soft armchair, he suddenly jumped up, a look of discomfort on his expressive face. He strode over to the fireplace, where the brilliantly glowing logs crackled sporadically, like frenzied fireflies.

His back to me, Chris peered into the flames, brooding. Periodically, his long, slender fingers would dart over his clothing, flicking something off his navy-blue blazer, then something else from one of the gold regimental buttons on the sleeve or from the open collar of his white shirt. At the time, I could not tell whether he was reacting to something actually there or was being driven to psychic discharge by a painful fantasy. But for the moment, that really didn't matter. Because this young man's anxious movements had the kinetics of a compulsion, the technical issue for me was to decipher correctly what the activity represented in terms of his reasons for coming to see me.

The conventional assumption would be that he was struggling with the problem of articulating those reasons. The report suggested that Chris was experiencing a great deal of psychic suffering. It was a companion he had known long and well, much more intimately than the numerous women he had slept with. Indeed, there is no consort more faithful to human experience than suffering.

I had been recommended to Chris because of my therapeutic experience with creative people who could not fully actualize their talents. Again according to the report, Chris had seen several psychiatrists but had been unwilling to trust his psychic vulnerabilities to any of them.

Apparently, he had not had much experience with life's practical matters either and usually fled when situations became difficult for him. Because his independent wealth supported a vagrant lifestyle, he did not have to concern himself with the realities of earning a living. After only a year of college, which he found intellectually stultifying, he wandered from one city to the next, searching for new excitement or breaking away from the latest troublesome romance.

Because his mother was uncomfortable with intimacy, Chris sought the nurturing she had not provided in one tempestuous love affair after another, dealing with his numerous lovers in childishly demanding ways.

These women soon tired of his insistence that they continually prove their love. According to one psychiatrist, Chris could not tolerate being alone. Quickly becoming despondent when he was no longer another's special love interest, he had attempted suicide at least eight times.

The first followed on the heels of his breakup with Jane, a fashion model in London. She ended the relationship, which was always stormy, when he slept with one of her best friends. The night Jane left the flat they had been sharing, Chris overdosed on sleeping pills and Valium. He awoke in a hospital, having barely survived. To the consulting psychiatrist called in to evaluate him, he expressed surprise that Jane would have been disturbed by his infidelity, much less upset enough to end their relationship. Surely, he said, she must have realized that he loved her nonetheless.

After other suicide attempts, Chris was also professionally examined, but he became annoyed with this intensive probing into his sense of emptiness and inadequacy. He tired of hearing doctors suggest that his fear of falling asleep because demons would pursue him in terrifying dreams might be linked to self-hatred. In fact, he was more comfortable consulting psychics, readers of tarot cards, and practitioners of black magic. He told one psychiatrist that he felt kinship with these guides to the occult because they lived by the conviction that the capacity for paranormal experience is a special gift, not evidence of psychopathology. After conferring with several of these psychics, he decided that he could set his life straight by pursuing an interesting career.

Thinking himself talented in drama and poetry, Chris returned to the United States and enrolled in an acting program. But his itinerant habits continued. After several months of interrupting his training by impulsively winging off to Europe or the Caribbean for rest and diversion, he was warned by his drama coach that his habits were professionally problematic. If he could not stay in one spot long enough to study on a continuous basis, she said, he would never be able to compete with actors who are more disciplined. It was because she recommended psychoanalysis that he had contacted me, purportedly to learn to deal with his poorly understood impulses.

As Chris stood staring into the fire, I recognized that I had to make some impact on him immediately, or the opportunity for fostering an analytic alliance would be irretrievably lost. Alerted by the report of his abortive relationships and his attempts at suicide, I knew he could not easily broach with me the painful secrets that, in fact, he had never revealed to anyone else. I was concerned he would flee my office, convinced yet again that analytic inquiry was useless in helping him come to terms with his psychic demons.

"What do you see in the flames," I asked Chris impassively, "that you are not sure you can entrust to me?"

His violent shudder took me off guard; it was alarming. It was as if my question precipitated a change in his consciousness. My uneasiness increased when he spun around and faced me.

"I used to dream about a demon chasing me. He had burning red eyes and a darting, dagger-shaped tongue, and he wore a black cloak. No matter how fast I ran, I could see that he would eventually overtake me. As he drew closer, we began to merge into one being.

"Right now in this room I have the same sense. Someone is chasing me, and I am becoming that person. What terrifies me now is that I know that I am not dreaming."

Evidently, my question had not come a moment too soon. Like other floridly psychotic patients I have worked with, he had been slipping away from the psychological confines of the room.

"Do you *really* want to know what I see in the fire?" he snarled, his nearly perfect teeth glowing with reflected firelight. "You have no idea what you are asking of me! Dammit, do you really want to know?"

"Try me and find out," I said.

His question had been rhetorical. He did not want to talk openly.

"As much as I desperately need to cast this living demon out of me," he said, "a voice pleads with me not to trust you or anyone else."

As he spoke, I became aware that my consulting room had subtly changed. Inexplicably, the polished wood and rich leather of the furniture now seemed weathered. The light had dimmed, and there was a faint damp scent.

Based upon similar experiences with strange patients,[1] I guessed that some vigilant part of my psyche was cautioning me to be careful with Chris. Nevertheless, I decided not to try to ward off these disturbances to my senses, and once my initial alarm subsided, I felt only curiosity.

Because psychoanalysts and other behavioral scientists know so little about the inner workings of madness, they cannot depend solely on scientific and clinical knowledge to treat profoundly disturbed patients. Something more is required. Like creative artists, they have to tap internal psychological processes unavailable to intellectual endeavor. In our beginnings as a race, our consciousness and the intentional language that became its eventual by-product were only rudimentarily developed. Each of us today, in common with other humans, retains the remnants of an archaic nonverbal language that consists of communication cues and signals evoked by smell, sight, and bodily vibrations. As a clinician, I have learned to use this shared primitive language to respond to badly frightened patients like Chris.

I realized that my breathing was now precisely in sync with Chris's. Apparently, I had without prolonged deliberation decided not to let him take his perilous journey alone.

I leaped up and demanded that he introduce me to his demon.

"Don't you see him?" he howled plaintively. "I am wearing his face."

"What the hell do you mean?" I asked, staring intently at his features.

"I mean that the devil has taken hold of me."

"Show me in the mirror the face that is not your own," I ordered, leading him to a full-length mirror on the wall.

"You damned creep," he shouted into the reflection, "appear in the mirror so you can be seen!" Obviously frightened, he averted his gaze from the glass.

I waited. In the glass there appeared no other face but Chris's, handsome and anxious in profile.

"What do you see?" he impatiently demanded.

"Well," I said, "I see your unhappy face. Nothing else."

He turned fully toward the mirror and stared into it long and searchingly. Suddenly, he jumped back and spun toward me.

"I don't know that face. Now, Doctor, you think you have all the answers. Tell me, what is that strange face doing in *my* reflection?"

Instinctively, I glanced back at the reflection of my patient's tormented face.

When Chris was somewhat calmer, I tried reaching him on another level.

"Mirrors are an inseparable part of our endeavor to create the self that we would like to be," I began. "Each of us uses our mirror to cover up what we feel inside. We don't want the terrors in the depths of our being to rise up, frightening and embarrassing us. That's why many people avoid gazing into a mirror when they are feeling most vulnerable to self-doubt.

"More often than not," I went on, "we approach our mirror defensively. We might say something like, 'I feel terrible inside . . . do I show it? I'd better look in the mirror to see if I have to hide some aspect of my inner being by external means—maybe with sunglasses, makeup, or a phony facial expression.' "

Drawing upon Chris's theatrical interest, I brought up Shakespeare's *Richard III*. Throughout the play, I explained, Richard seems to be watching himself in an invisible mirror, measuring his every emotion so as to appear both to himself and to us more well-intentioned than his treachery reveals him actually to be. Like him, we all want to know whether or not our mirrors can see inside us and reveal what cannot be seen by others.

The danger for any of us, I went on, is that the mirror can conceal too effectively. I explained that my clinical experience had taught me that many people are so highly guarded that they cannot recognize their own reflections in a mirror, even though they do recognize the reflection of someone standing beside them. In short, it is possible for us to lose the ability to see ourselves clearly to the extent that we fear what we may find.

Next, I suggested an idea that Chris found more provocative than I intended.

"Perhaps you don't recognize that pained face in the mirror as your own," I said, "because you are defending yourself from becoming aware of your inner conflicts."

Chris turned on me in a spasm of passion. He seized my arms in a viselike grip.

"This is the last time anyone will call me paranoid, Doctor!" he yelled. "I will not have it!" He abruptly pulled away and stood near the door, breathing heavily, but I could still feel the physical imprint of his feelings of hurt and misunderstanding.

His anger grew, actually changing the contours of his face. In rapid succession, what I believed was his usually melancholy expression became a sneer, then something very different, and so on, as numerous "faces" flashed quickly by. Occasionally, an expression lingered longer than others, as if a particular psychic force was struggling to remain on the scene as long as possible. Some expressions recalled figures in medieval painting; others looked like antique photos of inmates in nineteenth-century asylums.

Finally, one last face, pained and lonely, became fixed in place. Less horrifying than the series of kaleidoscoping expressions, it was yet sharper, paler than Chris's expression when he first entered my office. I was reminded of Gustave Doré's engraving of Satan as a withdrawn, brooding figure.

In my bookcase beside the mirror were several volumes on myth and magic. I quickly pulled out a book that discussed the writings of Birnsfeld, a German demonologist in the sixteenth century. He believed that earth is patrolled by seven separate devils, who rise up from the underworld to seek out victims. Each represents one of the seven deadly sins—pride, lust, anger, gluttony, envy, sloth, avarice—originally identified by Saint Augustine and later, thanks to the influence of Thomas Aquinas, condemned as "capital sins" by the Roman Catholic Church. Augustine chose these particular vices because he felt that they are the most likely to stimulate carnal appetites, weaken the will, and discourage the pursuit of piety and good deeds. In other words, the seven deadly sins are the most likely to entice the susceptible person into further sinning.

According to Birnsfeld, Lucifer was the devil who represented pride; Mammon, avarice; Asmodeus, lechery; Satan, anger; Beelzebub, gluttony; Leviathan, envy; and Belphegor, sloth. It was not precisely coincidence, then, that the prismatically changing faces of Chris's terrible rage had reminded me of a picture of Satan, the devil traditionally thought to represent anger.

Another of my books reproduces illustrations of the seven devils from a thirteenth-century French manuscript. When I handed Chris the book and asked if he had seen any of these faces in the mirror, he pointed without hesitation to Belphegor, the devil of sloth. This, too, made sense. Sloth, which is in effect the violation of one's own human potential for developing the positive, compassionate, productive attributes of selfhood, can be regarded as the most tragic of sins. According to the French philosopher Michel Foucault, pride was the original sin of humankind.[2] But after the fall from God's grace, insofar as much of the world is no longer fertile, the absurd pride of poverty, the sin of idleness, has taken on the mantle of supreme vice. As the American poet John Whittier wrote, ". . . of all sad words of tongue or pen, / The saddest are these: It might have been!" When our potential for creativity and compassion is denied, such other human vices or maladies as mistrust, anger, and despair soon follow. Sloth, then, can be considered a master emotion. So it had been for Chris. He was caught in a trap between his terrifying aloneness, on the one hand, and his inability to share his pain with anyone else, on the other. Joining the horns of this dilemma was his resistance or inability to examine forthrightly the causes of his unhappiness. In turn, his lack of self-understanding produced his idle, self-indulgent way of living.

Chris, still standing near the door, began to relax now.

"So," he said with a sigh of relief, "you *do* believe in the devil!"

"No . . . not quite."

"Then why did you show me that picture?"

"We can talk about that later. But sit down first. I have something important to tell you."

He virtually hissed in reply: "I was right, after all! I can't trust you. I knew you wouldn't believe me. You're like all those other psychiatric types who can't tell the difference between your theories and the truth."

"Oh? Like whom?"

"That shrink I saw in the hospital after Jane left me. He claimed I was a narcissistic hysteric, pretending to be possessed so I could feel important. He accused me of preparing my roles by going to see the medieval paintings in the British Museum. Another shrink said I was just crazy. I mean, she couldn't tell the difference between psychosis and actual possession by an evil power."

"And where do I fit in?"

"Coming to you has been a waste of time too."

"No, not quite, Chris." His eyes met mine. "You're convinced that the devil has hold of you. That's what you're telling me, isn't it?"

"Yeah . . . and so?"

"I'm not interested in convincing you that you're not possessed. It's clear to me that something malevolent has hold of your life. Can you reasonably ask me to understand more than that, at this point in our exploration of your situation?"

After a moment, Chris replied, "Well, maybe you do want to help me, but you can't, because you shrinks depend on using words and drugs. And *you* can't even prescribe drugs, because you're not a physician."

"Well, what's the problem with words? Why can't we try having a dialogue?"

Chris smirked.

"Your words are as empty and unreal as my mother's," he said. "But psychics and ministers don't need to use words, because they're in touch with the mystical presence of the spirit world. Too bad the psychics I went to see cared mostly about getting their hands on my money! And preachers! How could I trust one of those fakes after what went on between my mother and the Reverend John!"

The story he told me now, a truly gothic tale of childhood horror, occurred when Chris was nine years old. In a few months' time, he went from innocence to enduring feelings of betrayal and despair.

Early one morning, Chris was startled from a deep slumber by a violently percussive sound. Breathing rapidly in his fright, he shuddered and rolled over on his side, pulling the covers over his head. Yet he could still hear a resounding echo as the hefty metal lock in the front door was opened.

The boy heard forceful, menacing footsteps approaching steadily down the hallway outside his bedroom. They reminded him of a dreadful, unwanted presence that appeared to him in a recurrent nightmare. He glanced furtively at his bedside clock and shuddered again: his father had already left for work.

The footsteps paused just outside his door. For a long while, there was nothing but silence. Chris literally held his breath, terrified that any sound would endanger him.

Eventually, the unknown intruder strode on down the corridor. Chris heard the doorknob to his mother's room turn quickly. His mother's voice, strangely hushed and desperate, whispered, "Oh, Reverend John! My daring Johnny! I've been waiting all night for you!"

Every morning for several months, the boy heard the minister stealthily enter the house and march heavily down the corridor. Anticipating the man's approach was a stimulus to childish fantasies of forbidden embraces. Finally, the boy could bear it no longer. One morning, as the despised footsteps neared, he flung open his bedroom door with all the force he could muster and threw his slim body against the imposingly large minister. Smirking, the Reverend John knocked him to the floor.

Chris, weeping with rage, struggled up on his feet and began pounding the minister's chest.

"Leave my mother alone!" he shouted. "Go away! She doesn't want you here!"

The Reverend John growled, "You are an evil child. You've had things too easy because your family's rich and too lenient. You'll never amount to anything, and you want to do bad things to your mother.

"I'm here," he went on, taking his toll on the vulnerable boy, "because your father is too weak and frightened to stop you from doing wicked things. Your mother needs my counsel, my protection. Hear me well, child!"

Later that morning, Chris looked into the bathroom mirror. It had always been reassuring to look at his unusually winsome face, admired so openly by other people for its dark eyes and full lips. Now he was horrified to see an unfamiliar, rivetingly sinister face in the glass. He sensed immediately that it could read his innermost thoughts. He knew that he must turn away or risk being swept inescapably and eternally into an appalling maelstrom.

Bolting from the bathroom, Chris ran back to bed and hid under the covers. He solemnly swore never to speak about this apparition to anyone. For one thing, his mother had frequently warned her inquisitive, imaginative child to stop telling so many preposterous tales about himself and asking so many intrusive questions, or she would lock him up in a dark room. There, she promised, he could be alone with his boundless imagination for as long as he liked.

I tried to make sense of this disturbing, possibly overwrought, story. Based upon his psychiatric history, I had already surmised that Chris had been denied the conditions necessary to giving him a sense of self-worth and inner goodness. He and his only sibling, an older brother, never lacked for material or cultural pursuits. His family was quite affluent. The family money came from his mother's side. According to her son, she was "hard as nails," an action-oriented doer who repeatedly said that one has to be strong to make it in this world. By concentrating more on Chris's and his brother's actions than their feelings, she neglected a mother's crucial function in preparing a child for intimacy.

Ideally, the mother teaches her child not only how to love and establish intimacy with another person but also, and just as important, how to be intimate with himself. The mother's caring responsiveness, especially as communicated through her eyes and facial expressions, symbolically gives her child access to the mysteries of her psyche. He, in turn, feels the permission to witness his mother's relationship with her own inner being, which gives him leave to have a similarly intimate relationship with someone else—as well as to enjoy his own company. Lacking this emotional nurture, children like Chris perceive the world as persecutory and their innate longings for intimate contact as troublesome and painful.

In the psychiatric report, Chris's mother was described as a "Jocasta," a woman frustrated because she felt unfulfilled in a loveless marriage. When a mother this troubled tries to hide her fears and limitations from her child, she is apt to relate to him by controlling his responsiveness to her. For example, Chris told his London psychiatrist that he had always felt prohibited from curiosity about his mother's body. And indeed, he could not recall that she had ever held him close. Apparently, by withholding her mystery from him, she discouraged Chris from trusting his own body and psyche as places for discovering beauty and contentment. Unable to trust his inner being as basically positive, he paradoxically felt both malignant and empty.

On the other hand, Chris fondly remembered touching his father when they showered together when he was a child or when they hugged or clapped each other on the back in joyous moments. Unfortunately, his father spent much of Chris's childhood developing an increasingly successful advertising company and often had to fly off to Los Angeles and New York on business.

More difficult to understand than Chris's failures at intimacy, however, was the diabolic apparition in his bathroom mirror, which was not mentioned in the psychiatric report. But since I had by this time worked with Julius and other severely deluded, institutionalized patients, I had some intuitions about Chris.

All of us, to some degree, remain in the shadow of our own unsatisfied childhood. To the extent that a person is unwilling or unable to mourn the loss of the ideal parent and the cherished relationship he longed for as a child—by giving words to and consciously acknowledging his inability to achieve the desired relationship—that person cannot live fully and comfortably in the present. He lives a life of pretense.

According to the psychoanalyst Leslie Farber,[3] children who cannot express their upset over their lack of control over their lives are compelled to find ways of pretending that they are not as helpless as they feel. Moreover, the more parents treat their child's feelings of disappointment and loss as if they don't matter, the greater is the child's need to pretend that he can get whatever he wants. Thus, Chris was also forced to deny his feelings in a second way.

When powerful childhood emotions are suppressed because they threaten a child's relationship with his parents, they are consciously denied. But they remain dormant within him, potentially volatile energies waiting to react and infuse adult experiences during tense conflicts or when released by potent drugs. With some seriously disturbed patients, the unresolved tensions of personal identity take on a sinister character in the shape of a shrouded, elusive, hostile second self, so psychologically separate it is not even recognized.

Such patients are highly prone to acting upon the demands of this deranged, malevolent self during radical shifts in consciousness known as a *fugue* state. In this dangerous condition, people become disoriented in regard to their actual identity and their physical location. Later, I would learn that Chris had never been able to express his anger at his mother or his disappointment with his father over the frightening visits of the Reverend John. On the contrary, he held himself responsible for the minister's terrible accusations, because he believed he had poked his nose where he should not have. Because his sexual awakening had occurred in this climate of betrayal and contempt, he saw his sexual feelings as wicked. The "good" reverend became an internalized devil, continually reminding the boy of his "bad" self. Chris's alcohol and drug abuse as an adult was an attempt to ward off the hurt he felt, as well as his consciously suppressed anger toward himself, his parents, and the Reverend John. When he took strong drugs or found himself passionately in conflict with someone else, however, he felt yet again the presence of the menacing apparition in the bathroom mirror.

I was just beginning to see how I might help this terrified young man, when the office doorbell rang. Even though I had set aside an unusually long session for his first visit, it was time for my next patient. When I went to ask her to wait a moment, Chris ran past me and out the front door, into the night.

I was deeply concerned about him. As we talked, he had sounded like one of the Pirandello characters he said he was studying in drama class, full of sound and fury but unable to sustain a mutual dialogue. But we were not characters in a play representing reality; we had been dealing with the core of Chris's actual reality, a life-or-death struggle with madness.

But neither I nor anyone else can provide people like Chris with any kind of psychic equipment to ensure their passive survival. They do not, in the Dylan Thomas phrase, go gently into that good night,[4] essentially because they have so very few nights that gentleness could endure.

In short, because they cannot be protected from the consequences of their madness, they must be given the opportunity to transform it; this is to say, they must be provided with situations in which they can feel a sense of mastery and choice in coming to terms with their hateful second selves.

Concerned as I was, I had no way of contacting Chris, who had refused to come see me in the first place if I insisted on having his phone number. I accepted this condition because allowing him to be in control of our meetings obviously helped protect his psychic vulnerabilities.

After about a week, he called, leaving an odd message with my answering service:

"I've had more horrible experiences. If you don't believe in the reality of the devil, don't bother to call me back. If you do believe, but you can't stop him from possessing me, don't call either. But if you do believe, and you think you can handle him, call me and tell me what to do."

I called him immediately, but he was out. I left a message on his answering machine, giving him an appointment the following day and urging him to be sure to bring Belphegor with him.

When Chris arrived the next day, I asked him if he knew much about devils. He shuddered and said no. I explained that, thinking about his problem since our first meeting, I had done some research into the subject. As he sat quietly, I explained my theory.

While devils are regarded as embodying evil, I began, each of the seven devils representing deadly sins is actually a fallen angel, a rebel against a heaven that requires blind obedience to a supreme authority. Chris grinned and said that kind of heaven sounded like his childhood. I was relieved that he seemed to understand and appreciate my allegory. I went on, explaining that in my view, sin can entrap people who are too frightened to know themselves, not just those who harbor malevolent thoughts. At this, Chris began rapidly to blink his eyes. I continued, watching his reactions closely. Competent human development, I argued, requires courageously facing our limitations and vulnerabilities. Chris squirmed in his chair, his facial muscles taut, his fists repeatedly opening and closing.

At last, he said simply, "I am very frightened."

"Yes, I know. But what is crucial for you to recognize is that none of us, because of some imaginary moral obligation, have to learn about ourselves all alone. We are allowed, Chris, to have trusted friends."

"Will you be my friend?" he asked softly, like a shy child. "Will you take care of me?"

"No, I won't take care of you," I replied firmly. "I have enough work taking care of myself. But as your friend, I will teach you what I, and people I've worked with, have learned about taking care of ourselves. If you're willing to start this difficult process of learning about yourself, I *will* take care of Belphegor, for the time being. And I'll see that he doesn't interfere with your important work."

Taking Chris by the arm, I walked him over to the mirror and encouraged him to bring forth his devil in the glass. Whispering, I advised him to tell Belphegor that we were beginning to understand him, that we realized he wasn't such a bad sort but he must be feeling very angry and badly neglected. I suggested that Chris ask the demon to leave us alone for six months, so that we could learn how to meet his needs. In his own words, Chris conveyed these ideas to the mirror. After a few moments, I asked how Belphegor had responded.

"He said ninety days," Chris replied. "And not a moment more."

After some negotiating, Chris's demon agreed to five months. Not willing to gamble on the trustworthiness of an apparition, I got Chris to help me carry the heavy mirror to a storage closet in the next room. I locked the closet, placed the key in a sealed envelope, wrote the operative dates of our contract with Belphegor on the outside, and put the envelope in the bottom drawer of my desk.

Then Chris surprised me. He asked which demonologist had suggested the technique I had just used for capturing a devil. I had to laugh, because he was assuming that the ability to survive by adaptive cleverness requires intellectual acumen. On the contrary, the idea came from my experience working as a summer camp counselor with emotionally handicapped children when I was still in college. One phobic child, hoping to contain his fears until he and I found an effective way to deal with them, came up with the envelope scheme. When I told this story, Chris smiled broadly. For the first time since we had met, he looked relaxed.

In the five months of analysis allowed us by Belphegor, I saw Chris three or four times a week, but this is not much time for dealing with the inner conflicts of someone so bedeviled as he was. On the other hand, he was very bright. Ravenous for the companionship and mentoring of someone he could respect and trust, he became very adept at discerning—often before I could—that he was reflexively concocting some clever psychological dodge for avoiding unpleasant issues.

After some three or four months, there came a moment of great importance to our work. Uncharacteristically despondent when he arrived one afternoon, Chris said he was feeling worthless, despite the gains he had made in understanding himself. He still could not bear to be alone. The night before, he had drunk too much wine at a supper club and, ashamed as he was to admit it, had awoken in bed with a woman he did not remember meeting, much less following home. He was even more appalled to find that she didn't know his name either.

Making it back to his own apartment, Chris saw Belphegor in the bathroom mirror, laughing and calling him a fool for wasting his time with an analyst. When Chris snapped that he had broken the contract, the demon countered that naively trusting fools get what they deserve.

I considered all this for a moment.

"Why did he tell you it was foolish to trust me?" I asked.

Chris shrugged his shoulders. Belphegor, claiming that he overheard our sessions from the locked storage closet, catalogued a host of therapeutic mistakes I had supposedly made. He charged that I had misinterpreted the true messages hidden in many of Chris's statements and had misdirected our dialogue to issues that were less germane to my patient's concerns than interesting to me personally.

To share my vulnerabilities with self-contemptuous patients is risky, because they might be tempted to extend their feelings to me, scorning my competence.[5] On the other hand, our analytic alliance will suffer harm anyway if I am not as open with them as I expect them to be with me.

"Belphegor is right!" I admitted. "I have made mistakes with you." Although I felt somewhat foolish acting as if Chris's demon were some actual observer whose astute opinion I took seriously, I had to let my patient express his doubts in whatever way made him feel safe. Moreover, I hoped that my admission of limitations would help Chris gradually become more accepting of his own.

But he snapped back, "I'm not impressed with your willingness to admit trivial faults in yourself." In other words, he promptly rejected my unspoken advice for him to be less judgmental. "You have your act together, I assume. It's easy for you to sound modest. People depend on you. But I have to be sustained by other people. You've written books for other analysts, so I guess they respect you. I buy books. No one respects me."

Not surprisingly, his feelings were familiar to me, as they will be, of course, to many people who can clearly remember their early twenties. At his age, I too felt confused about my ambitions; I certainly was unsure how to fulfill my longings for achievement, recognition, and the caring of others. With Chris, as with many seriously disturbed patients classified as "mentally ill," I recognized that to some extent I can share certain of their moods and feelings that are inherent in being human. This bond of important psychological commonalities was a bridge of communication between us. It was the availability of our shared human bond that enabled me to reach Chris and to free his tormented, encrusted psyche from the rage, hurt, and malevolence that he had been unfairly shamed into believing was his inevitable destiny.

I told him that as with many others who become therapists and writers, my role in life had been cast for me long before my birth. I had been imprinted with the desires and worldview of preceding generations. My grandmother admired men of learning and compassion. As a small child, I loved to sit by her side as she served me wonderful meals at her diminutive chrome-topped kitchen table in her small apartment. Preparing the food, she told me exciting tales of the old country. I was especially fond of stories about her father. My namesake had been a lover of books and of the human spirit. People from all segments of society—Jew and Gentile alike—had come to him for encouragement and advice. From my grandmother I received the message that one could hardly do anything more worthwhile in life than be a compassionate and wise friend to people in need. That I was to become a writer was also impressed upon me from an early age. My grandmother's youngest son, my uncle, was an apprentice in a printshop at the time of my birth. A week or so before I was born, he crafted bookplates for my parents to put into the books they would buy me. One depicted a young boy writing at a desk; several others showed him reading in various outdoor and indoor locations.

I told Chris that my recent book in defense of narcissism was created from the sweat and passion of my self-examination of the role my family played in driving my career ambitions. To my surprise and deep disappointment, the very colleagues who had praised my previous books criticized this one, because in it I revealed unbecoming aspects of myself as analyst. Bruised, I retreated to a resort town south of the border to lick my wounds.

One balmy evening, a sympathetic friend and I made our way up a hill to an unpretentious local café. Our close communion required few explicit words about my glum mood. As we sat drinking cold beers in silence, a thin young man with dark hair falling across one side of his face began slowly to sweep the sawdust-covered floor. Apparently absorbed, he was very conscientious. His clothes were ill-fitting, his face a stolid mask. His lack of reaction whenever a patron crossed the threshold suggested to me that he was intellectually impaired.

Yet I found myself envying this young man. He did not seem to resent his job or, I fancied, aspire to something loftier. As I imagined myself exchanging places with him, I felt a sudden sense of relief, an unburdening of who I was. In this reverie, life now seemed safe and certain. As long as I accepted my destiny as sweeper and presumed no higher, I would have a comforting predictable existence.

But this was impossible. Cast out of ignorance by an accentuated awareness of possibility, I was a captive of my unfulfilled longings. I could not switch places with the sweeper. I recognized only too well that my wounded vanity was a transformation—that is, the respect and admiration I had not been able to win from my family I now wanted to earn from colleagues and patients. I could not be happy in simplicity and obscurity. Vanity drove me to prove to others that I am both sincerely caring and eminently wise.

And so it must be. From working with patients and continuing my own self-examination over the years despite periods of doubt, I have come to accept, and appreciate, the draw of the cards that made me what I am. My personal and professional ambitions may have been forged in psychic pain, but they have provided my life with meaningful purpose. I have been fortunate, in other words, in being given passion and drive. Many in my profession who have revealed to me far less hurt in growing up now suffer, it seems to me, for lack of passion and drive.

My story helped me understand Chris's problem. People like me, luckily, were encouraged as children to be curious about ourselves, to explore our inner being. In the search, our love of discovery eased most fears we might have had about the unknown in ourselves, and we were spared the life-and-death struggle with malevolence that deformed Chris's life.

By contrast, he and others like him do not seek to understand themselves unless impelled by pain. His stern mother instilled fear of self-exploration by shaming him for his inquisitiveness and his longing for intimacy and caring. As he discovered so memorably at age nine, she gave to a stranger the loving embraces she refused her own child. His father, good but weak, was also an aversive influence on Chris's sense of self, as he could explain quite perceptively.

"You probably don't know," he said to me, "that the worst thing about those terrifying mornings had to do with my father. He'd been my only ally. He was a very nice man. But he was a coward in dealing with business competitors. He called them 'wolves,' and he felt his wife was a 'bitch' he could not satisfy.

"The Reverend John mocked him that morning. I was furious. But I was not able, or maybe even willing, to defend him. His weakness put an unfair burden on me. All these years, I've had to protect him by keeping my mother's ugly secret to myself."

We know that every child must, so to speak, "choose" to emulate one parent rather than the other. Because Chris cared more about his father, he unwittingly identified with him, thus "borrowing" the man's fears of weakness, his sense of limitation.

As for the Reverend John, his role in Chris's life was a professional revelation to me. For the first time, I realized that people don't descend into madness only because they have experienced trauma and deep unhappiness. The presence of malevolence is also required. Absent the malignant influence of the minister, I believe—based upon my clinical experience with patients similar to Chris—he would still have become a fearful, shame-vulnerable person likely to live a slothful, unexamined life. But he would not have been further burdened with the conviction that he was both possessed by malevolence and capable himself of great wickedness.

On the other hand, Chris might never have sought my help in understanding himself, if the Reverend John had not disturbed him so. In other words, in a potentially beneficial sense, the presence of malevolence can cast light into the meaning of confused human striving.

Of course, traditional theologies tend to disagree with this reading. In the Christian worldview, which posits devils as forces standing in opposition to moral behavior, we cannot allow them to guide us toward understanding, lest they banish virtue from our lives, endanger our souls, and cast us into endless misery. In *The Jewish Bible,* beginning with the story of Adam and Eve, it is Satan in the disguise of a serpent who seduces humankind to commit the first sin by violating God's foremost commandment. Yet we should not fail to notice that the sin produces knowledge and self-awareness.

Among the many interpretations of the Eden parable, I mentioned to Chris the possibility that Satan approached Adam and Eve out of compassion, not malevolence.

"Isn't it possible," I suggested, "that Satan, in a Promethean sense,[6] was trying not to lead humans astray but to provide these innocent beings with enlightenment from the tree of knowledge, so that they could better understand themselves and the world around them? And so it was necessary for human understanding, perhaps, that all three had to sin against God's commandment?"

Chris seemed intrigued. I added that according to this interpretation, sin does not prevent self-enlightenment. Quite the contrary! His despair, I went on, seemed to me to be based upon his unreasonable assumption that human limitation and vulnerability are morally unacceptable. What he saw as sin, I saw as vulnerability. And it is our very vulnerabilities, I argued, that give meaning to our lives by providing us with opportunities to know ourselves—*if* we recognize the opportunities rather than turn away in shame from our weaknesses. By exploring our vices honestly, we can locate the fears that prevent us from finding out how to satisfy our longings in constructive ways.

Chris did not agree. He believed that his years of cowardice about life decisions proved that he was ill equipped to handle life as effectively as people whose parents were better role models.

I countered that he was not necessarily correct. Whatever the nature of our early experiences, we each can choose whether to move toward enlightenment or toward ignorance. It is the exercise of courage that gives us the power to make the choice. Pain, as every analyst knows only too well, is not sufficient to lead troubled patients toward self-understanding. Without courage, so necessary to the human condition, characterized as it is by conflicts and uncertainty, everyone would tend to avert the deeper concerns of human existence.

Our perceptions of courage, as of heroes, have shifted radically from past concepts. In ancient sagas and traditional legends, courage was seen as fortitude in dealing with external enemies or natural disasters. As we have become increasingly self-aware in the contemporary age, however, courage has increasingly come to mean psychological bravery, the will to face our divided urges and inner terrors in order to create a vibrant discovered self.

My views about human nature and psychotherapy have softened during the course of my career. I no longer regard disturbed patients as very different from the rest of us. I perceive people as rather similar in desires and concerns, differentiated only in their degree of honesty, their courage, and their ability to secure what they claim they want for themselves.

"You have suffered," I said. "But you don't have to continue to doubt your talent and your personal character. You don't have to continue seeing them as a metaphoric replication of your parents' flawed and intractable personality traits."

"But what choice do I have?"

"From the start, I've been impressed with your sensitivity and your passion. Your drama teacher and the other students tell you that you have considerable talent. Your passion gives you an important choice."

"How so?"

"If I were you, I'd make friends with Belphegor. Give him his due and admit that he's really offering you a double-edged tool. You can either use it self-destructively by continuing to regard yourself as weak and cowardly—in other words, remain afraid of examining your undiscovered self. Or you can become openly curious about yourself—and by doing so, explore who you are with passion and courage."

Chris began our next session by telling me he appreciated my speaking frankly about my own vulnerabilities. No one significant in his life, he explained, had ever been so open with him. He saw me now as an ally on a shared mission, and for that reason, he felt the awakenings of hope for living his life more meaningfully. For the first time, in sum, he felt free to explore his inner devil.

Chris did indeed stop running from his demons. During several sessions, he faced the mirror in my office and engaged in dialogue with the previously disowned parts of himself. He gradually came to realize fully that openness to who we are, though often painful, gives us the freedom to face the present moment with confidence and courage. Furthermore, it helps us confront where this moment will lead us in future.

Why did the mirror exert such a remarkable influence on Chris?

As we learn in the next chapter, the mirroring experience has the potential to register the most profound questions about the self, such as whether one is essentially a good or a bad person.

CHAPTER SEVEN

The Role of the Mirror in Human Suffering

A life lived out of fear is a life half lived.

—ANONYMOUS

THE SELF, AS CONCEPTUALIZED BY THE EMINENT AMERICAN SOCI-ologists Charles H. Cooley and George H. Meade, is a "Looking-Glass Self," created from the reflected appraisals of other people. In other words, the infant forms her sense of self from the responses of the significant adults in her life. Each serves as a mirror, and in these mirrors she invents her self.

My own work as an analyst makes abundantly evident that the earliest and most basic aim of social behavior is the striving for intimate relations with a caring other person. The capacity for intimacy develops in the infant by means of the mother's mirroring function. That is to say, the mother's responses serve to represent how other people, in subsequent years, will respond to the child. However, the mirror between mother and child is a two-way affair. Intimate connectedness is a mechanism of survival for the child. The infant who responds appropriately to what the mother wants and requires of him is more adaptive in pleasing her and more likely to be rewarded by her caring behavior than is the less responsive child. Reciprocally, the mother's smile evokes pleased responsiveness from the child because her countenance gives the child a sense of being present and cared about. The child *needs* to be looked at, smiled at, and approved of by an active, loving, and supportive caretaker. Without this emotional nurturance, Julius, Chris, and all the other people we will examine who have characteristics of a malevolent personality experience the world as persecutory and regard parts of themselves as unacceptable. Individuals who are subjected to an unresponsive or distorted mirroring relationship with significant others in their life will be handicapped to a greater or lesser degree by their limited capacity to experience their inner being freely, creatively, and courageously, as we will soon see.

Evidence from developmental studies of infants clearly indicates that the child learns to recognize himself in the eyes and facial expressions of the mother. It is the nature of the mother-child bonding that the mother offers her child one of three very distinct and important options in their relatedness. In their early relationship, as discussed in the last chapter, the child may be given unrestricted *permission* by the mother to look into her depths *through* her eyes and by means of her facial expressions. Such a mother metaphorically gives her child access to the mysteries of her psyche. Witnessing the mother's relationship with her own depths allows the child to have a relationship with the mystery of another person.

In sharp contrast with the first option, the child may be provided the opportunity of only looking *at* her eyes and facial expressions and, as a consequence, be allowed to perceive only his or her reflection as the mother's *restrictive* view of the child, as in Chris's upbringing. As we learned about Chris, when a mother is troubled, as was his, and tries to hide her fears and limitations from her child, she is wont to relate to her child by controlling the child's responsiveness to her. By fearfully withholding her mystery from him, she simultaneously discourages her child from trusting his own psyche as a place to find beauty and inner contentment. Those inner psychic urges that the child has access to will be experienced as painful and troublesome.

In the third option, the mother allows her child into her depths. But in the process, she *overwhelms* the child with her anxieties and fears. In my clinical work with very disturbed patients, this model seems to have been operative. The mother treats her child as if the child were her own imaginary parent, there to assuage her loneliness and desperation. Because she fails to recognize him as separate from herself, or even as real, she does not allow her child the freedom to have his own mystery. I would suspect, although I have no direct evidence for my assumption, that Julius's relationship with his natural mother approximated this bonding model.

Taking the three kinds of bonding options together, I am proposing that satisfying intimacy between mother and child in their early bonding requires the mother's ability to be intimate with her own depths. She must be willing to struggle with, or at least not to deny, aspects of her totality as a person. Significant in their relationship, therefore, is the child's witnessing the mother's fortitude in bearing pain and suffering in her caring functions. In Roy's case, discussed in the next chapter, and Gina's case, in this chapter, we see the devastating effect of the parent who tries to shield her anguish from her child.

Children who are denied the open, inner being of their mother for identification of their own internal experiences will be in continual search for external mirrors, such as strangers, to reflect acceptable aspects of themselves, thereby validating and justifying their existence.

But as we are all well aware, inanimate objects also participate in this mirroring process. When the glass mirror was invented, in fifteenth-century Venice, replacing the smaller and cloudier steel mirror, it became possible for the first time to examine oneself extensively, to rely upon one's own perceptions rather than the word of others. According to the French historian George Gusdorf, the aristocracy jealously guarded the glass mirror and originally kept it from the common people because of its reputed powers,[1] which gave rise to self-consciousness.

We continue inventing our selves by means of the mirroring process as long as we live. Our glass teaches us to see ourselves as we imagine others see us. Because the exposure of one's vulnerabilities to the eyes of others evokes the threat of suffering, the self may try to undo and remake itself, concealing its risky aspects in the process.

What is the nature of this vulnerability we can see in the mirror? Gina's story explains.

Graced with the sullen lips and coal-black eyes that inspire flamenco, Gina's face is captivating, but she abruptly lost all interest in her features during adolescence. One day, the vacant countenance of her reflection staring back frightened her; she did not look directly into a mirror again for many years. When she wanted to locate blemishes or check her make-up, she purposely focused on only one portion of her image at a time.

I met Gina when she was in her early thirties and living with her profoundly disturbed mother. When Gina was five years old, this woman, then pregnant with a second child, vanished one morning without warning. Unknown to her husband and daughter, she felt incapable of loving and caring for another child and went off to have an abortion. Ashamed, she never returned home.

Gina searched for her mother for years. Only the year before she began seeing me in analytic treatment did she finally locate the woman and bring her home to a quiet, secluded apartment in New York's Greenwich Village. Unfortunately, finding her mother did not put Gina's fears to rest.

Over the years, each of us fashions an image to conceal our doubts and insecurities; otherwise we might become overwhelmed and demoralized by our vulnerability to pain. We present this mask to ourselves and to the world, creating it with the help of our mirrors. Note that a mirror is, in this sense, reversible: it not only reflects our flaws but also helps us conceal them.

Although Gina very much desired the company of others, she intensely mistrusted their motives and could not risk contact without hiding behind a mask of concealment. The protective masks we use can take various forms. To shield herself from her terror of being taken by surprise, Gina would leave her answering machine on continuously, even when she was at home. That way, she didn't have to answer her phone without knowing who was calling and why. The voice of her taped message acted as her surrogate. Indeed, this second self was the only image of Gina available to many callers.

Her dependence on her mechanical double was based on an assumption many of us share about the mirror: that it transcends and may even replace physical reality. We can beg the question of what *is* and, in collaboration with a mirror, instead ask how we *should* appear. In effect, the phenomenon of the mirror poses the question "What is real?"

Viewer and mirror enter into a magical relationship in which we believe that the self or aspects of it can be reinvented, reversing the natural course of life. This hope springs from the recognition that mirrors are never absolute. Each mirror has its own peculiar characteristics and is influenced, to some extent, by its surroundings. Move a mirror, and the light affects how it reflects. Consider: many of us prefer using a specific mirror at a certain time of day, hoping to find always reflected there the special self we have invented.

For Gina, her taped "mirror" was an attempt to hide her narcissistic vulnerability—that is, her realization that her unusual good looks would eventually vanish. She had switched from glass mirror to magnetic tape in the hope that her youthful voice, recorded for all time, would magically preserve her beauty forever. She was desperately trying to believe that she would not have to examine troublesome, vulnerable parts of her self as long as some aspect of this beauty endured.

But what was the cause of Gina's terrifying vulnerability?

A psychoanalytic explanation of Gina's behavior would tell us that she unconsciously felt guilty for her mother's disappearance, believing that her mother left her because she was a bad child—a child too difficult to handle. Moreover, like so many children in a similar situation, Gina probably had hateful, perhaps even murderous, feelings toward her mother after the desertion. Psychoanalytic theory would further explain that Gina had probably transposed her feelings *after* her mother left to having occurred *before* she left and that consequently, since the age of five, she had guiltily believed there was something evil inside her that drove her mother away.

While the psychoanalytic explanation of Gina's behavior I have offered may have some validity, I will provide another type of reasoning, which I believe comes closer to the motives that influenced her unhappy life.

Several root causes were involved in Gina's terrifying vulnerability—all of them related to the psychological conditions that can foster malevolence—but the most pivotal was *inability* or *unwillingness to self-examine*.

We suffer primarily because we are aware of our vulnerability to pain and to death. In response, we design most of our daily activities as aids in denying or buffering our dread of nonexistence. In fact, according to recent studies of average Americans, the fear of death is a crucial determinant of how most of us live our lives.[2] Clinical studies of my patients suggest that this fear may play an even stronger role for the emotionally disturbed.

Death is the ultimate shame, revealing our essential helplessness and confirming our abject, lifelong fear that we largely have no control over what happens to us.[3] All of us, I believe, seek throughout life to deal with that fear by acquiring knowledge and making a special place for ourselves in the world, hoping to forestall if not defeat both death and its accompanying shame. In this sense, the experience of shame issues from a profound despair at having no infinite future as an existent being. It should be understandable, then, that the most painful sense of shame and despair I have found in my patients is the *shame of not being seen*—perceiving oneself as not worth noticing by others and disappearing for all time— rather than the embarrassment of being seen as flawed, as Freud and others have claimed. Not being seen, not being noticed by others, carries with it the curse of intense loneliness. My clinical experience has underscored my belief that the terror of believing that one will be alone forever, untouched and uncared for, is a major cause of human misery.

Perhaps the most excruciating articulation of this awareness is Tolstoy's novella *The Death of Ivan Ilyich*, which shows how the fear of death is central to the tragedy of living and dying without being understood or uniquely cared for by one's closest friends and loved ones. As the dying Ilyich deteriorates, his wife and children join in denying his condition. His chief torment is that they become annoyed when he is downcast, censuring him for suffering. As Tolstoy notes, Ilyich is condemned to painful solitude: "And he has to go on like this, on the brink of doom, all by himself, without a single person to understand or pity him."

Tolstoy dramatizes his hero's sense of death as the ultimate shame for two different, but related, reasons: death is undeniable evidence of human inability to control fate, and it brings humiliating disapproval from others for awakening their own inner fears. It is the second kind of shame, or "lie," according to Tolstoy, that causes Ilyich the most pain: "the lie adapted by everyone for some reason, which stated that he was only ill and not dying."

Such forces as this "lie," supported by societal myths, impose a major impediment to self-discovery. In other words, once self-discovery uncovers the truth that we are mortal and restricted by human limitations, our resulting self-knowledge becomes the estranged sibling, as it were, of the magical belief that we can defeat death and our inherent limitations. Consequently, if we can magically ignore the truth, we can continue believing that we are not on the brink of extinction. When we rationalize the postponement of self-discovery we may magically assume we will live forever and have limitless time to deal with the responsibilities of our existence. The problem of human alienation and malevolence, I submit, can be traced back to this fallacy.

Our greatest human achievements are derived, I believe, from our ability and willingness to accept our limitations. In doing so, we soberly confront our magical strivings for being *Übermensch*. Giving up these magical beliefs, however difficult, allows us to know love and create beauty, illuminating the preciousness of what we have, and providing access to the deepest strata of our undiscovered selves. There are, however, forces in our society that keep us from this recognition.

Certain venerable legends warn us of the dangers of peering below the surface of the image we present to the world. In the myth of the handsome Narcissus, for example, his mother asks Tiresias if the boy will have a long life. The seer predicts that he will, but only if he never sees and comes to know himself accurately.[4]

Eventually, of course, Narcissus falls into a pond and drowns while admiring the beauty of his reflection in the water. The standard interpretation holds that he falls in love with the image, thinking it another person, and dies when he leans over to embrace it. I disagree. If we recall Tiresias' warning, the tale suggests that Narcissus recognizes his reflection only too well. He surrenders to despair, plunging to the bottom of the pond when he comprehends the painful vulnerability that lies below the surface of his legendary beauty.

Similarly, each of us fears a full disclosure of our dark side. A few years ago, I conducted a research investigation of sixty-four highly experienced psychoanalysts and psychotherapists.[5] This group had a mean average of over thirty years of clinical experience. One of the questions I asked of them was their experience with self-analysis. The Socratic doctrine "Know thyself" is the ethos of the psychotherapy profession. Freud regarded it to be indispensable to the most profound understanding of any problem, recommending that the psychotherapist continue a regular process of self-analysis after personal analysis with an experienced therapist was completed. Most of the respondents, while admitting to self-examination's general usefulness for themselves, emphasized the highly elusive and deceptive nature of a process in which the seeker of inner knowledge may too easily fall prey to being satisfied with superficial and partial explanations of troublesome behavior. Still others admitted that they had not developed any great skill with self-examination, despite their having had considerable personal analysis or personal psychotherapy.

Thorough self-understanding, then, is only a philosophical ideal, not the achievable goal of any actual human being. Self-doubters, we feel the need to cover over what we don't know about ourselves. We fashion masks with the aid of our mirrors, rehearsing them daily in order to conceal our secrets and self-doubts.

But our protection can be lost in an instant. Like Chris, we can have an experience so frightening that it will expose our inner vulnerabilities, shattering the ruse of the mask. We all sense that day of reckoning and try to forestall it.

This conscious refusal to know ourselves, though temporary, provides a magical reprieve from our fears of our selves. Because the unconscious, as Freud stressed, is timeless, there is no sense of death (or negation of possibility) in the unexplored recesses of the psyche. By acting as if we will live forever, we rationalize our postponement of self-discovery.

In this regard, some of my disturbed patients have made a "magical bargain" with Providence in order to protect themselves against their fears both of death and of self-discovery. In this bargain, they are not allowed to experience themselves consistently as being *alive,* because, as the psychoanalyst Harold Searles has written, "one need not fear death so long as one feels dead anyway; one has, subjectively, nothing to lose through death."[6]

Does the fear of death that cripples profoundly disturbed patients have the same impact upon the perpetrators of malevolence? In a study of criminality, Yochelson and Samenow found that this fear is strong, pervasive, and persistent in the thoughts of wrongdoers. Most have expected from an early age to die young; many are preoccupied with the anxiety that their next breath will be their last. At the same time, they consider it cowardly, even equivalent to death itself, to *admit to any fear.* As a result, they have little tolerance for their own perpetual dread.[7]

Fear of death is abundantly evident in both the works[8] and the life of the infamous eighteenth-century Marquis de Sade. In striking contrast with the German philosopher Friedrich Nietzsche, who contended that some humans strive to find wisdom in order to become *Übermenschen* (extraordinary beings), Sade believed that one must act like a god to become a god, and gods have the power to use us humans as mirrors of their own capacities. Sade himself sought to quell his fear of mortality by striving to gain control of life and death. It is said that he tried to attain his goal by performing dehumanizingly cruel experiments on other people, including children.[9]

Sade died in chains in the Bastille, raving mad. I am convinced that his insanity was nourished by the grandiose lie of immortality that governed his life. It is the same lie that caused Gina to hide behind the mirror of her taped message, letting the recorded voice seem to be the real Gina, while her self remained hidden. Like Sade, she paid for her deception through increasing loss of contact with other people, along with the loneliness and desperation that result from the absence of caring from others.

And no more than Sade, in the end, could Gina transform her deficit of self-esteem into positive self-regard by having a romance with her mirror. Why not? Because we learn to regard ourselves benevolently only in our flesh-and-blood dialogues with real people—those we care about, those who care about us. Any romance with the mirror reveals a basic *mistrust* of other people's intentions.

Before Gina's mother left home, she told her impressionable little daughter that her growing beauty would one day entitle her to all the riches of the world; also protecting her from its miseries. The failure of this promise was experienced by Gina, of course, as a mother's betrayal. Consequently, she suffered not only because she feared the humiliation of revealing her frailties to others; more important, she faced the pain of having to admit that her mother's assumptions about her place in the world were untrue. For Gina, shame sprang from the realization that the life she had been promised was a *lie*.

On the other hand, she most feared the lie yet to be. That is, even while viewing her youthful beauty in the mirror during adolescence, she could simultaneously grasp that it was impermanent. Before she turned abruptly away from all mirrors, she asked one fearful question: could her mirror depict what lay within her, the self that could not be seen by others with the naked eye?

One of Freud's greatest discoveries was that people erect psychological defenses because of their fear of knowing themselves intimately. What he did not seem to recognize, however, is that we come to know ourselves in large part through the eyes of others. We are anxious that others might see us too accurately, again not so much because they might condemn us, as Freud believed, but because we are forced to see unsavory aspects of ourselves when these attributes are perceived by others. In other words, the person who knows himself best should have the least to fear from others because he has the least to hide from himself.

So for Gina, as for many of us, the fading of vitality and the resultant suffering do not become real until other people recognize our symptoms. Therefore, because we fear that mirrors will reveal magically unseen aspects of our selves, our fear of the mirror is the *fear of what is yet to be*. Realizing that we are fundamentally frail and limited beings, we resist making the effort necessary for attaining personal significance and unification.

The busywork of our daily endeavors can somewhat decrease our recognition of vulnerability. But at certain moments, as when we or a loved one comes down with life-threatening illness, we are baldly forced to confront the impermanence of human existence. Such moments evoke more than mere anxiety; often, they unleash sheer *terror*. Far from being focused solely upon the question of mortality, this terror includes questions about our achievements, our reputation, and the likelihood of our being remembered by others. It is a terror of shame having to do with fear of erasure or distortion of everything we've created and struggled for—in short, the meaning of our life.

Some of us experience this particular terror more acutely than others; certainly, Julius and Chris felt it profoundly. The continual terror most floridly psychotic people experience, in its ultimate sense, is an inability to defend against the prospect of total loss of meaning of oneself as a person.

Like Searles, the sociologist Ernest Becker argues that the psychotic feels more keenly overwhelmed by life, more conscious of finitude, more fearful of death, than others. In his important book *The Denial of Death*, he movingly explains why the patient might suffer so deeply from these realizations:

> . . . he has not been able to build the confident defenses that a person normally uses to deny them. [His] misfortune is that he has

been burdened with extra anxiety, extra guilt, extra helplessness, an even more unpredictable and unsupportive environment. [As a result, he can*not*] *confidently deny* man's real situation on this planet.[10]

This underbelly of terror, experienced by us all in at least a subliminal way, was the impetus behind Gina's attempt to reconstruct her image.

So far, I've been discussing shame solely in pessimistic terms; traditionally, it has been viewed as a negative emotion. But this perspective is both inaccurate and unhelpful.

Far from being our enemy, shame confronts the reality of our tenuous human existence. By direct contrast, guilt is an attempt to deny that terrible truth, misinforming us that all human distress is caused by violations of moral and/or civil law. In other words, guilt promises that our suffering will be resolved by reacceptance into the human community once we confess our sins or crimes and make penitence. Under this "vital lie," we act as if we do not need to try to better ourselves in order to improve our world. We assume, quite mistakenly, that all we need do for happiness and security is to obey the law.

If guilt tells the sufferer that he is at fault, shame reveals that he has *inhibited* a necessary, legitimate action. That is, by mirroring an awareness of the neglected conditions of our self-worth, constructive shame derives a moral imperative from the embarrassment we feel in catching ourselves in the act of trying to deny our existential responsibility.

In other words, shame is a kind of traffic signal—sometimes red, but often amber or green—that can direct our progress along an important if perilous avenue of the inner self. In short, shame is positive and potentially constructive insofar as it fosters the conviction that we have an obligation to take an *active participating* role in our existence, rather than merely obeying the law.

In sum, the destructive manifestations of our shame can be overcome, once we understand why it exists within us.[11] Were we instead to refuse to probe our potentially constructive shame, we would forever, in Hamlet's phrase, "lose the name of action."[12]

Before Gina was able to take legitimate action that would enable her to experience self-worth and pleasure in being alive, she had to learn to give voice to her terrors and shame. Eventually, she separated from her mother and moved to another city, where she derives great personal success and satisfaction from working with abandoned children.[13]

Of course, despite Gina's symptoms of shameful and negative personal identity, she was not a criminal or malevolent person. Can constructive shame help divert someone from the road to crime? The following stories provide an answer.

Early in my career, I worked as a consultant on group psychotherapy for Drug Central, an unusual grassroots organization in Washington, D.C., which brought together former drug addicts, alcohol-abuse counselors, attorneys, judges, psychologists, and journalists. Joined by their concerns about the local "drug scene," the participants meet once a month to pool their ideas and resources for setting up and maintaining effective drug information/treatment programs.

One "elder" in the group, previously addicted to street drugs for close to forty years, had been completely drug-free for almost a decade when I arrived. Moreover, he broke the habit on his own, an achievement so rare on the street that we all wanted to hear his story.

To pay for his very expensive habit, he told us, he often burgled houses and pawned the loot. Generally, he targeted the homes of relatives, because he knew when they were likely to be out and where they kept their valuables. One day, when his dealer demanded cash within the hour, he panicked and raced over to his parents' house when they were both at work. He went to the china closet and gathered up his mother's heirloom silverware, her most valuable and prized possession, stuffed it under his coat, and dashed to the front door.

But as he reached for the knob, he felt a sudden wave of heat extend from his neck over his entire body. A voice that sounded like his own, but was entirely separate, scolded him:

"How can you steal from your own mother? Have you turned into a selfish savage?"

He replaced the silver and never again felt the temptation to take hard drugs.

On the other hand, his character had not been completely transformed by this experience. Still creatively manipulative, as he had been as a thief and con artist desperate to pay for a fix, he used his cunning for socially constructive ends. He was brilliant at persuading federal and private agencies to fund the effective drug-treatment program he operated for inner-city youths. His "street smarts" were also invaluable in communicating with these alienated, troubled young addicts.

He explained to our group that his drug-free decade had given him pride, for the first time in his life, in his self-sufficiency. His phrase for the incident in his parents' house was "maturing out." I call it "constructive shame."

Why "constructive shame" rather than "constructive guilt"? First, feelings of shame and guilt are highly susceptible to each other. In other words, shame often evokes guilt, and vice versa. Moreover, shame may be disguised, denied, or bypassed by a host of subtle psychic mechanisms. For example, some people with a particularly tenuous self-regard cannot tolerate even the slightest sense of shame and, unwittingly, convert being humiliated into feeling guilty for having done some wrong. Consequently, in the ex-addict's case, I would not deny that some guilt might have been present; nevertheless, shame was the far stronger and more profound of the emotions present.

Guilt, in contrast to shame, pertains to the violation of a *specific act* or some circumscribed aspect of behavior. Essentially, feeling guilty expresses the fear of corporal punishment for violating the laws, wishes, or morality of those whom one *fears* and believes will cause *abusive* punishment. This understanding was the basis for Freud's castration fear metaphor in showing how guilt feelings serve the child as a deterrent against immoral behavior.

However, it should be pointed out that the ex-addict, similar to many drug addicts I worked with at a federal hospital, didn't fear his parents—and probably never did, to any considerable extent. His shame, I believe, was representative of the sense that he was living his life contrary to the values of the parents he loved and respected. In the accentuated, disturbed sense of self that we call "shame," it is admired figures from our past (in this case, from the present also) who are experienced as disappointed by our behavior. In other words, whereas feeling guilty comes from the recognition that one is at fault (affirming that the ex-addict probably experienced some guilt), shame is derived from having inhibited a necessary action, preventing one from defining one's personal identity with self-esteem and pride. Moreover, the feared punishment for shame is not abuse from others, as in other people's reactions to one's guilty behavior, but loss of the loving connection with significant others, who are believed necessary for one's psychological and/or physical survival.

It would be instructive to examine another incident in which a malevolent criminal felt guilt but insufficient shame to recognize the malignity of his actions.

A few years ago, I spoke about the problem of malevolence to a synagogue congregation in Santiago, Chile. The rabbi, who had trained as a clinical psychologist in the United States, told me about an experience he had while working in a mental health clinic in his native Argentina.

A distinguished-looking middle-aged man entered his office and, after some difficulty, told him that he had come for psychological help in getting rid of his guilt feelings, which prevented him from sleeping and getting on with his life.

What had caused these feelings? As an Argentine Air Force pilot, he had flown planes from which prisoners of the state were thrown into the sea.

He was asked what he had done about his heinous behavior. The former pilot looked at the psychologist without comprehension, then answered, "I was in part responsible for some awful crimes. And now I feel terrible about what I've done. Isn't this enough? I want to rid myself of these feelings, because they are driving me insane. Will you help me?"

The psychologist took a deep breath, then told him that the only sane thing about him was his conviction of guilt. However, feeling disturbed wasn't sufficient. What he had done was to divorce his deeds from his central being. These deeds had not bored into his soul, as was necessary if he was to examine authentically the attributes in his character that had permitted his involvement in the crimes. Only with this insight could he change his life for the better and regain self-esteem. If he had a sense of shame, he would recognize this. Since he apparently didn't have this, he would be told the right thing to do. He must report to a judge and be imprisoned for his crimes. Only in jail would the psychologist agree to provide psychological counseling.

We will see in Roy's story to follow how the groundwork is laid for malevolence to emerge when we are unwilling or unable to examine our inner selves. The person who becomes cruel and destructive is seeking to dispel the disturbing realization that he is neither invincible nor likely to be superior to other people. For particularly self-contemptuous people like Roy, it can precipitate the transition from "child of the devil," or Stage II of the development of the malevolent personality, to Stage III, "perpetrator of malevolence" toward others.

But the lies of the malevolent are only aberrant forms of the vital lies that most of us tell ourselves. As that insightful observer of human character Henrik Ibsen pointed out, if one deprives the average person of his saving lie, his happiness will also disappear.

CHAPTER EIGHT

Transition from Victim to Perpetrator of Malevolence

We cannot do evil to others
without doing it to ourselves.
—JOSEPH FRANCIS DESMAHIS

I NEVITABLY, THE PSYCHOANALYST'S OFFICE IS A PLACE OF SHAME.
On the one hand, the patient seeking treatment is ashamed, perceiving his visit as an indication of incompetence as a person, and this
shame is magnified by the very presence of the analyst, which forces the
patient to reflect upon unworthy and mortifying aspects of himself as he
reveals his secrets.

On the other hand, his shame is capable of shaming the analyst. Unable to reach and heal a suffering patient, any caring practitioner is also
vulnerable to feeling shame. This inexorable shaming will awaken the
analyst's personal concerns and conflicts as well.

When Roy came to me for treatment, he was thirty-five years old. The
youngest of five siblings in a working-class family, he exhibited some of
the classic Lombroso characteristics of criminal physiognomy: thick neck,
barrel chest, powerful torso.[1] Well over six feet tall, square-chinned, with
piercing pale-blue eyes, he wore his blond hair cropped short, and had a
tattoo on his left forearm.

When Roy was five years old, his father deserted the family. Starting at age seven, the boy spent half his life in psychiatric and forensic institutions. Usually, the incidents that led to his detention involved the sadistic intimidation of women, stopping just short of rape.

Although he was a high school dropout, Roy was a facile conversationalist, with an exceptionally wide vocabulary. He was also cannily observant of other people and could analyze their motivations quite plausibly.

He had come to me, he said, because he sincerely wanted to straighten out his life. Fair enough—but the route he had taken was bizarre. Some time before, I had helped train the paraprofessional staff of a county "hot line" crisis service. Afterward, I continued to be available as a consultant for unusually difficult or risky situations. One evening, Roy called the service to say that he was worried because he had been making obscene telephone calls for years and couldn't force himself to stop. The obscenities he repeated, together with his frequent allusions to violence alarmed the volunteer who took his call. She asked him to hold for a moment while she consulted with her professional consultant.

Roy shot back, "You can't help me, kid? Just give me the doctor's number!" She tried to put him off, but he became insistent. "Little girl, I know who you are. I'll have no trouble finding out *where* you are. And when I do, I'll come over there and rape you again and again."

She promptly gave him my home number.

Roy called me for an appointment, explaining that his finances were limited, even though he was a skilled cabinet-maker, but he would find a way to pay my standard fee. We met several times in preliminary sessions—with more than a little misgiving on my part about his motivations—before I agreed to work with him. In the first place, despite his claim that he wanted to examine his life closely, his history was checkered with numerous short-lived forays into various treatment programs. Second, my office was in my home, so it was possible that Roy might be using the pretext of visiting me to "case" the neighborhood for targets of theft, or even rape.

Why, then, was I willing to risk treating such an intimidating person in my home? Even today, I'm not entirely certain, but it had something to do with my need for an intensive challenge. For some time, I realized, I'd been feeling apathetic toward almost all areas of my life other than psychological work and intellectual activity. This situation was at odds with the person I had been in adolescence, a "jock" so deeply absorbed in sports that I had entered college expecting to become a professional athlete.

Now I was recognizing in myself the very malady I was struggling to help my patients transcend: the foreboding sense that I might never actually live my life well. This existential malaise demanded some means of resolution, and practicing psychotherapy was one of the few areas in my life that had recently given me some sense of actual accomplishment.

Roy was evidently a very difficult person, but it seemed likely that dealing with him would generate a resurgence of my vital energies. In addition, I felt a partial identification with him, because we had both played highly competitive football. Fantasizing a physical as well as a psychological combat with him recalled the days when I matched my youthful daring against intimidating opponents on the field.

To my dismay, however, Roy did not cooperate with my need for accomplishment. On the contrary, he was resistant to analysis and threatened my overvalued persona as a highly competent practitioner. He laughed at me whenever I tried to relate his present conflicts, such as being frequently fired from jobs because of his violent confrontations with supervisors, to events and feelings in his early life. His brutal snicker conveyed unmitigated contempt for me and my technique, but his words were hardly less upsetting.

"Who are you trying to kid, Doc?" he would say. "You're no better than me. If I stay around long enough, maybe I can help *you*. But what can *you* do for me?"

These frequent attacks made me feel embarrassed and exposed. I began to wonder what he suspected about me. Surely, I thought, he had not been able to detect my own personal dissatisfactions.

Finally, about six months into Roy's therapy, we encountered a serious crisis. For about a year, a serial rapist had been loose in the county, luring women out of their cars at night by pretending to be a police officer. I started to worry that Roy might be this rapist, though I didn't want to confront him directly, because he'd be likely to suspect, despite my pledge of confidentiality, that I'd go to the police. Suspicion alone could cause him to mask, distort, and lie about his past behavior—as well as about the feelings attached to those harmful events in which he remained pathologically mired. I felt that my main therapeutic responsibility was to work with his *neurotic guilt,* not the possibility of his actual guilt as a rapist.

One afternoon session, contrary to my usual practice, I spoke first. Referring to his menacing conversation with the young woman volunteer on the hot line, I asked Roy if he had ever raped anyone. I felt that he would probably be less reluctant to admit more remote crimes than the current attacks. And since serial violence rarely begins as such, there would most likely have been previous sexual crimes if he was the Beltway rapist.

To my great surprise, the usually glib Roy sat for a long moment with his eyes downcast, and for the first time, I realized that my willingness to accept him as a patient meant a great deal to him. Until then, I had assumed that therapy gave him the so-called psychopathic or secondary gain of securing, and temporarily savoring, the exclusive attention of someone he believed to be a successful professional. Consequently, I was taken aback by the real pain in his reply.

Looking up, he said, "I think you're afraid I'm the Beltway rapist." In a troubled tone, he continued, "If I was that mug I would tell you so. Why do you keep trying to make me have a guilty conscience? I don't! That's not what's bothering me!"

He went on to say that he'd already been punished for many things he had done that most people would regard as immoral. He felt no resentment.

"That's the way the game of life is played," he said.

What was bothering him, he continued, was more difficult to confess than any crime.

"Look," he said, "I'm a real big, powerful guy. People are scared of me. And I've never been afraid of anyone or any situation, but inside, I'm scared shitless, lonely and sad, all the time. It's strange, because I can have just about any woman I want and get her to do what I want. Like, for example, getting the woman I hang around with to pay my bill to you when I run out of money. . . .

"But what bothers me most is that I'm going to die, I'm going to leave without having really been here. I'm more ashamed to admit that I don't know how to live than of anything immoral I've done. I don't know what's missing in me. That's why I keep coming here. And I've trusted you. Why the hell can't you trust me!"

At that moment, I felt unprepared to address his anguish. My professional training had emphasized that unconscious, neurotic guilt—usually of an incestuous nature—is the major cause of human unhappiness. But I suddenly realized that there was a real difference between Roy and my other patients, who harbored identifiable feelings of guilt.

I recalled Harold Searles's poignant article, "Schizophrenia and the Inevitability of Death,"[2] which argues that psychosis is the defensive strategy of fictitiousness. In other words, the psychotic pretends that he is neither alive nor dead, for to be alive is to be launched down the pathway to death. To someone like Roy, convinced that he has not yet fully lived and will never live well, the prospect of death is especially terrifying.

But I also saw that the dread of death Searles describes is undoubtedly true of all of us, an identification I would have to closely examine in terms of myself if I expected to reach my patient effectively. And yet there was something shameful about trying to become more fully identified with the unsavory Roy. As long as I continued to work with him, it would be impossible for me to find refuge from the self-doubts and concerns we had in common.

Fortunately, clinical experience had taught me to recognize when my reactions are being induced from patients. In this case, therefore, my feeling shameful with Roy probably indicated that he was feeling shameful with me. Once again, I was encountering a case of unrecognized shame. Until this critical session, I had not given either his shame or mine its proper due.

The psychoanalyst Erik Erikson[3] asserted that shame is produced by a crisis of trust between mother and child. In order to ascertain whether or not conflictual aspects of Roy's relationship with his mother were deeply implicated in his shame, I needed his *personal story*. That is to say, I could not effectively treat his despair (and other psychological conditions) without understanding how he saw himself and his experience of being-in-his-world. For this exercise to be meaningful, he needed to describe himself with personal statements drawn from the deep recesses of his psyche rather than as someone might perceive him from the outside.

Not surprisingly, many patients find it very difficult to reveal their personal stories. Otherwise articulate, highly thoughtful people are suddenly at a loss for words when asked point-blank to convey a full, coherent sense of themselves. One of Freud's most important discoveries was that the fear of what we might learn if we take an intimate look at ourselves is the single greatest cause of emotional disturbance. It follows that despairing, shame-afflicted patients want to hide their sense of incompetence not only from me but also from themselves.

To deal with this problem, I suggest that patients draw upon the thoughts and feelings we form early in childhood and then continually revise throughout our lives. I never question or challenge these stories so long as they sound heartfelt and uncontrived, but I do intervene occasionally to make comments and ask for clarifications in order to understand how they are feeling while talking about themselves in this way.

We are, after all, meaning-oriented beings. We create our personal identity in the *stories we tell ourselves* about what has happened to us. We may not have one favorite story that "says it all," but we can each tell stories that reveal a paradigm of how we see ourselves in relation to the world, its opportunities, and its obstacles. Because we cannot empirically discover any absolute truths, we derive our stories from a wide variety of sources—the events, legends, and myths of family and society—in order to create a reliable guide for living.

In fact, these myths can show quite succinctly just how my patients navigate through life's straits and vicissitudes. At least as a working hypothesis, they help me clarify what my patients want from life, which obstacles they fear, and what resources they can use to attain their desired selves. I begin by asking for a story that best represents what life has been for them. When they come to the end, I ask them to go over the events again, describing as much as they can about the thoughts, feelings, and actions of the other people involved. Finally, I ask for the *moral,* or significant message, exemplified by the tale.

When I asked Roy for his personal story in the structured way I have just described, he spoke more openly about his mother than he had about her or any other person during previous sessions. He seemed to be seething with resentment, claiming that his violent temper came from being "done in" by women like her and his sister.

As a very young child, he recalled, he always looked forward to seeing his mother; he felt safe with her. But she died when he was only seven, and his sense of security vanished. His circumstances forced him to live with an older sister, who did not want him around; she was having enough trouble raising her own brood after her husband deserted her.

Forever afterward, Roy felt alone, unguided, and severely shaken. Naively, like most children, he had believed that his mother could keep his world safe, predictable, and just, so long as he returned her love with unquestioning devotion. When she died, he was left feeling bitter and betrayed, by her and, indeed, by the entire world.

Trust in ourselves usually develops together with trust in our physical surroundings. If we fail to perceive or predict correctly the events of the external world, we can lose trust—often permanently—in ourselves and in those who have cared for us.[4] Roy's feeling of self-worth was overthrown when he found out that his confidence in his mother had been misplaced.

Life is not always reasonable and fair. In each child's life there will inevitably be disappointments and misunderstandings. Nevertheless, the child must be protected from experiencing too frequent and too prolonged emotional pain. On the other hand, if there is too little stimulation in the child's life because he has been thrown on his own when he is still too immature to care for himself, he may develop an unrelenting hunger for excitement. Children who develop precocious restlessness, fed by a craving for stimulation, rarely form the appropriate sensitivities to the subtleties and nuances of life. They can perceive the world only in bold black or white dimensions. These children are compelled by an unrelenting obsession: "I've been cheated. I won't stand for it! I must have my own way! If not, others won't have their way with me again!"

I refer to the emotional unavailability of parents and caretakers—depriving the child of attention, vigilance, guidance, and compassionate concern—as *benign neglect*. It is a factor no less lethal in the development of the malevolent personality than are physical and sexual abuse.

Benign neglect thinly conceals the parents' ambivalence about being parents and adults, as well as their rage and hostility toward each other.

When young children have to create their own morality because their parents have left them to their own devices, the result is usually children who are out of control. This is one of the messages of William Golding's novel *Lord of the Flies*.

Roy's story was an important revelation to me: for the first time, I saw that the shame ordinarily at work in our lives does not necessarily arise from malevolence, intentional cruelty, or even the ill wishes of another person. Roy's shame had its origins in his mother's love; for the more fervently we have believed in the benevolent qualities of love, the more grievous are our pangs of shame and despair when we are disappointed.[5] Roy's mother tried to shield him by keeping her fatal illness a secret. As she lay dying, he was not even allowed to help her in the small but important ways available to young children. Consequently, he felt betrayed by what seemed to be her lack of confidence in his ability to care for her. Roy's expressions of intense anger toward others as an adult were actually unsuccessful attempts to expunge the morbid impotence he had felt as a child after this traumatic event.

His hurtful shame, therefore, derived to no small extent from his inability to protect the person he loved most, and the loss of his loving bond with her crushed any yearning for loving or caring for anyone else ever again. In short, his shame was caused by his separation from loving relations and his feeling inadequate to carry on by himself.

Until this session, Roy had never been willing to examine the hurt, resentment, and contempt that arose from his painful experiences with his mother and sister. Instead, he angrily and brutally acted upon his agitation, deftly rationalizing his contemptuous behavior toward women and his violence toward men.

"I have the balls to do what other men just fantasize about," he would boast.

All of his adversaries were displacements for the people who had hurt him in the past. Understanding *displacement*—a psychological defense set up when someone who has hurt us is no longer available or too powerful to confront—is essential to understanding malevolence. Roy and other wounded people, who are at least partly aware of what they are doing, "choose" to harm victims whose suffering will resemble their own original hurt. Seen from this perspective, the malevolent person can be intimate with himself—at least, with the hurt self he disavows—only during these acts of displacement. At all other times, he keeps in place a callous defense that denies any identification with his pain.

"Since life is cruel and mean," Roy frequently said, "I'll be cruel and mean too."

In other words, he had transformed himself from abandoned child, a victim, into victor of an ongoing struggle with others for dominance. At the same time, by becoming a master manipulator of women, he subtly flaunted his sense of superiority over his father, who in Roy's view was *not man enough* to handle women because he allowed his wife to die and had abandoned his own son.

Roy and I shared a common bond. If betrayal was the symbol of shame and anguish in Roy's life, it was in mine as well. My despair was the product of feeling betrayed by my professional life. Many analysts develop a sense of fraudulence about the examined life. They feel that their commitment to analytic understanding of themselves has not harvested the savory fruit of the well-lived existence that their faith in psychoanalysis had promised. This is a subject that few analysts are willing to talk about publicly, instead deferring their nihilistic feelings for conversations with close trusted colleagues or for their return to the analytic couch.

Meaningfulness does not wane categorically for the analyst who is in despair. Confidence and the sense of well-being depart bit by bit. Therefore, through the skills and tricks of the trade, the seasoned practitioner may still carry out his professional duties almost competently, even when his convictions about the theories he subscribes to and the illusory benefits of pursuing the examined life trouble him. For the seasoned practitioner, these disturbing effects may first reveal themselves in a crippling manner for his private life. For me, the experience of being a seasoned therapist undoubtedly gave me skills in enhancing my relationships outside my clinical work. On the other hand, preoccupation with clinical problems gave me a "legitimate" excuse to avoid responsibilities to my family and my marriage. Inevitably, of course, these effects of disturbed meaning will manifest themselves in clinical practice.

If I dared to look back honestly over my career, I had to admit that the years did not seem well spent. But like other disillusioned practitioners, I thought it was too late to recover what was lost.[6]

Why did I feel such despair? I had come to realize that analytic expertise and insight into human affairs are not always finely attuned, dependably rational tools. Originally, I had believed that I could rely upon the wisdom of the examined life to succeed in both my professional and my personal affairs. But now I was convinced that knowledge and analysis had not actually done much to help me live any more fully and satisfyingly than someone who was less self-examined. Moreover, I had similar doubts about the significance of my work.

This existential malaise, as I suggested earlier, had grown over the years as I shifted from being an active participant in life to spending most of my time observing it. I had hoped that my scholarship in books and articles would provide lasting meaning in my life. By contrast, of course, clinical work is written on the wind, since it is largely unobserved and subjected to the mercurial nature of my patients' lives.

In short, my writing was an attempt to deny my own vulnerability and mortality, but we cannot continuously fool ourselves about the truth of impermanence, as I was reminded when I interviewed for an administrative position at a large teaching hospital. The process of meeting with various staff members went well until the end of the day, when the director of the outpatient clinic looked up from my résumé and stared at me quizzically.

"What is this all about?" he asked. Since I clearly had no idea what he meant, he pointed to the list of my fifty or so publications. "Why do you need to write so much?"

Of course, I felt immediate resentment, since he seemed to be reducing my publications to little more than some unresolved childhood conflict. Then I became considerably anxious, instantly recognizing once again, as most of us do from time to time, that the conditions upon which our hopes and aspirations depend are fundamentally and terribly fragile. At such moments, we also realize how quickly and easily our apparent achievements can be taken from us and how our desires, even when they seem satisfied, may prove to be empty.

One force motivating my writing, although I had not consciously acknowledged it until then, was my shame in regard to my father. This was evident in one particularly vivid memory.

While still in analytic training, I wrote a book about my clinical work. It was well received professionally, and I proudly gave my parents a mint-new copy the next time I visited them. My mother opened it excitedly, glanced over practically every page, and said that she was impressed that I could write about such a difficult subject. My father gave my book a brief look and shrugged.

"You should write a novel instead," he said. "People like to read about ideas in a story rather than an academic book." Then: "Are you making any money yet?"

I nodded. (Untruthfully, of course, since I had only just begun to practice.)

"Good! Good!" He walked off to watch television.

The shame I then felt about wasting time writing a book recalled my shame about athletic and literary activities I pursued in my teens, when both parents worked overtime at strenuous jobs to give me a first-class education at a boarding school. Because I did not want my father to feel that his years of toil and sacrifice had come to nothing, I decided to write a better book next time, one that would show him at last who I was and why I had chosen my career. I was never able to write that book, though I wrote many others, before he died.

It was in that boarding school, with its German accent and the conveyance of the love of books, Mozart, and the outdoors, that I first heard mention of psychoanalysis. Also, there I first experienced the capacity of the psychoanalytic mind-set to reach the inner recesses of the psyche. My teachers, non-Jews who had fled the Nazi Holocaust, were well educated and trained in psychoanalysis and Gestalt psychology. They conveyed an understanding of human behavior that was for me mysteriously powerful. They seemed able to put into articulate words the intrapsychic messages that sustained periods of silence for my classmates and me.

My experience with these European teachers is related to my reasons for becoming a psychotherapist. At some subliminal level, psychological knowledge presented to me a means of both understanding and escaping the confusing conflicts of my nuclear family. In other words, studying psychology led me to a career in which I found the financial and psychological means to separate successfully from my family.

Because psychology had such a salubrious effect on me, I was, as a beginning therapist, somewhat uncomfortable about being paid. My most gratifying clinical year was my internship. I assumed that the clinical skills I was developing would enable me to experience the world in a way that ordinary people could not. The fact that I was paid a minimal wage, less than half of what I had made the year before and so low that I was actually eligible for welfare benefits, was no problem for me; my sacrifice was my investment in the future.

Contrasting how I experienced myself in my twenties, a beginner having an unforeclosed future, with my perspective of midlife, its future more limited, I felt betrayed by myself and by those mentors I had trusted.

Accepting my malaise, or in effect dealing with my tragic sense of the existential condition, is no less onerous for me or any practitioner than for a patient. Session after session, I have to face aspects of myself that I would rather deny or evade. But it is necessary for me to use myself as a mirror to help my patients learn to integrate themselves, even though the mirror is dangerously reversible, a potential threat to bearer and gazer alike. That is, I may encounter my own sense of vulnerability in the eyes of my patients, and this bold sight of my frailties may evoke the discomfort of shame.

But no matter how deeply the therapist suffers in these circumstances, he must continue to try to help the patient work toward healing. In essence, this is the agonizing existential dilemma for the shameful practitioner: the analyst-patient bond requires that he help someone whom he might resent for bearing witness to his own vulnerabilities.

During the most difficult moments of my critically important session with Roy, I felt myself losing connection with what was familiar and safe. I could neither escape nor control my pain; there was no place to hide. Time seemed frozen, endless.

Even so, my shameful awareness was strangely illuminating, and I began to see that the key to my impasse with Roy lay in the *untranscendable* sense of shame. I realized that we were struggling with shame in *existential time.* In other words, the shameful feeling that we are incompetent to find purpose in life is important to us only because our time is limited and we will one day cease to exist. Our most disturbing experiences are those that threaten our relation to time; the most painful aspect of them, as in Roy's case, is the inability to imagine a future moment when we will be free of our anxiety or depression.[7]

I also became aware that our most profound human experiences—joys and dejections, ecstasies and fears—are heavily influenced by differing dimensions of time. To my knowledge, no theorist has yet described the crucial phenomenological distinctions among the three existential anxieties: guilt, anticipatory anxiety, and shame.

Guilt is experienced as an act already committed, an event in the past. The culpable person experiences his guilty deed as one which he has *chosen.* Moreover, he may haggle or negotiate with the internal representatives of authority within himself as to when he will address his culpability. The victim of neurotic guilt, for example, chooses to remain in the past.

Anticipatory anxiety, by contrast, is struck in uncertainty about some future moment. Obsessive concerns about what may lie ahead prevent him from concentrating on life's immediate demands.

But in my impasse with Roy, I was suddenly, startlingly aware that my feeling of vulnerability was occurring in the moment: there was no sense of time. I had no choice but to be who and where I was. I was the shame. And I could not transcend myself. Time had stopped and I felt engulfed by the prospect of the pervasive shaming moment remaining everlasting.

Shame results when we try to avoid the present, because the constructive role of shame is to teach us the reality of time, how to enhance our lives in the present because our time is implacably limited, and how to release the past in order to stop harming our present and our future.[8] Too much emphasis on guilt, therefore, compels the patient to discuss superficial, often irrelevant material. The result is that he and the practitioner will evade the profound concerns they both harbor about the conditions of their own self-worth in the present moment.

With Roy, I had the option: would I, or would I not, keep my vulnerabilities concealed from him? To the extent that I ceased concealment, I realized, I would be free to explore the factors crucial in having a meaningful alliance with my patient. Most important, we needed to examine how each of us was allowing the other to be perceived. I asked Roy how he experienced my treatment of him.

"You've always used the word 'discount' to explain how people put me on the defensive when I was a kid," he answered. "But that's what *you* do to me."

He was hurt, in other words, that I had not confirmed his feelings as legitimate and real. Evidently, I had allowed my own shame to stand in the way of responding to his in the present, preferring to keep our therapeutic encounters focused on the remote shadows of his past. By working with his transferential distortion—how Roy might be confusing me with conflictual people in his background—I was denying my participation in the present and giving no importance to what he needed right now. In the same vein, I had been relating to him as if I were an objective, detached scientist on an archaeological quest rather than a fellow traveler suffering similar despair over not having lived fully and well. I had been ignoring the mutual shaming that existed between us.

Roy needed me to bear witness to the unfairness of a life ravaged by

shame. I recognized that my feelings of shame in the presence of my patients were not only a manifestation of my own unresolved issues. They
were also a testimony to my conviction of *what ought not to be* in my patients' lives. At the same time, as a professional guardian of *what can be,* I
recognized that I had to remain actively alert to the constructive aspects
of Roy's shame.

To reach the deeper sources of our existence, we need to have a dialogue
with a responsive other. Sharing shame experiences, though painful because they produce a disturbingly accentuated self-consciousness, are
moments in which we become aware, however fleetingly, of the ambitions, longings, and sentiments that are valuable to our sense of who we
are. By providing a mirror to reflect aspects of our selves that are usually
hidden, shame confronts us with the reality of our tenuous existence, as
opposed to the "vital lie" described by Ernest Becker.

Any practitioner who chooses to acknowledge both his own and his patient's shame clears the way for discovering important options for living
one's life. Experiencing my shame with Roy taught me that I have a personal as well as a therapeutic obligation to take an active role in my encounters with other people. Those of us who become psychotherapists
typically share our patients' exquisite sensitivity to suffering, but we also
differ from someone like Roy, for example, in having found that human
conflict can be successfully handled by psychological means.

Quite to the contrary, Roy had felt deceived and betrayed by the many
regimes of psychological treatment he endured. He was especially bitter
about the electroconvulsive therapy forced upon him at one institution.
Having spent most of his life in one form of psychological treatment or another, he well knew that ECT was clinically contraindicated in his case
and therefore constituted abusive psychiatric treatment. Because of this
and other incidents, Roy had severed his empathic identification with others in order to develop a characterological shamelessness toward his own
feelings, thus shielding himself from his psychological vulnerabilities.

I needed to offer him some existential choices based upon the constructive influence of psychological examination, but paradoxically, in my
malaise I now found the examined life deficient. And yet, as I have indicated, my growing understanding of shame showed me that sharing my

own feelings of impotence, vulnerability, and transparency might be the critical sine qua non of healing Roy's devastating despair. Furthermore, if I could not feel compassion for myself, how could I genuinely feel compassion for my patients? Rather, by regarding my own emotional struggles during a session as the pangs of caring and concern, not as weakness, I might be able to provide a significant therapeutic experience. In short, I concluded, only when a practitioner and a patient share their common humanity can they actually begin traveling down the road to finding meaning in human existence. Until they trust each other in the present, they cannot deal effectively with the shame and guilt of the past. This suggested a reversal of the usual psychological procedure, but my consideration of the role of shame left me no other reasonable conclusion.

And so my therapeutic task with Roy was clear. First, I had to demonstrate that we can all work toward emotional maturity by engaging in psychological examination and then using the psychic data as signposts in our struggle with the unbecoming aspects of our selves. Second, I had to acknowledge to him that I had just as much investment as he did in making ourselves known to each other. Third, I had to offer a psychological scrutiny of myself as a means of repairing our therapeutic alliance.

I told Roy about my experience at the job interview, explaining that from subsequent self-examination I had come to realize that my sudden anger had sprung from the painful recognition that I was living a lie. In other words, my frantic efforts to give my life permanence had been futile; for me, as for everyone else, such attempts were illusory sand castles in the dunes of time. On the other hand, I went on, I could now recognize that my life is given meaning by my relations with other people, albeit a kind of meaning that is always shifting, mercurial, and subject to the whims of circumstance. I said that I was willing to offer this understanding of myself as a means to help him make sense of his own life.

Eyes are the windows of the psyche, we've been told. We avert our eyes to conceal the desolate domain of our inner self or, similarly, to avoid having to concern ourselves with the tribulations in the psyche of the other.

It was not until I allowed my eyes to meet and lock with Roy's that I knew that the shaming between us was indeed the key to his healing. When we looked frankly at each other, I sensed his wish to assure me that I need not feel ashamed of what I had just revealed. Then I asked, to be sure, and he nodded. In return, he said that he wanted to feel he was an acceptable person in my eyes, even though he had never contributed anything of value to anyone.

I replied that each of us was a separate person who would someday go his own way. Therefore, the more openly we made ourselves known in the present moment, the more accurately we could appreciate the feelings and concerns we were sharing and the great value of the present moment. No, we would never fully understand each other or agree fully on everything, but if each became able to recognize and respond to the humanity of the other, the process would be worth the effort.

A couple of weeks later, I had to leave town for a month or so. When I returned home, there was a message from Roy on my answering machine. He had decided to turn himself in to the police for a criminal act he had committed some weeks before beginning his treatment with me. Because he had always felt the need to impress others with his mature sexual prowess, he had been ashamed to tell me about an incident that involved exposing himself to young adolescent girls sitting in a parked car. From our sessions, he said, he had learned that the only thing to be ashamed of was not living his life openly and to the best of his capacity. He had decided to confess the truth and take his punishment, then get on fearlessly with the rest of his life. The last sentence of his message sounded like a quiet resolve.

Some readers may be puzzled that the patients described in previous chapters, each exemplifying one of the initial two steps in the forging of the malevolent personality, seem to be less reality-oriented than Roy, who exemplifies Stage III. Conventionally, the earlier ones would be diagnosed as "schizophrenic," Roy as "psychopathic."

In the next chapter, we will see why such standard psychiatric concepts and clinical labels do not help us understand the malevolent personality. By focusing on madness rather than psychosis, I am suggesting a new perspective for understanding disturbed behavior.

Madness
and Malevolence

So farewell hope; and with hope farewell fear;
Farewell remorse: all good to me is lost;
Evil be my good.
—JOHN MILTON, *PARADISE LOST*

To BE UNDERSTOOD IN DEPTH, MALEVOLENCE HAS TO BE SEEN IN the context of its relationship to virtue. On the one hand, Niccolò Machiavelli made the remarkably cynical assertion in *Discourses* that people will always prove bad unless necessity compels them to be virtuous.[1] But Socrates, supposedly that wisest among ancient sages, is shown in Plato's "Protagoras" contending that no one willingly acts malevolently. The person who knows what is good, he continues, will be unable to choose wickedness.[2]

We know very well that people do horrendous things to themselves and to others, things that are clearly avoidable. Can we account for these acts and also accept Socrates' belief?

Setting aside the metaphysical causations of evil, we can reasonably propose only three possible explanations for wicked acts, if we concur with Socrates:

1. Malevolence derives from ignorance of what conventional morality regards as good as well as ignorance of those actions that violate conventional morality.

2. Questions of morality rest on cultural values; therefore, societies differ in their judgments of what constitutes wickedness.

3. The malevolent person's capacity for recognizing what is proper has been intellectually and morally impaired by either a lifetime aberration or a psychological trauma later in life.

At first glance, ignorance must be ruled out as the operative factor in most serious crimes. We have ample evidence, from the statements of Jeffrey Dahmer and Westley Dodd to Colin Wilson's extensive investigation of criminality[3] and the clinical studies of the behavioral scientists Yochelson and Samenow,[4] to show that heinous crimes are usually committed in the full recognition that they are violations against conventional society's idea of acceptable behavior.

There is general merit in the "cultural relativist" thesis that the acceptable and unacceptable latitudes of normative behavior vary to some extent from one society to the next. For example, not all cultures hold the same attitudes toward work, sex, and child-rearing practices. Nevertheless, the condemnation of extreme behaviors involving cruelty and destructiveness differs only rarely and under special circumstances among different societies.

Consider, for example, the Nuremberg war crimes trials. As reported by prison psychologist Gustave Gilbert in *Nuremberg Diary*,[5] Julius Rosenberg, the Nazi party's fervidly anti-Semitic ideologist, defended his own role in the Holocaust in terms that suggest it was deemed socially acceptable: "Of course, we didn't expect it to lead to such terrible things as mass murder and war. I was only looking for a solution to the racial problem."

Similarly, Hermann Göring, the second-most-powerful person in the Third Reich, tried to justify his acceptance of genocide because it was recognized domestic policy:

They ask me why I didn't turn against him [Hitler], if I couldn't persuade him to take a more reasonable course. Why, naturally, I would have been executed on the spot. But aside from all that: the German people would never forgive me for that. It is not a question of dying but of my reputation in history. And if I've got to die, I'd rather die a martyr than a traitor.

But the malevolent behavior of such men was acceptable to only a minority of the German people. The majority fled Europe, were imprisoned, or remained a part of society by *denying* the terrors that were taking place. Indeed, according to Robert Lifton, virtually everyone felt an enormous reluctance to acknowledge what state officials were perpetrating, ostensibly on society's behalf.[6]

And sociologist Lewis Coser affirms that this reluctance was not at all based on ignorance:

> [The German] people ..., though they had a somewhat vague knowledge of the fact that some horrible things were done in the concentration camps and elsewhere, nevertheless managed to hide this knowledge from themselves. They knew and yet they didn't know. They saw themselves and were seen by others as "good people"—they would never have done any dirty work themselves—and yet they were dimly aware of some dirty work done by others and even in one way or another condoned it "as necessary."[7]

In other words, most Germans did not view Nazi actions as "good" or "acceptable" but, according to Coser, might have found them "necessary." Living in a society that regards cruelty as "necessary," one is forced to choose among options less desirable than one might ideally prefer. Given this situation, a malevolent act becomes a good choice, because it is preferable to an even worse solution. Such choices are not made, therefore, in terms of any absolute morality.

Logically, if we do not knowingly choose bad, then whatever we choose must be, in our eyes, good. The choices available are between competing values, competing obligations, or both, but these concepts are defined by the *parties to the conflicts*, not by outside observers or analysts. To describe the opposing sides of a conflict as "good" and "bad" is to impart our own values to the situation.[8]

We need to ask what psychological factors would have led some of the German people to believe that the mass degradation, torture, and murder of helpless people is a "preferable" option. Since we have ruled out the first two possible explanations on my list—ignorance and cultural difference—we are left with the third: something interfered with the normal human capacity to make rational decisions.

In the case of Nazis who actively participated in malevolent actions, was this interference, this impediment to appropriate behavior, a form of mental illness? That is, more or less, the commonly perceived wisdom about malevolence in our own country, where a number of forensic hospitals are filled to overcapacity with convicted criminals who have been determined by the courts to be suffering from diagnosed mental disturbances. On the other hand, Westley Dodd, Jeffrey Dahmer, and Adolf Eichmann were never declared insane. Moreover, half a dozen psychiatrists examined Eichmann before his trial in Jerusalem, and no one discerned any serious abnormality in his intellectual functioning. In fact, one of them, emotionally agitated from having to be with this architect of genocide in close quarters for several hours, commented that "[Eichmann] is normal, more normal, at any rate, than I am after having to examine him."[9]

British political scientist B. Clarke wrote that what concerned him most about Eichmann was not his madness but his sanity. Eichmann's tragedy, Clarke claimed, was "that he did not inherently lack the faculties of understanding, judgment, reason and will but merely gave up the active and individual use of these faculties—that he deferred in all important aspects to the faculties of others."[10]

Other Nazi officials were examined by behavioral scientists soon after World War II, as part of the preparations for the Nuremberg trials. In order to determine whether the personality organization and psychological functioning of these war criminals were affected by some form of psychopathology, they were given a psychiatric interview, an intelligence test, and a Rorschach.[11]

The results were surprising. The team of psychologists who evaluated the Rorschach tests reported: "From our findings, we must conclude not only that such personalities are not unique or insane, but that they could be duplicated in any country of the world today."[12]

Common sense surely finds a remarkable discrepancy between the psychologists' findings and the barbarousness of the acts instigated or condoned by Nazi leaders. Only two explanations seem possible. One, we could choose to believe, as many apparently do, that the reports of the kinds and number of atrocities were greatly exaggerated—that is, the defendants at Nuremberg were not guilty of heinous crimes, after all. Two, we can doubt the adequacy or appropriateness of the psychological tools used to evaluate these malevolent criminals.

Since the empirical evidence of the Holocaust cannot be denied by rational beings, we are left with the second conclusion: the tests and interviews at Nuremberg failed because they were not designed to recognize crucial signs of intellectual and emotional dysfunction necessary for understanding malevolent criminality. In the early years of my career, I spent a considerable number of hours administering psychological evaluations. For the most part, I found, these tests were based upon unproved and, in my view, dubious psychoanalytic assumptions about the unconscious processes in mental functioning.

Where, then, do we begin to look for these indicators of malevolent criminality? I believe Erich Fromm was on the right path when he asserted, "Some people have no freedom to choose the good because their character structure has lost the capacity to act in accordance with the good." In effect, he is casting aside such assessments of abstract psychological functioning as Rorschach inkblots. Instead, he stresses the *moral development* of the malevolent personality.

Unfortunately, most psychologists who work in the areas of moral and cognitive development have traditionally shown little interest in the study of malevolence. They have confined their investigations of aberrant behavior to why children lie and steal. Virtually no important study has been made into the psychological development of children who become involved in serious violence. Consequently, no significant information about the impairment of moral and cognitive development has been found that might reveal a possible link between malevolence and moral and intellectual deficiency. Nevertheless, as the vignettes in this book should convincingly demonstrate, such data is available.

People involved in acts of extreme cruelty and destructiveness, though they may not be discernibly psychotic, are yet caught up in their own *madness*. For what is madness, after all, but a *rage* in which reason has been disturbed.[13] As we have seen in earlier chapters, early experiences of humiliation and shame ensure that self-contempt becomes an integral part of someone's negative personal identity. When the contempt becomes so overwhelming that it endangers the integrity of one's ability to survive, it is cast out in the form of acts of retaliation against everyone who has inflicted, witnessed, or stood by idly during the individual's terrible suffering.

Madness has little or nothing to do with illness—at least, not with disease as we understand it in the medical model: that is, as an affliction of a bodily organ. After all, which organ would be involved in malevolence? In fact, the "illness" model is an inappropriate explanatory metaphor, based upon the clinician's moral disapproval of the behavior of his patient, which is as true of other emotional disorders as it is of malevolence.

Even today, after centuries of study, observation, and treatment, emotional disorders remain mysterious to us. We know little more about schizophrenia, for example, than the ancient Greeks, who explained aberrant behavior on the basis of a diseased liver, demonic possession, or freely chosen iniquity. Despite our extensive research on the brain chemistry of diagnosed schizophrenics, we have yet to provide definitive evidence that brain physiology is involved in any demonstrable way, as it is in aberrant behavior caused by known organic disease.[14]

Psychologist Morton Schatzman has succinctly summed up the thesis that designating someone "mentally ill" is actually a moral judgment:

> All that is certain about "mental illness" is that some people assert that other people have it. Epistemologically, "mental illness" has the status of an explanatory concept or a working hypothesis. No one has proven it to exist as a thing, nor has anyone described its attributes with scientific precision and reliability.[15]

MADNESS AND MALEVOLENCE: A THEORY

The madness involved in malevolence is a *moral malaise*, an impairment of the ability to feel good about one's self or confident in one's relationship to others.

The madness of malevolence is a protest against the inhumanity of what the sufferer believes has been done to him by caretakers and others in his past.[16]

The greatest philosophical writers—Sophocles, Shakespeare, Goethe, Dostoyevsky—understood intuitively that madness is not an illness but an affliction that issues from a severely pained, anguished conscience. Unfortunately, their brilliantly intuitive insights involve characters who are adults, already suffering from the pangs of conscience and despair after committing shameful crimes. Only rarely are we given glimpses of these writers' understanding of the childhood influences and conditions that have contributed to the behavior of their adult protagonists. My case vignettes have been selected to provide that understanding.

But these great writers do offer us a perspective from which we can view madness as a self-imposed excommunication from human company. Because the mad are not actually guilty of anything, they can realistically do little or nothing to change their moral condition. As unaware victims, they are shamed by their incapacity to deal with the world, and they use madness as a way of hiding from it and keeping others away from their vulnerable selves.

In Chris's case, as we have seen, the devil in the mirror was a disturbing reminder of the secret he was forced to bear, signifying his entrapment between terrifying loneliness on the one hand and inability to share with anyone his painful travails on the other. From his story we see that madness is a reaction to a sense of shame about one's personal helplessness, just as fear of death has inspired religious beliefs that promise immortality. Madness as a state of being uncared for and alone is the punishment for one's personal inadequacies.

In Dostoyevsky's *Crime and Punishment*, the young intellectual Raskolnikov's gradual progression into madness is a powerful illustration of the effect of shameful helplessness in emotional disturbance. Unable to forgive himself for his inability to earn enough money to support his widowed mother and younger sister, he feels devastating humiliation when the latter enters a loveless marriage so that he can continue his university studies. Soon thereafter, he murders two miserly old sisters for their money, rationalizing that they are of no value to anyone, while he has a keen intellect that requires upkeep.

Subsequently, Raskolnikov, separated from human company, is unbearably lonely. Such a terrifying conviction that one will be alone forever, in conjunction with a personality that is unexamined, cultivates a vulnerability that enables powerful forces and people to take control of one's life. As a very disturbed patient explained to me early in my career, "Being paranoid, so that I hear voices accusing me of evil acts, means that I never have to be alone and disregarded." At the time, I did not understand that his ironic humor masked a message that is critical for understanding madness and malevolence.

We all have unknown aspects of our personality, and if we neglect them, we are as much in peril as anyone else of having an encounter with "the devil." To repeat Jung's warning: That which we do not bring to our consciousness appears in our lives as destiny.

Faust's encounter with Satan in Goethe's famous drama can be viewed as a depiction of the tragic hold of toxic shame in the lives of those who do not know themselves well enough to find the inner wisdom and interpersonal resources that can help establish a constructive purpose for their lives. Because Faust has not discovered his hidden self, he can never recognize what he actually needs to find fulfillment. Like all unexamined people, he wants more and more.

Someone who believes that she is possessed by evil is too vulnerable to psychic pain and suffering to be able to break her pact with the magical forces that are supposed to protect her from the suffering and death that befall ordinary people.

Of course, it is not only the unfortunate few who are shamed. As humans, we are all bound in a state of shame because we suffer a lack of equilibrium: a disharmony between our animal, carnal appetites and the search for meaning that is motivated by our spiritual nature. When we fall short of our spiritual ambitions, we incur a sense of shame and despair.

Therefore, it is never the devil who tempts us to wickedness; it is we who seduce the devil. Satan could approach Faust only when petitioned. He could take control only when Faust inadvertently exposed his vulnerability by asking for magical solutions to free him from his failure to obtain romantic love, friendship, honor, and eternal youth.

To build upon Fromm's view, once a person sets foot upon the road of malevolence, his character becomes his fate, and he can only with increasing difficulty, choose to act benevolently. But how do we explain, from a psychological perspective, the act of choosing?

FREEDOM AND CHOICE: THE PSYCHOLOGICAL MEANING

Acts of atrocity, especially those involving serial violence, do not come out of the blue. They are detectable in the types of choices used by the perpetrator to justify his earlier acts of insensitivity and cruelty. This perspective speaks to the problem of human freedom. The fundamental question philosophers have tried to answer through the millennia is whether or not we have freedom of choice over our actions.

Unfortunately, even the finest philosophical intellects of each generation have posed the question in such a way that the problem could be answered only abstractly. That is to say, the focus of the dilemma of choice has been to ascertain whether an individual has freedom of choice at the moment of a crucial moral decision. The emphasis in stating the problem this way is to examine the character of some abstract notion of human nature and not the concrete, specific series of actions of a particular person. On the basis of abstraction, the determinist can argue persuasively that the behavioral forces bearing upon a person from the past inevitably compel the person to take a predictable action at the point of decision. Abstractly, as well, the alternativist can convincingly show the many potential alternatives available to the person at the point of moral decision.

More so than philosophers, psychoanalysts have typically adopted a deterministic position—that is, they tend to attribute only a minimum of freedom of choice to our decision making. To reach this conclusion, they have arrantly devalued the governing powers of our conscious mind, contending that the unconscious is the relentless ghostwriter of our life script.

Quite simply, my personal experience confirms my clinical: they are wrong. The unconscious mind dominates only with the permission, or at least the tolerance, of the conscious mind. As we all should know from our everyday experiences, the conscious mind is the actual author of our thoughts and deeds. It seethes continually with feelings, ideas, urges, and images, which range from pleasant to unpleasant or remain unjudged. Usually, we choose to ignore or suppress or attempt to evict some of these mental occupants, while encouraging or cherishing others. It is from these decisions that we form our feelings about ourselves.

Of course, our choices are not entirely inventive, for they are grounded in past judgments made for us by others, particularly our caretakers. If we examine closely which thoughts or urges we ignore, we can see that our choices are based on *shame* considerations more, because they provide us with a sense of ourselves that may or may not be in keeping with our positive personal identity. For example, suppose that we encounter a street beggar, sincerely feel sympathetic to his plight, but rush onward because we're late or otherwise preoccupied. Immediately, we begin making excuses for ourselves. Yes, we are really kind and decent, we really want to help deserving people, but that guy might have been a con artist. Or perhaps we think that he was too aggressive in his approach, offensive in his manner, and so forth. In other words, to justify this compromise of our ideal positive personal identity, we suppress the odorous feeling about ourselves and attribute the "badness" to the beggar, since he was the one who evoked the situation that threatens our self-image.

Nevertheless, to the extent that we suppress those feelings and urges that comprise our self-esteem, we experience the unsettling feeling that something is wrong with us. Worse, we might also feel that some aspects of our hidden selves may be so unsavory that they are best left unexplored. This region of imprisoned, abandoned thoughts, feelings, and urges is what psychoanalysis calls the "unconscious," pictured as operating separately from our consciousness.

As we have just seen, however, we do not unwittingly censor the material that is shifted to the unconscious; we shelve it there by conscious choice. Of course, as we continue to ignore and abandon certain of our mental occupants over time, they move to the periphery of our minds. There, they operate more or less independently of our ready awareness.

RATIONALIZATION AND DENIAL

But what accounts for the chain of choices that eventuate in the perpetration of malevolent acts? My clinical studies strongly suggest that the psychological mechanisms known as *rationalization* and *denial*, when used in conjunction with contempt for and manipulation of other people, are the psychodynamics that justify and perpetuate a chain of choices that tend to malevolence.

Denial is the defense mechanism used to disavow unacceptable motives. Rationalization is a psychological strategy that provides quasi-legitimate, seemingly rational reasons to justify behavior that does not fit an individual's perception of his personal identity and values. Each must be viewed in light of the key role justification plays in all societies. Because our behavior always has reference to some standard or set of guidelines that legitimizes our actions, we continually rely upon such concepts as "deservingness" and "reasonable" or "fair" behavior in our conversations, to say nothing of our thoughts.

The Existential Basis for Rationalization

What seems most basic to human endeavor is that each of us craves a sense of meaning and unification for our existence.[17] In order to survive, we attempt to bring some semblance of meaning to our experience by creating standards to live by, thereby regulating and ordering an otherwise inexplicable world.

For this reason, Oedipus put out his own eyes even though, in a particularistic sense, he could not be held culpable for the tragic slaying of his father. He had acted only in self-defense, killing a man unknown to him. But in a universal sense, as Oedipus realized, patricide was unpardonable. A price had to be paid, and he found it just.

All societies, subcultures, and groups establish normative systems that regulate exchanges among their members. Without such systems, which may be regarded as psychosocial formulas for social utility, interpersonal relations would be bombarded with haphazard, chaotic, unpredictable demands and consequences. When the standards of the system are no longer shared or cease to function as intended, individuals have difficulty communicating with one another. Unable to experience their existence as having been lived harmoniously and well, they begin to feel shame and despair.

Even among social deviants, as has been well established, the need for justification exists.[18] By using the special kinds of justification known as rationalization and denial, they provide mitigating circumstances that allow them to bend or break social codes. For example, the drug addict justifies his habit on the grounds that he was born weak; the alcoholic her drinking, because she is misunderstood; the criminal his lawbreaking, because he has the courage to do what others dare only in fantasy.

In addition to self-justification, rationalization can serve as a form of social *sanction*, providing malevolent people with a sense of omnipotence. How did Hitler justify his brutalization of the Jews and other peoples? He regarded the indifference shown by the rest of the world, such as few nations allowing the Jews to enter their borders, as grounds for believing that he was being given permission to treat these people any way he wanted.

According to psychoanalytic conceptualization, the function of rationalization, as of all other psychological defense mechanisms, is to protect a person's vulnerable sense of personal identity from becoming overwhelmed by unacceptable unconscious thoughts and urges. But also like all other defense mechanisms, rationalization is adaptive only so long as it is a *temporary* measure for easing difficult situations. For the malevolent, however, rationalizations are rarely adopted only temporarily; they become self-sustaining.

The psychodynamics that compel rationalizations are among the most invidious and tenacious of defense mechanisms, as can be seen in several patients I have treated recently.

A forty-three-year-old businesswoman who claims that one of her goals in seeing me is to stop smoking asks one afternoon if I will allow her to light up. She intended to start a "stop smoking" program on her own that very day, she explains, but since she unthinkingly smoked a couple of cigarettes already, she feels it would be better for her morale if she just enjoys her smokes for the rest of the day and inaugurates her program afresh the following morning. She would fail in this program, of course, as she had frequently failed in the past.

A forty-five-year-old social worker with a long history of relationships with abusive men asserts that her major goal is to end a year-long affair in which she feels seriously neglected. She quickly adds that now is not the most opportune time, however: "At least he is safe as a sexual partner. It would probably take a considerable amount of time to find someone who's an emotionally appropriate partner and sexually healthy too."

A thirty-two-year-old stockbroker has convinced himself that he has overcome his weekend cocaine addiction. In order to test this assumption, he buys bags of coke from his dealer. He explains to me that he can't be certain he's cured unless he has evidence that he can resist temptation. He will not resist the temptation.

Above all, rationalizations reveal disturbed motives. People addicted to rationalization are shame prone, more painfully plagued by their vulnerabilities than are others. At base, addiction to rationalization is a refusal to come to terms with human limitations.

Apparently, clinicians who study criminals have not yet recognized that their rationalizations are a component of *magical thinking*, a thought process in which a person suspends critical assessment of her behavior.

Rather than make efforts to improve her character, she convinces herself that she is already perfect.

To this end, malevolence and madness share a common mission, for neither is capable of securing a personal identity that provides a sense of goodness and worth. Faust, therefore, uses magical thinking to try to transform his sense of being frail and vulnerable into a position of invincibility. One is reminded of the Irish poet William Butler Yeats's explanation that the ultimate objective of magic is to obtain power over the sources of life, a level of power that eludes normal exertions. Reinhold Niebuhr, the American theologian, pointed out that malevolence and madness arise from the tragic arena defined in a memorable aphorism: "Man is mortal. That is his fate. Man pretends to be immortal. That is his sin."

THE MALEVOLENT TYPE OF MAGICAL THINKING

As I hope I have made clear, rationalization takes hold only after one feels the need to excuse shameful, guilty behavior.

Magical thinking, on the other hand, begins long before a child is aware of any such need. Indeed, according to the work of British psychoanalyst Melanie Klein, among others, magical thinking is common in infancy. As we mature, it remains in the background of consciousness, neither good nor bad in itself. In fact, magical thinking can serve admirably as an imaginative source for innovative ideas that will enrich our being-in-the world. But it can just as easily get us in trouble if we make assumptions about others based upon what we wish or fear from them rather than upon actual experiences and our rational analyses of them.

The specific kind of magical thinking that is a product of the addiction to rationalization however is neither innocent nor fanciful. Rather, it is *hard-edged*, forged from the pains and suffering of childhood, a vehicle for expressing contempt toward those who caused hurt and those who did not intervene to help. The magical thinking involved in malevolence creates a moral and emotional distance between perpetrator and victim. This feeling of alienation, in which the malevolent person feels as if he lives in a different world from the targets of his rage, starts long before the first acts of cruelty.

As we have seen, children who learn during the age of belief that they cannot depend upon caretakers decide early on that they can survive only by not becoming overly dependent upon other people. As we have also seen, feelings of self-worth cannot be acquired, generally speaking, without the availability of caring and supportive others. To compensate for the pain of abandonment, children may employ denial in the form of a narcissistic *reaction formation*, denying their wish for care and intimacy by acting as if they harbor an opposite wish. That is to say, they invest no effort in establishing satisfying interpersonal relationships because they decide that they are very special and don't need anyone else. Their subsequent behavior, characteristically boastful and expansive, belies the fearful, shamed inner lives in which they suffer considerable inner pain.

Psychologists refer to this replacement of real people with a magical conception of one's superiority as *grandiosity*. It is a kind of characterological scar tissue, hardening as the result of ongoing deprivation of emotional and social nourishment. Once grandiosity pervades a person's life, the only problem he can admit to is that other people don't recognize his uniqueness often enough.

Grandiosity is typically a dominant character trait in the malevolent personality, as we have seen with Roy, and an unmistakable sign of inner trouble. It is a ploy used by people addicted to rationalization as a bogus indication that their behavior is under rational control. From our understanding of shame, we should recognize how wrong they are. Like all the rest of us, they can learn only by doing. Impulses to self-examine our motives and actions, on the one hand, and impulses to avert and deny the forces that steward our behavior, on the other, occur continuously throughout our lives. Generally, they pop up in small matters; even so, the way we respond to all earlier decisions shapes our significant moral and emotional choices down the road. An addiction to rationalization, though it develops gradually, facilitates an advance along a continuum of refusals to come to terms with our limitations.

The private shame that accrues from our sense of cowardice in facing these realities fosters a very painful negative personal identity. In turn, more extreme rationalizations are required to bolster a feeling of security. In sum, each decision to rationalize erodes our freedom of choice until inevitably an addiction to rationalize becomes forged into a way of life. For this reason, those addicted to rationalizations—whether in regard to smoking, abusive relationships, drug inhalation, or malevolent acts—find it difficult to end their aversive behavior.

In malevolence, the hurtful awareness of vulnerability unleashes a desperate delusion of magical invincibility, and the consciousness of superiority turns vicious. Madness, or the effort to gain magical powers, is a necessary precondition for malevolence. Both malevolence and madness, then, are refusals to come to terms with human limitation, as well as expressions of contempt for the world. As the Roman philosopher Tacitus observed, it is a principle of human nature to hate those whom you have injured.[19]

Unlike the earlier stages on the journey toward malevolence, when the self-contemptuous person passively tolerates shame and humiliation by others, the malevolent person actively directs his contempt toward everyone: both those who have mistreated him and anyone who tries to get close. We are all held responsible for permitting his humiliation and shame.

Such contempt toward the entire world diminishes the ability to self-examine. Unlike the depressed and/or self-contemptuous patient, who can self-examine because she retains some sense of responsibility for what has happened to her, the malevolent hold others responsible. Self-examination is impossible because it is believed to be unwarranted.

DIFFERENCES BETWEEN PSYCHOSIS AND MALEVOLENT MADNESS

There are obvious differences, of course, between perpetrators of malevolence and "autistically mad" people caught up in their own self-contained psychosis. Ronald Markman, a forensic psychiatrist who has been involved in many of the most sensational murder trials in the United States over the past twenty years, warns us to keep the distinction clear: "Our society is leaning awfully close to the idea that you have to be mentally ill in some way to commit a crime. This is not so. Most crimes—even grisly murders—are not committed by mentally ill people . . . most mentally ill people are not dangerous."[20]

In fact, the autistically mad are more likely to be talking harmlessly to themselves in their rooms than malevolently involved in someone else's life. The social world is too bewildering and frightening for them to be able to deal with it effectively. Although they are dominated by feelings of grievance and resentment, like the malevolently mad, they feel unable to

express any desire for revenge by attacking those who have psychically injured them. Some are so traumatized by violence that they fear it in any
form; others fear that their revenge would be so excessive that it would
invoke shame and guilt they could not handle. Still others fear that any
act of revenge on their part would provoke excessive retribution—that is,
people in the social world would destroy them.

More comprehensible to the autistically mad than the world of other
people is their private world. There, their delusional, fantasy cohabi-
tants regard them in ways they understand, consistent with how they
were treated by their early caretakers. In these private worlds, the autis-
tic are involved in continual self-examination, desperately seeking ways
of redeeming themselves for the sins their caretakers accused them of
committing.

During my apprenticeship as a clinical psychologist in a municipal
psychiatric hospital, I was assigned to work with a severely disturbed
young man of my own age. Above average in intellectual functioning, he
was unable to keep a job and had few friends and social contacts. Teased
and psychologically seduced by an Orthodox Jewish mother who dressed
and undressed in front of him when he was a child, in preparation for her
extramarital dates, he was obsessed with the fantasy of becoming sexually
involved with a beautiful older woman. Whenever he felt intense desire
for a woman, he believed that there sat on one of his shoulders a devil of
temptation and on the other an angel of deliverance from sin. Compelled
at those times to return home from wherever he was and sit alone in his
bedroom, he felt violently polarized by what he perceived as the theological agents involved in a struggle for possession of his soul. Although he
was terribly frightened, he was no less fascinated by the debate over his
soul, in which over time he became an active participant.

But the malevolent, as we have seen, are incapable of self-examination,
because their internal world and its undiscovered self are more frightening to them than the social world they share with others. There, because
they often possess superior physical, social, or intellectual skills, they are
able to play a dominant role. More important, they have developed an accentuated capacity for denial and rationalization of their insensitivity and
unkind behavior. Ironically, their lack of self-monitoring provides them
with the means of taking advantage of or controlling others. For example,
most of us would pause to reconsider any impulse to harm someone else

seriously, no matter how justified our anger, but the malevolent do not. The rationalizations they have used for their previous cruel behavior will justify and facilitate any new act of malevolence. Indeed, their lack of control over their impulses contributes to their social dominance.

Like the development of the malevolent personality, the profile of the violent person follows a series of distinct steps in regard to how the perpetrator loses control over his impulses. It might be asked: if the violence a person commits has distinct steps, why have psychologists had so much difficulty selecting out the people who are likely to become violent and, by doing so, helping to prevent their committing brutal acts?

For the most part, future violence is predicted by psychologists on the basis of a person's past acts of outrage. On this basis, psychologists cannot provide much assistance. A considerable amount of the violence in our nation is not carried out by hardened criminals or violent types; it is committed by people who have "broken" under situational stress, few of whom have violence in their background.

Does the absence of violent outrage in a person's past mean that we cannot accurately assess his potential for violence? Not at all! As I show in the following pages, the factors that compel people toward violence are predictable, but only if we know where to look. Every violent act is driven by compelling forces and decisions. No act of violence is senseless, if "senseless" is meant to imply that the act was without understandable motives. The central message is that acts of violence seem senseless and unpredictable only if we don't recognize the vicious influences that bear upon people in our contemporary society and how people respond to these threats.

Any one of us, even among those who have led a decent and reasonable life, is capable of violence. But—and this is the important point—the way the average person becomes involved in a violent act differs from that of a person who is already initiated in violence.

The average person who is normally controlled and well behaved will become violent only under the combined extreme circumstances of fear, confusion, stress, and traumatic hurt. The specific stages he will undergo in order to commit a violent act can be highlighted by the following outline:

1. *Quiescence.* The person feels in harmony with other people prior to a painful intrusion in his life.

2. *Intrusion.* An outrage is done to him or to someone important to him.

3. *Injustice.* He experiences the act/event as unfair/unjust.

4. *Anomie.* He experiences a startling upheaval in his sense of trust and confidence in the social order.

5. *Shame.* He feels considerable shame and humiliation for having been a victim, or a helpless observer.

6. *Inarticulateness.* He is unable to express his feelings of hurt and unfairness/injustice.

7. *Self-contempt.* He feels self-contempt for how he dealt with the outrage.

8. *Panic.* His feelings of self-contempt are intolerable; he undergoes strong autonomous nervous system reactions of panic, fear, confusion, and intense anger.

9. *Contemptuousness.* Feelings of rage are directed at those who are held responsible for the outrage and/or those who did nothing to stop it.

10. *Rationalization.* Because acting contemptuously is not a customary way of behaving, he needs to justify his angry impulses.

11. *Dehumanization.* Justifying his contempt makes it possible to dehumanize temporarily those he holds responsible or unhelpful.

12. *Numbing.* Dehumanizing the victim(s) allows him to become indifferent about his actions toward the victim(s); the transformation of consciousness he incurs is similar to that which a butcher might assume in cutting up the carcass of an animal.

13. *Attack.* Violence is directed at the victim(s).

14. *Agitation.* Following the attack, the perpetrator feels shame, regret, and remorse.

For those who are characteristically violent, how does the commission of violence differ from that of the progression outlined above?

As I have stressed in this chapter, our characters are formed by the choices we have made in the past. Each decision to act on an angry and hurt feeling narrows the range of choices, so each choice is less subject to moral scrutiny.

Jeffrey Dahmer's life history, as told by his father,[21] supports my thesis. From early childhood, Dahmer experimented with cruelties he inflicted on small animals, then later with other children. Finally, he graduated to brutal rape, torture, murder, and cannibalism.

The recidivists who commit the horrible crimes we read about in the newspaper daily do not require the same number of steps as those who have led decent and reasonable lives. The former no longer have to rationalize their contemptuous feelings or anesthetize their brutal actions. Why? Because the noxious repository of injustice, shame, and self-contempt they carry around with them fuels their feelings of contempt against the world. As a result, for those who are already contemptuous, the steps toward violence are accelerated. Their steps toward violence can be outlined as follows:

1. *Shame.* Chronic feelings of shame and humiliation have been turned into self-contempt.
2. *Inarticulateness.* The person who will commit the violent act has difficulty expressing his shameful hurt verbally.
3. *Agitation.* The self-contempt has been turned into intense contemptuousness, and he is restless and excitable.
4. *Excitement.* He feels energized as he searches for opportunities to express his contempt.
5. *Frenzy.* He experiences a heightened excitement in finding a vulnerable victim. This is often a person who reminds him of his own shame and hurt.
6. *Attack.* He violates his victim with minimal deliberation.
7. *Quiescence.* The perpetrator feels serene and superior to his victim(s).

In sum, a violent person is someone whose previous choices have pushed him into narrower and more restricted ways of dealing with painful discoveries about himself. His insensitivity, indifference, and increasingly cruel and destructive behavior have become fully justified as an acceptable way of responding to the difficult circumstances of his life. Other options for dealing with his hurt, if still considered, are seen as strange and not reconcilable with the person he now experiences himself to be.

Stated another way, violence is a madness—whether it is rageful or cool and calculated. It is a madness predicated upon the desperate reasoning that holds that those who are denied their humanity by the social order can heal their injured humanity and gain full presence in the world only by forceful assertion. In this sense, violence is both a dangerous and pathetic communication. The violent man wants to be consoled and reassured that he is safe and cared for—and in this way regain faith in the social order so that he can pursue his life fully and well. But he dare not, because he is too hurt, frightened, and cynical to trust anyone or anything again.

In sum, then, we see that the disturbed and disturbing rationalizations of magical thinking that direct the lives of malevolent people are hallmarks of madness. In Jason's story, we can witness these dynamics in action.

CHAPTER TEN

Experimental Malevolence

When the devil cannot reach us in
spirit, he creates a woman beautiful
enough to tempt us in the flesh.
— OLD SPANISH SAYING

N O ONE BECOMES BONDED TO MALEVOLENCE EXCEPT TO INURE himself to some great suffering. The problem the behavioral sciences have had in dealing with malevolence is in recognizing the precise ways in which such suffering is psychologically transformed in malevolence.

Jason, a writer in his early thirties, explained in our first session that he had come to me because of his problems with intimacy. For as long as he could remember, the important people in his life scolded him for living solely for the moment, neither building bridges to others nor showing them sufficient compassion and concern.

Still, he was doubtful that psychoanalysis could really help him. Having been in analysis for many years, he knew that the process depends upon words, and he had come to believe that words cannot accurately convey immediate personal intent. Like Pirandello, Jason felt that each of us has within himself a special world of meaning, and even though we believe that we understand what another person means in his words, in fact we never do.[1]

On the contrary, Jason went on, words are used in the vacuous pursuit of a reality that is treacherous. That is to say, we all use words to make definite-sounding commitments, such as pledges of eternal love, for a future that is uncertain. Without words, we cannot make these false promises. Words are inherently ambiguous or ambivalent; actions are not. Jason reasoned that his inability to love resulted from his having to use words to declare and commit himself in a relationship.

His specific reason for contacting me was a series of deceptions he had committed in collusion with Sonia, a beautiful married publisher with whom he was sexually involved. Sonia demanded that during sex he declare his love, but she didn't expect him to pretend any love for her afterward.

Yet the mutual deception troubled Jason: "I thought at the moment: what does it matter what I say to her, in the heat of passion? After all, the affair won't last forever. But something kept telling me that we should scrutinize our every word to each other, as if we will live together forever and have to bear each other's suffering. Nevertheless, to my surprise—because it's contrary to my usual personal proclivities—I was compelled by my sympathy for her dependence on my words to tell her each time we were passionate that I would love her forever. It disgusts me that I told her what she wanted to hear."

An unfortunate lifelong legacy for many patients I have treated born to wealth and privilege is that their parents gave them therapists in childhood instead of nurturing emotional responses. Jason was introduced to the world of psychoanalysis and the power of language at the age of five; when he came to me, he was a veteran of twenty-five years in analysis.

I learned that the second of his many therapists felt the need to write for advice about the boy's problematic behavior to a world-renowned British child psychiatrist. The letter cited Jason's lack of compassion for others, his violent temper, and reveries in which he spent hours imagining himself to be the heroes of the classic novels given to him by his parents. Unfortunately, the analyst failed to mention that Jason's lack of empathy resulted from his parents' making impossible demands upon him to save them from their suffering.

According to behavioral science studies, destructive behavior is linked with difficulty in forming empathic bonds with others. If one is unable or unwilling to take into consideration how someone else feels—in effect, psychologically take the place of the other person—one tends to treat others as objects of no importance rather than as beings like oneself, with feelings and concerns and the right to be treated with decency.

Perhaps using this reasoning in response to a letter that provided an incomplete patient history, the British expert wrote back that Jason was evidently a child schizophrenic in need of extensive psychoanalysis. Jason, of course, was told about this assessment.

His actual story suggests an alternative diagnosis. His European parents, understanding the implications of Nazism early on, had scrambled frantically to smuggle out their jewels and gold certificates, taking little thought of their equally threatened relatives. In the United States Jason's father combined this stake with his astute technological sense and business acumen to make a fortune in industry. Such success, of course, could not assuage the parents' gnawing sense of guilt and shame for abandoning their relatives to horrible fates in the Holocaust. They desperately sought for evidence that their flight to safety had produced some socially redemptive consequence.

To Jason's mind, they had criticized him virtually from birth for any perceived faults, their anxious, demanding attentions implying that only if their precious child became an exceptional, flawless person could they be forgiven. In Jason's daydreams, he tried to imagine ways of escaping from their desperate emotional focus on him.

The adult Jason was tall and powerfully built, with dark, wavy hair and chiseled features. With a very high IQ and verbal fluency, he became a successful writer, well regarded in literary circles. Yet, not surprisingly, he felt alone in the world, having no close male friends he could turn to for support. Probably one of his strongest motives for continuing analysis in adulthood was that the therapeutic session was the only place where he could achieve even a modicum of intimacy with another man.

To satisfy his inner emptiness, Jason became a sexual athlete. A new woman was like a drug; he experienced the same "rush" he did with cocaine. Unfortunately, this heightened excitement waned immediately after a successful seduction, and he became depressed. Although he felt trapped by this addiction, the sexual "highs," short-lived as they were, energized his will to live. When there was no new candidate in sight, he was not interested in returning to previous conquests; he felt intensely agitated and self-punitive.

In short, Jason was a "stimulus addict," the kind of person who does not feel alive unless involved in encounters that are risky and uncertain. He was incapable of securing pleasure or harmony from close, intimate relationships, fearful that any woman who really came to know him would discover that he was a schizophrenic. Throughout his childhood and into the present, he harbored a deep resentment toward all women, convinced that they considered him physically attractive but emotionally impaired.

Rationalizations for Jason's increasing indifference, insensitivity, and cruelty toward women were easy to find, given his sharp intelligence and practiced imagination. When he tired of a partner, or tried to initiate a relationship with a highly unstable woman, he would precipitate some sort of crisis in order to deal with his feelings of "deadness." He coolly rationalized such contemptuous behavior as putting a pillowcase over his lover's head during sex because he had convinced himself that he was superior to conventional morality. By boasting about his cleverness in manipulating others, he was actually trying to reverse the humiliated status he suffered. As we have learned, each rationalized choice of insensitivity toward others eroded his freedom of choice, and thus his cruel behavior inevitably became unassailably justified.

Pivotal in Jason's unstable life was his unwillingness to take responsibility for his difficulties. For example, he could not bear to consider the possibility that his inability to reach out and form close relationships was a sign of incompetence. Rather, he portrayed it as a virtue—that is, his dedication to a relentless pursuit of knowledge precluded becoming involved with other people's sensibilities. This quest for knowledge, of course, was directed almost entirely outward and only rarely included examination of his own hurt psyche.

Jason's torment fueled a serious addiction to cocaine. At his publisher's Christmas party, he insulted Elyse, an editor who was a longtime friend, by proposing that they make love in the office washroom with the door ajar. She was not entirely surprised, having heard many rumors about Jason's seducing women, then subjecting them to degrading experiences. In one tale, he had allegedly spent the night with some new woman in a hotel, pushed her nude out into the hall the next morning, and bolted the door, evidently enjoying her frantic efforts to get back in. It was said that she later committed suicide. Elyse, who was a patient of mine, decided that her friend needed immediate help. It was she who recommended me to Jason.

Soon after our sessions began, I became aware that Jason would sometimes take on another persona, whom he referred to as "Stud." Jason explained that this second self was the part of him that did not age and lived in accord with Nietzschean philosophy—that is, Stud regarded his behavior as beyond the strictures of conventional morality. He justified his belief on the basis that he was sufficient unto himself, needing no one else.

"I don't give a shit," Stud said. "I enjoy myself and indulge any whim or desire I have. Anything else in life is too dull and uninteresting, or it requires too much effort."

Stud took over or was heard from when Jason felt inadequate or apprehensive about making the correct life decisions. He argued that society's highest possible morality would be to allow people like him to exercise their superior capacities to the full. If lesser people suffered thereby, that would be regrettable but unimportant.

It would stretch credibility to maintain that a *superiority philosophy* is a major cause of malevolence. Undoubtedly, however, it serves as a lethal fusil for the other factors I have already discussed as constituting the malevolent personality. Few people can live without the support of some person or social structure to sanction their behavior. In other words, malevolent people are drawn toward belief systems that justify their responding to the powerful contemptuous forces inside them. Every superiority philosophy has an adjunctive requirement: hatred of those who don't possess the alleged attributes of the superior. After all, one can only be superior if there is someone who is inferior.

Throughout his growing years, Jason had experimented with the "technicalities" of morality. As a young child, he purposely strode across lawns with Keep Off the Grass signs. In adolescence, he parked his car in spots reserved for the handicapped or people with special permits. He cheated on college exams even though he was always well prepared and usually the brightest in class; he was "turned on" by the thrill of outwitting the teacher. In adult life, he intentionally lit up cigarettes in No Smoking sections or carried on distracting loud conversations during concerts or lectures. In all these situations, his facile, glib charm usually spared him the wrath of the people he annoyed.

Eventually, when his grandiosity convinced him that he could talk his way out of virtually any kind of trouble, he graduated to more serious offenses against conventional morality.

The degrading acts against women were rationalized as uncompromising scientific curiosity about human behavior. According to Stud, Jason had pushed the naked woman into the hotel corridor in order to enact authentically the disturbing legacy of schizophrenia bestowed upon him by the psychiatric profession.

"I have been told all my life that I'm incompetent to do the right things," Jason was in effect saying to his second self. "Maybe they were right! Someone else will have to make decisions for me. I'll let that other part of me, the confident part, take charge."

Not surprisingly, given this analysis, Stud first appeared to Jason during a cocaine "trip." During the subsequent months of continuing drug usage, however, Stud made himself known quite apart from any chemical inhalation. Soon it was Stud who bought the drugs, Stud who planned Jason's escapades with women.

In their extensive study of criminals, Yochelson and Samenow pinned down the drug factor: "More than the nonusing criminals, the users [of drugs] lacked courage to take responsible initiatives and make the required efforts. Drugs always offered a rapid and effective way of achieving the desired mental state of being 'ten feet tall' and simultaneously dispelling the tedium of responsible living."[2]

Colin Wilson, based upon his own study of criminals, believes that each of us has a "shut-off" mechanism that allows our other self to make decisions about the choices we face. Suppose, for example, that we are feeling some strong biological craving but suddenly hear a voice cry out, "Help me, I'm hurt!" Most of us will push aside our own need and focus on the crisis facing the other person. This is not an automatic process; we deliberately choose to control our own needs until a more appropriate moment.

But the criminal, Wilson found, makes a *decision* not to abandon his own needs and concerns: "He can see no sound reason why he should waste his time establishing a higher level of self-control [than what seems to him to be in his best interests]. Let other people worry about that."[3]

This description fits Jason. When he had decisions to make that involved the welfare of others, he pushed those concerns out of his consciousness.

Jason's parents continually told him that he need not worry about the practical aspects of life. Others could tend to such mundane matters, while he concentrated on developing his superior intellectual and creative talents. In truth, at the time I first treated him, Jason felt incompetent to handle practical matters. When a difficult decision had to be made, his mind wandered off and Stud took over, carrying out the necessary actions.

Jason's rationalizations in regard to the woman who reportedly committed suicide are particularly revealing about choice and responsibility in the malevolent personality. The night of the incident in the hotel, he had taken a large dose of Ecstasy before leaving home. From articles in medical journals he had read and his own experiences, he was very familiar with the often violent side effects of this drug, once thought to be a "wonder drug'" for heightening erotic arousal and prolonging sexual endurance. He had taken Ecstasy several times previously and gone "out of control," endangering himself and others.

On this occasion, as on many others, he justified taking the drug on the basis that women did not offer themselves for his private delectation because they expected straitlaced, conservative behavior. They wanted excitement. And he was looking forward to the best possible sexual encounter, rationalizing that his previous loss of control was a result of his inexperience with this particular drug. Since he had learned how to handle cocaine and other psychoactive drugs by not allowing himself to become too fearful of their harmful effects, he believed that he could also control his experience with Ecstasy and luxuriate in its aphrodisiac qualities.

In fact, as Jason later realized, he was deluding himself. Almost immediately upon reaching the hotel, he felt irritated and annoyed in some unfathomable way. He set those feelings aside for later examination. In a manner of speaking, he gave Stud tacit permission to act upon him, without knowing what Stud might do.

Because pushing the woman nude into the hallway was not the action of the person he was raised to be, Jason provided himself with a highly convoluted set of rationalizations.

In the first place, he claimed, he became angry because his partner accused him of needing to sleep with a great many women, then relented and said it was all right with her, for the present. Once he got his head straight, she went on, he would realize that he cared more for her than for anyone else. What enraged Jason was that he had never professed love for this woman or discussed his addiction to serial sex, and yet, ironically, many of his lovers had excused or explained his womanizing in much the same terms that she had.

Obviously, Jason was terribly conflicted in his attempts at intimacy. Intimacy with another requires the capacity to be intimate with one's self. Acts of intimacy demonstrate a willingness to suspend certainty and allow the self to plunge into the unknown, experiencing in unison with the other what the self cannot experience alone.

In order for this to happen, the self needs a sense of confidence that what it has within is basically good, therefore ensuring that the qualities of its coming together in synthesis with another person will be essentially positive. Those who feel empty experience themselves as being at the mercy of the stranger. Those who feel malevolent fear that they will be destroyed by the other. In other words, those who were unable in their early psychological development to share the mystery of their caretakers fear both the unknown power of the stranger and their own impacted rage. Jason felt compelled to humiliate and degrade those with whom he was intimate and sexual lest they overwhelm him by asking for the caring behaviors he felt incapable of rendering.

In his emotional and chemical-induced agitation, Jason told himself that women who claimed to find his womanizing unacceptable but also condoned it had no integrity. They didn't merit his consideration. Therefore, he could—and would—do as he pleased with these shallow women. His many experiments with breaking the rules, beginning with walking on the grass, proved that rules were only for others. What conventional morality regards as wicked as he rationalized into a "philosophy of good": his experiments, then, had a socially redemptive value.

As this set of rationalizations might suggest, Jason's course of treatment with me was difficult and demanding. Intensely competitive, he could not easily accept the role of patient, which he defined as having to pay me money because he was weak and inferior and needed to be cared for by someone superior. Virtually snarling, he said that his twenty-five years of shameful indoctrination at the hands of analysts were enough.

I realized that Jason would continue to battle me and there would be no therapeutic progress if I continued to play the role of "knowledgeable analyst." Besides, I had been shouldering all of the therapeutic risks in our sessions by trying to deal with the contemptuous, irrational Stud. By contrast, Jason had assigned himself the easier role of "intellectual observer," standing aside and criticizing me for failing to outwit Stud in my office or to curb his malevolent behavior outside.

I threw the ball into Jason's court.

"You seem to know it all!" I said, again and again. "If you have the answers, then *you* have to tell me how to deal with Stud."

At first, Jason was stunned that I refused to grapple with him and his second self intellectually. Then he became infuriated, taking moral offense. He pointed out that, if he had the answers, he wouldn't be paying me. I countered that he seemed to take morbid pride in acting as if he knew how to deal with Stud but refused to let me use this insight in a practical way.

As Jason kept repeating that I did not understand him, I recognized him as an "anti-hero": that is, the sibling rival of the hero. As I had seen often enough by now, Jason felt jealousy, envy, and resentment toward the ideal image of himself that others held up to him, the self they wanted him to be. If the hero stands for hope, courage, and risk, Jason was a depressed version of the hero, so irritated by those values that he not only rejected them but also took a morbid pride in acting against them.

Being *misunderstood* is a central theme in the life of the anti-hero.[4] Jason preferred to be misunderstood, because being fully understood by his parents, previous therapists, or me would be dangerous. He had an urgent need to differentiate and hold himself apart from others. Because malevolent irritants are hard to endure, Stud served as a defense against his being consumed and incorporated by others.

I shared this observation with Jason, explaining exactly how he, along with Stud, had effectively taken control of all our therapeutic sessions.

From then on, Jason focused on his apparent command of situations in which he was involved, not only in my office but outside. As he did so, he slowly but steadily became in touch emotionally with his deep hurt and despair. Often, he would plead with me to understand him.

"Why don't you understand me?" he'd complain. "You're making me feel the way I always did with my family—helpless and incompetent. They expected me to do something no one realistically could."

I urged him to elaborate, but he refused.

A few sessions later, he tried to explain, perhaps in reaction to the disappointment that he read in my face at being unable to reach him.

"I remember the look my mother would get whenever I said or did something she didn't like," he said. "Her face froze. And I felt all alone in the world. I feel that way right now with you."

At this point, we were able to begin working on the force that generated his self-contempt.

Those who feel inordinately flawed or shamed are constantly escorted in the background of consciousness by a vigilant, rarely silent "judge," who examines and comments upon their every thought, feeling, and action. This "critical voice" has been scripted and incorporated into the self from among the myriad of interactions with parents and significant figures in the past. Leaping upon a bare minimum of information and experience in any given situation, this judge decisively forms a condemning opinion, thus intruding, impeding, and aborting behavior. In this way, the critical voice obstructs any effort made toward self-discovery, exploration of possibility, or any other deepening of experience. Rather, its moral judgments advise the ashamed individual that his behavior and actions are contemptible, then insist that he defend and justify himself.

In short, the behavior of shame-prone people demands continual justification.

I've found in my clinical work that people addicted to rationalization can take a critically important first step toward healing, once they are willing to spend the time and effort taking note of how often and in what ways their critical voice demands justification. Most begin by taking daily notes in a journal.

Then they become able through their observations to take the second step: confronting and disarming the critical voice just as they would an actual person who might try to abuse or humiliate them.

Third, they define themselves both to the critical voice and to themselves in terms of their desired self.

Fourth, they learn to dissuade the critical voice from making disparaging remarks about their thoughts, feelings, and actions.

Fifth, the first four steps result in an increasingly fewer number of rationalizations, since the gradual cessation of critical inner judgments presents fewer obstacles to new, exploratory behavior. Now patients learn to make more penetrating discoveries about themselves: for example, the revelation of one's deeply buried despair about human limitations. The bracing new opportunity of dealing with such discoveries helps patients learn to live more legitimately as purposive people and to develop a courageous, creative consciousness of human possibility.

A complete description of the steps required to heal shame and despair is presented in Chapter Fourteen.

To sum up, Jason's inability to empathize with others was forged in childhood, when his parents made impossible demands upon him to alleviate their guilt. As we have seen, the predilection to malevolence comes from a variety of sources in addition to abuse or neglect. It is very high among people like Jason, who have been subjected to unreasonable expectations they are not equipped to meet.

In traditional clinical practice, Jason would undoubtedly be diagnosed as a *psychopath*.[5] As with other so-called psychopaths, however, his emotional difficulties arose not from an absence of feeling for others but from too much. His childhood identification and empathy with his parents was too painful to sustain. Therefore, he felt forced to cut his bonds with them, and subsequently with everyone else. Eventually, his impotence to help others in combination with his image of himself as a psychiatric patient imbued him with shame and self-contempt.

Self-hatred, one of the most virulently destructive forces visited upon humankind, leads to all of the malevolence that plagues our world.

The shame Jason felt, so subtly inflicted, is more common in children than most people realize. His parents did not physically or psychologically abuse him, they were clearly decent people by any standards, but they were anxiously overconcerned about appearances and firmly discouraged their son's natural curiosity and sense of wonder. Consequently, Jason learned that he could not reach out toward people simply for the intrinsic pleasure of intimacy; rather, people were there to be used in his unending search for knowledge. And since his parents had suppressed his curiosity because it was too suggestive of personal limitations they found abhorrent, he sought knowledge primarily from the outside, rarely turning inward to examine his damaged psyche.

Jason was shamed into compliance with parental expectations by the conviction that being less than perfect is equivalent to being malevolent and undeserving of human company. People like him, when they reach adulthood, convince themselves that there is a mitigating greater good behind their malevolent acts that renders such behavior not only justifiable but necessary.

Nevertheless, Jason's parents' overindulging him, even taken together with their making unreasonable demands, cannot totally account for his cruelty. A colleague who heard me discuss this case at a professional meeting suggested that Jason may have suffered humiliation from his parents' cowardly, indifferent behavior in turning their backs on their endangered families in Europe and investing their concerns instead in acquiring affluence. Certainly, despite their large contributions and active participation in charities, their accusations that Jason was self-centered must have struck him as hollow. The only moral code his parents actually lived by was dictated by selfishness and the desire for material comforts. It follows that words came to have no real meaning for him. In response to his parents' disavowed guilt and shame, Jason may have developed a highly cynical attitude and *an identification with aggressors* who cruelly humiliate others. According to Anna Freud,[6] who first described the concept, a person identifies himself with the behavior of a dreaded person in order to transform himself from someone threatened and powerless into a capable, powerful person. Through his aggression and cruelty, Jason may have been trying to show that he was not a victim, like his Jewish relatives who perished during the Holocaust. Neither was he like his parents, forced to lie to himself and others about his motives.

Jason believed that he and his family could save themselves from the pettiness of ordinary human weakness by being brutally honest about their desires. And so he justified his cruelty with the assumption that his frank submission to his desires, even when they led to aberrant acts, was a greater good than the willful intellectual dishonesty of the women he met. In this way he assumed the attitude of a Don Juan (Don Giovanni).

Like this legendary character, Jason is a man searching for the "enabling-reparative mother." He wants a constant companion. He tires of always having to be Don Juan—i.e, always having to be prepared for a new adventure. He would like to let down his guard and reveal his psyche openly and completely. The stranger he seeks to find in sexual encounter is his own shadow, his soul mate.

Jason's cynicism covers both his deep hurt and his desperate desire to find a woman willing to journey with him as an equal—a partner who will engage him, confront him, and enable to face up to the responsibilities of a meaningful relationship. He has found it painful that no woman can be his friend without trying to possess him. Women who say that they will accept his friendship alone, without possession, eventually lash out at him for denying them his exclusive love, for being interested in other women, and for doubting himself.

Yet, like Don Juan, Jason recognizes that he needs perpetual confirmation. No matter what his previous conquests have been or how lovely the woman he has just left, he feels abject and worthless as soon as he is without a woman or sees another man with a woman.

Again like Don Juan, he is on a perpetual quest to find the woman whose touch and emotional intelligence will finally rid him of the curse of having issued from the "damaging mother." In childhood, he was deprived of a sense of well-being. His mother's milk was sour and unsettling. In other words, his mothering was characterized by staccato upheavals and persistent anxiety. He never felt safe, quietly cared for, or secure in the dependability of his surroundings. He feels resentful for having been thrust into a world in which his mother would tell him that he need only smile and be brilliant to get anything he wants. Even though his father said that it is vital to be cared for, Jason cannot trust this caring. His life has been forged within these two confusing messages. Sadly, he can find redemption in no woman. Since he cannot trust adoration, each woman he seduces will lose her value to him shortly after she begins to adore him. The admiration becomes untrustworthy as soon as it is bestowed. Jason loses interest in the woman and feels compelled to continue his quest for the reparative mother. Don Juan, Rank tells us, is a man who seeks the ideal woman and cannot find her. So it is for Jason.

Over the course of treatment, as Jason learned to deal with his shame and with his mad counteractions to his lifelong inner pain, he was able to share his vulnerabilities with others. In this way, he came to recognize that his personal growth would require continual sacrifice of his false securities. Previously, he had preferred to "look good" to others rather than be actually competent as a human being. To find healing, however, he had to relinquish this image; he couldn't pretend to have all the "right" answers.

As we continued to work together, Jason grew more curious about the undiscovered parts within himself and the feelings of other people. Eventually, he established a fulfilling and intimate relationship with a woman.

His case shows that seriously malevolent personality patterns can be transformed. But the corrective process depends upon a cogent understanding of the conditions that produce these patterns, along with a capacity and willingness to work with intersubjective shame; that is to say, the mutual shaming taking place between therapist and patient.

In working with Jason, I became aware of eight "tip-offs" for detecting potentially dangerous people in personal relationships which I describe briefly below.

1. More than other people, a malevolent person is likely to shift radically in his attitude and behavior toward you, almost in the blink of an eye. One moment, the two of you are having a warm, pleasant conversation; the next, he lashes out at you with a bitterness that seems completely unrelated to your interaction. My clinical experience suggests that this startling behavior is sparked when you unwittingly communicate a word, idea, or feeling that has a strong shaming effect upon him. Once this happens, there is no easy way to reason with and disarm his anger.

2. Apparently, this person is trying to draw you into a scenario that is based more upon some exciting and/or disturbing fantasy about you than upon your actual likes or dislikes. One giveaway might be his accusing you of being so cowardly, cold, or afraid to take chances that your life is boring and meaningless. He suggests that he has the ability to bring excitement into your life.

3. No matter what you do or say, it isn't right. He accuses you of attitudes and motivations that are not consistent with how you experience yourself feeling or behaving. If you protest or defend yourself, he is unmoved, acting as if he believes that he knows you better than you know yourself.

4. Clearly, the dangerous person regards people as having little worth as well as being very different from himself. You should be

especially concerned when it becomes apparent that he is unable to recognize that others, as much as he, should have their vulnerabilities protected.

5. His attitude and behavior reek of contempt and a desire for revenge. Resentful for not having achieved his desires, he rationalizes his contempt as justified. He claims that he is not responsible for any previously destructive behavior—in other words, his victims get what they deserve.

6. He seems to take pride in admitting that his values and morals are regarded by conventional society as heinous. In fact, he justifies his morality as the product of strength, cleverness, and superiority, while disdaining society's as the product of fear and inferiority.

7. He admits only one discrepancy between his ideal personal identity and his present identity: others misunderstand him.

8. Unable to tolerate his own hurt and vulnerability, he tries to hide his personal weaknesses from himself as well as from others.

As I noted earlier, lone wolves like Jason are not typical of malevolent personalities. In fact, most of them are foot soldiers in groups that indoctrinate them to values that deviate from conventional morality. We will next examine the crucial interrelationship between the psychodynamics of a deviant cult group and the magical wishes of its members.

CHAPTER ELEVEN

Courage and Fanaticism

I want you to be like me. I want you
to become what I am. I want you
to enjoy the fearlessness that I have,
the courage that I have and the compassion
that I have, the love that I have,
the all-encompassing mercy that I am.

—JIM JONES

IN APRIL 1993, AGENTS OF THE FEDERAL BUREAU OF INVESTIGATION and the Bureau of Alcohol, Tobacco and Firearms, heavily armed with assault rifles, flamethrowers, and army tanks, raided the headquarters of the Branch Davidian religious cult, on a ranch near Waco, Texas. To their surprise, cult members were waiting for them, armed with state-of-the-art assault weapons of their own.

For several weeks, the two sides took potshots at each other, while a horrified global audience, thanks to television satellites, watched what was happening minute by minute. In the early days of the siege, some federal officers who tried to enter the compound under cover of darkness were shot and killed. A long lull in the action followed. Several attorneys hired by relatives of cult members became involved in behind-the-scenes negotiations with cult leader David Koresh, hoping to convince him to surrender without further bloodshed. Meanwhile, frequent media reports seemed to give grounds for pessimism. Koresh was repeatedly described

179

as a dangerous megalomaniac who enjoyed a demonic hold over the minds, hearts, and souls of his followers. We were informed that they would dutifully carry out whatever he ordered.

The trend of the actual negotiations was not fully or accurately reported. In any event, this side of the story was overshadowed in an instant, as raging flames, whipped ever higher by fierce prairie winds, engulfed the compound. Nearly a hundred members of the Branch Davidians were killed, including a number of small children. As of this writing, investigators have not unequivocally determined how the fire started.

Many people want to believe that the madness and destruction at Waco is explained by a famous biblical prediction, Revelation 6:8: "His name was Death, and Hell followed with him." In other words, David Koresh was a demonic person able to coerce others into following him meekly to a fiery hell. In this chapter, by exploring a similar tragedy, which occurred fifteen years earlier in an obscure community in the jungles of Guyana, I explain why this belief is both wrong and disingenuous.

MODERN RELIGIOUS CULTS

Cults command our attention. There are reportedly 2,500 quasi-religious groups in the United States, with a membership widely estimated at between two and ten million.[1] These cults are regarded as the fastest-growing spiritual movements in the world. Each has been reputed to use various psychological means to control effectively their followers' thoughts, feelings, and actions.[2] Most of us are likely to encounter these cultists daily, for they are found throughout public life, begging at airports, on street corners, and in restaurants. Many groups are able to generate large revenues. The Unification Church, for example, claims to raise about twenty million dollars annually in the United States alone.[3] Such substantial income enables cults to retain the services of the best legal, political, and business professionals in promoting their mission.

Where have these cults sprung from? They have arisen from the dissatisfaction of adolescents and young adults who have experienced limited options in American society for pursuing what they consider to be meaningful lives. It is symptomatic of the tenuous values of our turbulent society that the struggle for a livelihood has been replaced by the struggle to discover one's self.[4]

Our youth live in conflictual, distrustful times. The ordered society of yesterday has dissipated, leaving behind eroded structures and clouds of cynicism and disappointment. Young people feel immobilized by complex social problems that appear insoluble. They yearn for the warm regard and assurance of others. They wish to touch others deeply and caringly but instead draw back in fear of their own malevolence no less than that of their neighbors. They do not feel themselves responsible for the destructive actions for which they blame others. They have tried to act as best they can to survive—and to survive with their integrity intact.

Aleksandr Solzhenitsyn, the defiant advocate of human rights, has bitterly depicted the Western world as plagued by a loss of courage and by a freedom that is destructively irresponsible because it has been granted without limitation. In a word, we live in an era in which people find it onerous to accept responsibility for their own actions and for the embittered, hollow course their existence has taken. Our guidelines for living stand broken, disjointed, in disarray. No longer do we have clear reasons for living and endeavoring. The magnitude and comprehensiveness of modern technology are such that a relatively few scientists and technicians can serve the physical requirements of the entire population. We have been informed that God is dead; indeed, in our ignorance and despair, we may have slain Him. Nonetheless, we need not fear a dead God. Many find that they are no longer held responsible for the children they have produced, nor the spouse to whom they were once committed. Our existence may be freely egocentric and asocial to a degree not tolerated but a short while past. We are not actually required, other than in terms of a tenuous moral sense, to maintain a trade and lifestyle forged on supporting immediate and extended family. In the past, one's destiny had always been family. It was the root and essence of existence. This is no longer true.[5]

YOUTH'S SEARCH FOR A BETTER WORLD

Modern religious cults concentrate on recruiting the adolescent and young adult offspring of middle-class families, manipulating the vulnerabilities of this accessible generation. According to a study by M. Galanter and his associates, members of the Unification Church tend to be young (a mean age of 24.7), white (89 percent), and unmarried (91 percent).[6] In another study, Galanter and Buckley found that 76 percent of the Divine Light Mission sect had attended college, as had 71 percent of one or both of their parents.[7] Reports of other cults tend to confirm these figures for cult followers in general.

The nature of youth in modern society renders young people an especially cogent population for recruitment by religious cults. Each of the cult sects has put together a marketing program in terms of its own brand of mission that appeals to the youths' unique combination of idealism and optimism no less than to their particular narcissistic striving.[8]

The primary responsibility of young adulthood is the creation of a viable value structure that will give the youth substance, support, and meaning as a person in the adult world. During his transition from adolescence to adulthood, he is struggling to shape for himself those values that separate the adult from adolescence: financial independence, enlightened citizenship, and parenthood. In a society that is itself changing at a galloping pace, the youth is caught between what his elders regard as the excessive idealism of adolescence and what his peers view as the overly conservative pragmatism of his parents' generation. His status in several overlapping social worlds is marginal, because these various social systems are philosophically at variance with one another, eroding his identity as a person and subjecting his self-concept to abrupt shifts. He is continually frustrated by the variations between his own aspirations and whatever is afforded and expected of him by the present social order. He gravitates toward peers in order to establish a viable purpose and the creation of a personal identity in the image of his own times from among what he perceives to be the pressing social priorities he has inherited from his parents' generation. Youth's immersion in and conversation to a peer group that is at variance with his parents' generation, as William James long ago observed, "is in its essence a normal adolescent phenomenon incidental to the passage from the child's small universe to the wider intellectual and spiritual life of maturity."[9] It is, however, the often insidious nature and implication of this conversion that concerns us in this chapter.

The cult phenomenon is an especially complex one. It defies simple explanation and definition. The argument I will develop runs counter to what I have read to date about cult groups. My thesis is that the cult leader, guru, or whatever he (rarely she)[10] is called is not a Svengali figure who forces followers to act contrary to their own wishes. Indeed, although the charismatic cult leaders vary greatly in wisdom, articulateness, persuasiveness, and authoritarian appeal, their common attribute is a certain absurdity, like that of a melodramatic character from a novel like Joseph Conrad's *Lord Jim* or *Heart of Darkness*. I will argue that the aberrance of cults derives from an intersubjective factor: despite the money and marketing tactics of the Reverend Moon, the political skills of Jim Jones, and the recall to fundamental religious doctrine of David Koresh, these leaders could not attract a large following if they did not encounter youths who actively sought lapses from reality and constantly reindoctrinated each guru in his own bizarre doctrine. Journalists Conway and Siegelman write about the crude, if not primitive, tactics of manipulation Jim Jones used on his followers in the People's Temple.[11] Outside observers and ex-members of this cult consistently agreed with the following point: "I cannot understand how so many bright, college-educated people could have been taken in by a thing like this."[12]

I attempt to explain this observation in this chapter by showing that each of the cult's followers, unwittingly but no less pervasively, is seeking out a leader and a movement in which he can be involved in extreme behavior, even when the emotional motivation is a need to avoid responsibility for having to make decisions for himself. The accentuated passivity of the cult members appears to be a defense against uncontrollable rage, concomitant with the fear that one's dependent needs can never be met. It is then understandable that the use of a rattlesnake to attempt to kill an attorney investigating Synanon, the famous drug-rehabilitation-center cult, was condoned by members, or that the blatant use of blackmail, physical threats, and brutal beatings and torture of former and current members of the People's Temple was tolerated by the followers of Jim Jones.

I do not attempt to describe the entire proliferating cult phenomenon. Rather, I examine the cult most widely known by virtue of the bizarre and tragic events that marked its termination—the People's Temple. I explore the development of this extraordinary cult in terms of the social and existential conditions that led to its emergence. Further, I attempt to explain its continuance and its tragic end by examining the role of charismatic leader in directing his followers toward a fanatical rather than a more open direction of their personal concerns and intentions.

As I will show, destructive cults operate from a code of morality that includes the following assumptive principles:

1. The ends justify the means. Behaving with decency, compassion, and caring are not justified if they interfere with the goals of the cult.
2. The leader knows his followers better than they know themselves. He has a divine ability to read the hearts and minds of other people.
3. Because of his divine insight, the leader knows best how the followers should live their lives. And by following his dictates, the followers will have all existential concerns about right and wrong removed from their lives.

In recent times, we have seen a dramatic rise in the pernicious, frightening influence of cult leaders around the world.[13] Many of them come from obscure backgrounds and remain little known to the general public. But one about whom we have considerable documented information is probably the most fitting subject possible for examining the power of a malevolent leader over his emotionally vulnerable followers: James "Jim" Warren Jones, of the bizarre and horrible Jonestown massacre in British Guyana.[14]

Jones was responsible for the deaths of more than nine hundred members of his People's Temple sect, including two hundred sixty children.[15] These devoted followers, who had been laboring for their leader under conditions of extreme physical and emotional abuse and deprivation beneath the hot tropical sun, were poisoned or shot to death by Jones and his lieutenants on November 18, 1978.

LIMITATIONS OF PSYCHOHISTORY

It is intellectually tempting to try to reconstitute the metamorphosis of Jim Jones's personality decompensation—a personality deterioration resulting from severe trauma and the inability to continue to effectively use his typical personal attributes—from a "crusading idealist to messianic monster"[16] who was responsible for "one of the most bizarre and awful massacres of our time."[17] To do so, I must psychologically examine a person I have never met—indeed, had never heard of prior to the tragic "White Night." Moreover, in being concerned with a social movement that has ceased to be, I am like the historian or the philosopher who is limited to the examination of events and circumstances beyond his ability to study directly or from within. (Because of the difficulty of confronting rather complex problems, no more than a handful of field studies have attempted to study the dynamics of a turbulent social movement like the People's Temple from within.[18])

Fortunately, several reports and a book have been written by former members of the cult. In the latter,[19] Jeannie Mills includes what she claims are letters written by Jim Jones and transcripts of his telephone conversations. Investigative journalists have produced an abundance of eyewitness accounts of the massacre and the events leading up to it. Since I have greater access to information about Jones's interactions with his followers, I can speak with more conviction about what he manifested in his behavior toward them than about what prompted him to behave as he did.

CULTS AS PSEUDORELIGIOUS MOVEMENTS

If cultism has become the new religion of the second half of the twentieth century, as the mass media claim, it is necessary to examine the religiosity of the cults—their purported intent and the effectiveness of their actual achievements—in order to understand why they have proliferated with such vigor in recent years.

Religiosity is the ostensible purpose of the cult group. Sixty-seven percent of the followers of a cult studied by Galanter and his associates regarded themselves as at least moderately committed to their family's religion prior to age fifteen.[20] At some time thereafter, 34 percent became at least moderately committed to one of the Eastern religious sects, while 19 percent identified with fundamentalist Christian movements. Moreover, 90 percent reported some prior confluence with fundamentalist sects. Yet despite the initial attraction of religious doctrine in the new cults, these groups are merely pseudoreligious political and paramilitary movements. They claim to be religious sects largely for the respectability and the legal and financial protection and benefit that accrue to religious organizations. I will be arguing later in this chapter that religious cults specialize in a particular type of politics and militancy.

Numerous eyewitnesses confirm that Jim Jones not only was an extraordinarily gifted political manipulator but, in fact, frequently disclaimed his religious role, ridiculing and condemning religious believers. According to an article in the *New York Times,* Marceline Jones described her husband as a Marxist:

> [He] held that religion's trappings were useful only for social and economic uplift. "He has used religion to try to get some people out of the opiate of religion," she said. Once, in his wife's presence, Jones slammed down a Bible with the exclamation, "Marcie, I've got to destroy this paper idol."[21]

The United States is a fertile climate for the emergence of pseudoreligious cults like the People's Temple, which seem to have considerably more difficulty surviving in other countries. Here, organizations involved in exploitative manipulation of their followers have realized the facility with which they can avoid paying taxes on their revenue and escape official probes of their account books and activities by declaring themselves to be religious orders. As Robert Lindsey of the *New York Times* has pointed out, in discussing various Supreme Court rulings:

> A religion legally is any sincere, meaningful belief that occupies "a place in the life of its possessor, parallel to that held by orthodox belief in God." As a practical matter, virtually anyone can establish a religion and get the legal advantages that go with it.[22]

To operate effectively from a loosely defined religious structure, Jones employed an impressive array of lawyers, business advisers, publicists, tipsters, spies, and strong-arm guards to intimidate anyone who actually threatened his mission or who he feared might attack it. Furthermore, as the head of a religious organization, Jones was not only virtually immune from governmental probing but, no less important, could ask more from his followers than as a political leader. Jones's talents as a politician, however, were reciprocated by the laxity of the various California, United States, and Guyanan governmental agencies under whose aegis the People's Temple operated. His cult flourished in a laissez-faire climate. Abundant evidence suggests that he enjoyed a quid pro quo relationship with local California politicians. In the face of rumors and reports of brutal and bizarre activities at the People's Temple, they continued to write him complimentary letters, make speeches on his behalf, and appoint him to community positions that carried considerable financial and political clout. In return, Jones demonstrated a remarkable ability to bring in votes for his favorite candidates.[23] He also had a considerable flair for defaming and blackmailing people who would not cooperate with him.[24] It is reasonable to argue that these political sanctions served to reinforce Jones's delusional system. He came to believe that he could virtually get away with murder.

On the other hand, California Congressman Leo Ryan's visit to Jonestown and his discovery of the adverse conditions there undoubtedly triggered the "White Night" massacre because his drop-in was a startling attack on Jones's narcissism. In fact, Ryan's visit appears to have been one of the few—certainly the only substantial—face-to-face confrontations with the People's Temple leader. The absence of cooperation among the various governmental agencies concerned with Jonestown gave Jones a virtually free hand for his tyrannical and bizarre activities. In the end, those temple members who stood up to their leader in order to defend themselves or monitor his brutality received no support from fellow temple members[25] or from governmental agencies.[26, 27] They either backed down and gave in to Jones's cruelty or left the church.

To understand this modern charismatic leader's appeal, we need to appreciate that he operated, paradoxically, in a climate of both cynicism and hope.

CYNICISM

Present-day youth have become rather cynical about how other generations have responded to the problems and social ills their world faces. Cynicism is a reaction to societal permissiveness, absence of firm values, and lack of commitment to anyone or anything except the pursuit of egocentric aims. Jones's ability to get away with his bizarre activities may be attributed, in no small part, to his realization that cynical people are drawn to self-indulgent leaders; in this regard, George Bernard Shaw supposedly was an early admirer of Joseph Stalin. Jones's personal refrigerator was stocked with the best-quality fruits and meats; he did not labor at all. His rank-and-file followers, on the other hand, gave up all their savings and valuables to the People's Temple, then toiled laboriously, sixteen hours or more, under a tropical sky, while subsisting on a nutritionally poor diet. Jones also smoked, drank, and boasted openly about both his hetero- and his homosexual affairs. All of these activities were strictly forbidden to all but his most trusted lieutenants. In fact, violations prompted severe and brutal punishment for Jones's followers. Accounts suggest that he learned some of his cynicism from the legendary black cult leader, Father Divine, who advised him that it was his "religious obligation to take possession of his flock and to satisfy the sexual cravings of the female members."[28]

In a true spirit of cynicism, Jones could forbid his followers from engaging in sexual relations with their spouses while forcing a female lover to watch while he seduced her husband.[29]

HOPE—THE RECONSTITUTED FAMILY

An inspirational source for the emergence of cults is a renewed interest in psychic phenomena. Through the widespread experimentation with drugs in the 1960s and 1970s, many young people incurred varieties of experience not readily accessible to ordinary consciousness. Together with a desire to foster a new world of brotherhood and understanding, such experiences of altered consciousness rendered these youth more susceptible to external influence than were their peers. This is especially cogent when influences are predicated on messages contrary to common sense and reason—the hallmarks of a secular world these youth have come to distrust and sought to reject.[30]

One also cannot fail to notice that the concept of "family" plays a crucial role in each of the cult groups. For many youth attracted to cults, the requirement that the sect followers live in communes is the fulfillment of the hope for brotherhood and understanding. In these settings, ex-members have reported that they felt an intimacy with their fellow members that greatly surpassed their experience in the world outside.[31]

Ungerleider and Wellisch discovered similar reactions when they examined cult members:

> [The cultists] revealed clinically an intellectual and philosophical bent that resembles what Lifton has termed "strong ideological hunger," regardless of their status in relation to the cult. These cults appear to provide, at least for a time, nourishment for these ideological hungers as well as relief from the internal turmoil of ambivalence.[32]

Philip Slater asserts in *The Pursuit of Loneliness* that American cultural institutions are structured for the most part to make intimate relations difficult.[33] In reaction to the dissolution of the modern family, youth are in search of a more formable, sustaining, and caring surrogate family. Parents and societal authorities no longer provide meaningful value orientations and guidelines for living. According to figures published in *U.S. News and World Report*, 40 percent of United States marriages since 1970 have ended in divorce. Youth today are searching desperately for someone who will stand strong and lead them out of their bottomless existential anomie and exhaustion. They erect a person or a group to do this for them and attribute strengths and virtues to their leaders, whether or not the leaders actually possess them. In order to give their lives some direction, they obediently follow these leaders. Cults have flourished in our day because they teach their followers, in rather clear dictates, "how to live": what is important in life and what the followers should do with their time and energies.

RELIGIOUS SOCIAL MOVEMENTS

According to Freud, religion was born in the attempt to help humankind ease the anxiety of feeling helpless before the powerful forces that direct our fate.[34] In our long journey through history, we have erected, worshiped, and then discarded countless images and conceptions of these invisible forces. In each era, it seems, at least some people have gone against the grain, unable to identify with or make firm commitments to the dominant religion and ethical value system. To the orthodox faithful, of course, such persons have been regarded as marginal.

Alone, no man or woman can transform society or create an improved separate world. Marginal people are likely to feel unfulfilled and dissatisfied with their lives and to suffer from anxiety, frustration, confusion, and the urge to seek redress.[35, 36, 37, 38] The most desperate of them search for others who harbor a similar unhappiness with the existing norms and have similar hopes for a better world.

Herbert Blumer, one of the most respected interpreters of collective movements, sums up this dynamic succinctly: "[Social movements] have their inception in a condition of unrest, and derive their motive power on the one hand from dissatisfactions with the current form of life, and on the other, from wishes and hopes for a new scheme or system of living."[39]

Accordingly, a religious social movement can be seen as the consequence of social ferment that arises from the failure of mainstream religious groups and the various social orders to meet adequately the spiritual needs of a segment of the population.[40]

Once the stage is set for a movement, the appearance of an inspired and inspiring charismatic leader is necessary. Otherwise the movement dies down or at least comes temporarily to a halt. Centuries after they lived, such enlightened historical figures as Socrates, Buddha, Jesus, Mohammed, and Confucius still profoundly influence the lives of others. Many other charismatic leaders, however, have been rageful, deluded people who wreaked havoc with the lives of their followers.

In admitting the new religious cults as social movements, we have to examine closely the particular form these movements have taken. Stoner and Parke have defined a religious cult as "a minority religious group regarded as spurious or unorthodox [in which there is] great or excessive devotion or dedication to some person, idea or thing."[41]

They explain that these groups have a doctrine based upon a living leader's revelations, which usually supplants rather than supplements or accentuates traditional religious scripture and doctrine.[42] The cult leader is always the sole judge of a follower's dedication to the cult and enjoys absolute authority over the life of the group. He lives in rich splendor, while his followers toil in abject poverty. The doctrines of the cult, unlike traditional religion, not only offer to revitalize the being of the cult followers but also promise a system in which a believer may work to save all humanity. Ungerleider and Wellisch found that the cult members they interviewed had higher mean average scores on the performance scales of the Wechsler Adult Intelligence Test (116) than on the verbal scales (111).[43] This tends to suggest that many cult members better demonstrate their intelligence in performing tasks than in critically thinking out problems and concerns. Many ex–cult members have come to realize that despite the grandiose promises of their leader, cults actually sponsor no community improvement programs. Cult religions are exclusively social clubs, promising that their followers will achieve salvation and happiness.

The Psychological Climate of Cults

A study by Pattison and his associates on faith healing indicated that the conversion process to a cult doctrine is not congruent with improved psychological functioning. By employing psychological inventories, these investigators discovered:

> A typical constellation of personality traits was found, including the use of denial, repression, projection and disregard of reality. Faith healing does not result in alternative symptom formation, nor does it produce significant changes in life style. The primary function of faith healing is not to reduce symptoms, but to reinforce a magical belief system that is consonant with the subculture of these subjects.[44]

This is advantageous for cult leaders, who seem to be highly adroit in inducing altered states of consciousness in their followers. As I discussed in Chapter Five, modern brain research indicates that each of the brain's hemispheres has separate neurological functions. Moreover, each side of the brain is seen as having distinctly different ways of apprehending reality. If this is valid, then it would appear that each hemisphere participates in a reality different from the other. The left side is rational and analytic; the right speaks the language of movement, imagery, and metaphor. By utilizing such tactics as "loading the language,"[45] as Robert Lifton terms it, the cult authorities may begin to block out the critical faculties of the left hemisphere. Through speaking in metaphoric phrases and clichés that relate to the typically unsophisticated, undeveloped right hemisphere of most individuals, they gradually take over the thought processes of their flock. Lifton describes the process in detail:

> The language of the totalist environment is characterized by the thought-terminating cliché. The most far-reaching and complex of human problems are compressed into brief, highly reductive, definitive-sounding phrases easily memorized and easily expressed. These become the start and finish of any ideological analysis. . . . For an individual person, the effect of the language of ideological totalism can be summed up in one word: constriction. He is, so to speak,

linguistically deprived; and since language is so central to all human experience, his capacities for thinking and feeling are immensely narrowed . . . [his] uneasiness may result in a retreat into a rigid orthodoxy in which an individual shouts the ideological jargon all the louder in order to demonstrate his conformity, hide his own dilemma and his despair, and protect himself from the fear and guilt he would feel should he attempt to use words and phrases other than the correct ones.[46]

Moreover, cult rituals and practices are frequently deleterious psychologically and dangerous physically. According to one ex–People's Temple member, Grace Stoen, Jones was able to get away with so much because the oppressiveness of his demands was increased very gradually over time.[47] According to Mills, Jones was a "genius"[48] at stripping the defenses of his parishioners at all-night "catharsis" sessions.[49] During these evenings, members would be accused of offenses, humiliated, and beaten. The accusations and punishment began gradually, then increased. Anyone who expressed displeasure would also be called forth for punishment.

The intersubjectivity factor (see p. 42) is crucial to understanding the cult phenomenon. In my view, leaders like Jones could not have attracted such large followings if they were not encountering potential converts, especially young adults, who actively sought lapses from reality and constantly reindoctrinated the leader with his own bizarre beliefs. Unwittingly and intensely, many cult followers, no matter how intelligent or well informed, seek out a group in which they can become involved in extreme behavior. To repeat, the emotional motivation of a cultist can be as simple, in fact, as no longer wanting to be responsible for having to make serious life decisions.

Jones also relied on psychedelic and mood-altering drugs, nutritionally deficient diets, and sleep deprivation to control his followers in mind, body, and spirit. Taken all together, these practices induced a state of psychological confusion and dependency on the leader and his doctrines.

In short, the use of tactics such as "loading the language," skillfully phrased metaphors, and physical and emotional deprivation renders the follower highly accessible to suggestion and command. This comes about as a cult member is caught up in a series of existential paradoxes imposed by the interface of both overstimulation (e.g., repetition of ritual and doctrine in sessions and church services that were experienced as unending) and understimulation (e.g., intellectual and physical deprivation). In this paradoxical climate, the follower is susceptible to interhemispheric brain conflict. One hemisphere inhibits the other in an attempt to repress contradictory perception. It is as if the follower is not able to ascertain whether he is rejoicing in paradise or suffering in hell.

It is small wonder that under these conditions the followers of the People's Temple typically accepted such absurdities as Jim Jones's unselfconsciously presenting himself like one of Conrad's megalomaniacs: "I resent the implication that you make that I am unfair. If you really believed in the cause, you would accept my decisions about these things and not expect me to explain them."[50]

His followers apparently went to considerable lengths to deny what they saw and thought. Fear, punishment, contradiction, poverty, and continual labor formed the backbone of Jones's utopia.[51] It was a paradoxical world in which the leader enticed his parishioners with his virtuous ideology and compassionate charisma, then humiliated them and reduced them to a state of abject religious serfdom.[52] As we have seen, Lifton indicates that what has been referred to as "brain control" becomes possible when a leader has complete control of communication in an environment.[53] Support for the hegemony of the cult over its followers comes from Ungerleider and Wellisch, whose study indicates that forcible removal of members is extremely difficult when they have belonged to the group for more than a year.[54] In a talk before a committee of the Vermont legislature, John Clark, a psychiatrist who has treated several ex-members of cults, documented the cognitive deterioration he has found in these young people: "Formerly bright, fluent and creative individuals are rendered incapable of the use of irony or of metaphor, and they speak with a smaller, carefully constructed vocabulary filled with clichés and stereotyped ideas."[55]

THE PARANOID LEADER

Throughout the reports of those who knew Jones over time there is a consistent and insidious theme: he was typically involved in duplicity, coercion, and rank denigration of others. He lied to people immediately upon meeting them; he lied to them after favorably impressing them. He continued to lie, manipulate, and humiliate followers who questioned him or his practices. But more important, Jones lied to and humiliated those who did his bidding devotedly and without question.

What seems central to Jones's character was his extraordinary need for control. He had more than enough personal charm, cleverness, and seductiveness to captivate others and get his way, but he wanted more. Throughout his leadership of the People's Temple, he seems to have been in danger of flying out of control. Evidently, then, his need to control was actually directed inward; the duplicity, coercion, and humiliation inflicted upon others were indications of a war between his own internal processes. He was, of course, desperately hiding his vulnerabilities from others, and perhaps also from himself.

Again and again, it seems, Jones tried to escape from a gradually diminishing ability to compensate for his inner disturbances. He moved an early congregation of his cult from Indianapolis to Ukiah, California, because of an alleged vision of imminent nuclear holocaust. Northern California, according to the divine message, would be spared. Soon, feeling unappreciated by the citizenry of Ukiah, he took his followers to San Francisco, because it was more "politically relevant." The flight to Guyana was precipitated by rumors that *New West* magazine was preparing an investigative article about the People's Temple. Jones was obviously grandiose enough to believe that he could continually flee without surrendering possession, power, or control of his flock.

These endeavors required considerable manic energy. One is especially struck by the instability of Jones's moods and the wide fluctuations in his demeanor. Sometimes he would appear to be kind and sensitive; at other times, he would brutally demand obedience. One factor might have been his apparently regular use of amphetamines and heroin, but for reasons I will discuss shortly, his drug ingestion was probably not the major player in his bizarre behavior.

At any rate, the accelerating progression of his decompensation was obvious in Jonestown. As the climax drew nearer, his moods seemed to shift with increasing abruptness and flicked from one extreme to another in an instant. Whatever he had been trying to control was apparently overpowering him at last.

I believe that he had always been facing one terrible and specific task:

to control the shame he felt because his early caretakers had demanded unrealistically that he save them from the ills and offenses of the world. At the same time, he was mocked by his misanthropic father for being "a psalm singing little creep." For most of Jim Jones's life, his father, who had been gassed on the battlefield in World War I, was unemployed and active in the Ku Klux Klan. Jones's mother was a fanciful dreamer, as is clear from John Nugent's account:

> Even when she was a factory worker she had time to spin fantasies during the monotonous bus rides each day to her job twenty miles away. In one of her daydreams she was a young anthropologist working with primitive tribes in Africa, trying to decide between career and marriage. Then from the far side of a river, her dead mother called to her and told her that she was to bear a son who would right the wrongs of the world. She soon accepted a marriage proposal, bore a son, and was convinced that James Warren Jones was the Messiah. That dream, told often by Jones in solemn tones with his mother in the audience, is best understood when one understands that Lynetta Jones also believed herself to be the reincarnation of Mark Twain.[56]

Ironically and tragically, the young Jim Jones's relationships with his parents led him to pursue a course of action that resulted in his becoming a messiah for hundreds of people who believed that he could free them from "the wrongs of the world." Apparently, neither his parents nor his followers were able to tolerate the possibility of his being an ordinary person.

"Everything that Dad [Jones] does is all right," said one of his followers, a reformed prostitute, "as long as he keeps on being a saint."[57]

According to an ex-follower, C. A. Krause, the cult leader often exclaimed, "Threat, threat, threat of extinction. I wish I wasn't born at times. I understand hate; love and hate are very close. They can have me."[58]

Yet the Jim Jones who could see so accurately into the hearts of other people could not look into his own heart. In an important sense, the Jonestown tragedy resulted from Jones's inability to locate and then silence or appease the cruel internal master he served. It was a disastrous dilemma, and therefore he viewed anyone who defected or criticized the Temple as part of a conspiracy to destroy him and his mission.

THE CHARISMATIC LEADER AND HIS FOLLOWERS

The possibility of demonic involvement is a seductive explanation for many people faced with events of massive human exploitation. Just as most of us prefer to believe that human disasters are caused by natural forces, not people like us, we create monsters of inhumanity to distance us from the dark, destructive proclivities we fear in ourselves.

In the preliterate mind, any attempt to understand or master the natural world is an impious violation of the spirits who control the universe. Consequently, it was believed to be more proper, and more effective, to barter for protection against the unknown through homage and sacrifice to these forces.

Not so dissimilarly in contemporary times, we try to manage our fate through denial. When we create monsters of Jones, Koresh, and other erratic charismatic leaders, we return to the prehistoric mentality that serves incomprehensible forces. Unless we recognize these gurus as the vulnerable people they were, we cannot recognize ourselves and come to terms with our own disturbing motives. Their followers need to be understood as actively and continually reindoctrinating themselves to the leader's messages, which are actually their own silent wishes that defy common sense. In short, it is both erroneous and dangerous to view cult members as passive victims. The monster created of Jim Jones was the repository of collective denial and the silent but dynamically alive wishes of his followers.

Eric Hoffer explained an aspect of this relationship in his famous study of the "true believer":

> No matter how vital we think the role of the leader in the rise of a mass movement, there is no doubt that the leader cannot conjure a movement out of a void. There has to be an eagerness to follow and obey, and an intense dissatisfaction with things as they are, before the movement and leader can make their appearance.[59]

Weston LaBarre, a psychoanalytically sophisticated anthropologist, came to a related conclusion in diverse cultures:

> Every religion is the dramatization on a cosmic scale of the fears, loves and longings the child felt in his experiences of his parents in

the nuclear family . . . "Charisma," that supernatural animal magnetism that seems to stream compellingly from the sacred vatic personage or religious innovator [who has an ability to predict as if led by divine guidance], is really a quite secular circumstance psychologically. The compelling force comes not from the great man as he voices new supernatural truth: he speaks only to the powerful anti-commonsense fantasy already in the unconscious wish of each communicant. . . . The whole of the vatic has an "'uncanny" consistency with each one's private wishes; . . . some psychopathic leaders can release psychopathic behavior in mobs that is usually repressed in the individuals composing the mob.[60]

Consequently, it is crucial to recognize that paranoid leaders operate from a matrix in which they and their followers simultaneously indoctrinate and reindoctrinate one another. Such a leader is as much a creature of his followers as they are his. It follows that the leader's charisma, no matter how compelling, can evoke only those behaviors that are already present in his followers. Indeed, as social psychologist Leon Festinger and his associates have shown in their investigation of prophecy-seeking cults, followers will go to considerable lengths to continue believing in their leaders and the cult dogma, even when bedrock prophecies fail to come true.[61]

The cult leader well serves the purposes of those who are afraid to live courageously on their own. Jeannie Mills persuasively shows that the cult members had sufficient evidence of Jones's hypocrisy, cowardice, duplicity, instability, and malevolence. In fact, Mills believes that perhaps hundreds of people inside and outside the cult had direct knowledge of his sadism and cruelty, but they apparently made a considerable effort to deny or ignore the evidence of their senses: "not one of them would speak out publicly. Each person had, in some way, been silenced by his threat or by his money."[62]

Of course, people believe what is convenient to believe. For most of his life, Jones was a consummate racist, but he was able to present himself to the followers of the People's Temple as an enlightened social reformer. With impressive showmanship, he wove together various appeals to the yearnings and vanities of those whose cooperation he sought: "To the religious, Jones offered religion; to the ideological, he offered politics; to the ignorant and gullible, he offered miracles."[63]

Above all, Jones gave his followers a direction in life. Mills recalls that she and her husband, also a member, believed that their lives had been meaningless until they met the cult leader and he took away their existential difficulties, installing them with "a sense of purpose." Because he gave them a reason to exist, they dedicated all their financial and emotional resources to pleasing him: "We believed that he loved us. We were certain that as long as we stayed in his group our lives would continue to be blissful."[64]

In recent years, psychologists have learned a considerable amount about the dynamics of obedience. On this basis, one might argue that cult leaders operate their regimes with military discipline. For all of Jones's followers, much as for soldiers, obedience to the leader is not only expected but required. Psychologists have found that ordinary citizens will commit brutal acts contrary to their own conscience with remarkable ease if they are commanded to do so by a person in authority. In a series of experiments with university students and with ordinary people from all walks of life, social psychologist Stanley Milgram was able to get about 65 percent of his subjects to deliver what they believed to be painful, dangerous electric shocks to innocent victims in an adjoining room. Despite the victims' pleas to stop this punishment, administered when the victims failed to give the correct answers to a learning test, almost two thirds of the subjects continued to administer shocks.[65]

Jones's followers, as we have already learned from the written reports of ex-members of the cult, were burdened with rather denigrative opinions of themselves. They flocked to him eagerly to become his disciples, and his victims. Many of them felt strongly repressed rage and were seeking an authoritative figure who would give them permission to enact consciously disavowed hateful aspects of themselves without having to acknowledge their motives. By continuing to stress themes of suffering, forced obligation, and vengeance, Jones became the repository of his followers' dark feelings, thus serving their unacknowledged purposes no less than they served his.

THE LOYAL LIEUTENANTS

Were Jones's pessimistic themes sufficient to maintain his hold over the many articulate, well-educated professionals who joined the People's

Temple? Probably not, but he provided them with other attractions, as Nugent reports:

> In 1968 Jones's movement had attracted almost a hundred and fifty members, mostly white and young and with specialties and skills that the Temple needed. There were accountants, writers, printers, social workers, lab technicians, executive secretaries, teachers and street organizers. They also knew how to handle hustling, ghetto riots, peace marches, draft dodging and even jail. . . . They understood politicians, and had studied Nietzsche, Freud, Marx, and Engels. Some held Phi Beta Kappa keys; some had done graduate work abroad; others were classical musicians, journalists, and students working on doctorates. . . . These were the talents Jones could muster to move into every important structure in the city of San Francisco.[66]

Without these bright and talented young people, the cult might not have survived to reach Guyana. Jones selected his most loyal and able lieutenants from this group, again recalling Hoffer:

> The uncanny powers of a leader manifest themselves not so much in the hold he or she has on the masses as in his ability to dominate and almost bewitch a small group of able men. These men must be fearless, proud, intelligent and capable of organizing and running large-scale undertakings and yet they must submit wholly to the will of the leader, draw their inspiration and driving force from him, and glory in their submission.[67]

The lieutenants, according to Nugent, were attracted to Jones by his supposed commitment to action under the banner of social justice, not by his religious themes:

> For the young new members, it was a time of tremendous excitement. They were being given two things sorely missing in their lives: challenge and responsibility. It was like working on a political campaign with a charismatic leader who drew rousing hysterical cheers

from the crowd. Jones satisfied their egos: cheers for him in an audience confirmed his lieutenants' ability to make things happen. . . .
They were in a twenty-four-hour strategy room making monumental
decisions for their world. To them, their world was *the* world.[68]

If their world had become *the* world, it is understandable that Jones's
delusional system became totally contagious to anyone who needed him
to express their fears and ambitions. In his famous confrontation with
Congressman Leo Ryan, he appeared to act out the rage and impotence
felt by his followers.

"By calling me bad you make me bad," his behavior seemed to say.
"Therefore, I will hurt myself and others and it will be *your* fault."

Potentially, we are all capable of tolerating this kind of violent, deluded behavior, but some personalities are undoubtedly more susceptible
than most of us, as LaBarre has written:

> True believers are authoritarian personalities because they are in-
> fantile dependents on the divine authority of the Shaman,[69] not ma-
> ture assessors of their own judgments. Fundamentalists abjectly
> depend on part tribal culture, not on their own contemporary com-
> mon sense. Every fundamentalism is an intellectual lobotomy.[70]

THE NEW MORALITY AND SEXUAL POLITICS

Mills tells us that Jim Jones taught his followers a new set of "situational
ethics"—i.e., "The end justifies the means." To church members, this
meant: "You do whatever Jim says because he knows what is needed for
the cause."[71]

The followers of the People's Temple professed to believe in social justice
and human worth. Yet they permitted Jones and his cohorts to brutalize and
humiliate them, their spouses, their children, friends, and neighbors.
They gave in to Jones's relativistic morality, lacking the courage to maintain their values and insist that there are some things that are inherently
right and others that are undeniably wrong. What was the payoff for the
toil, suffering, humiliation, and dependency that these followers derived
from their identification with Jones's "new morality"? Mills reports that
she and her husband were amazed at how little disagreement there was

among the members of the People's Temple. Jones had virtually taken the existential difficulties out of their lives.[72]

For most people, securing meaningful, intimate relationships with others is a difficult endeavor. According to investigative reporter John Nugent, sexual liberation was the central dogma of Jones's new morality.[73] To understand the power that Jones held over his followers, the issue of sexual politics in messianic cults in general should be examined. Jones used sexual tactics and programs to dominate, blackmail, and humiliate his followers. Sexual politics, of course, is not singularly involved with physical intercourse. It includes all forms of power tactics, such as seduction, sadism, brutality, and humiliation, to control the minds, bodies, and spirits of other people. Mills tells us that no follower was allowed to refuse a direct order from Jones.[74] In his doctrines, considerable attention is given not only to his parishioners' belief system but also to how they feel and are reacted to and treated in terms of their bodies and body images. Plato indicated that the great error of his day was to treat the person as if the body were separated from the soul. Jones also recognized the tremendous power he could derive from his parishioners by manipulating their body images. Having done this, he was able to establish himself as the only legitimate object of sexual desire and activity in the cult. He had a secretary who arranged his sexual affairs. At the same time, he would order brutal punishment for his parishioners who involved themselves in sexual activity he had not arranged.

Metaphorically, Jones demonstrated that he was the only person of worth in the sect. By utilizing unconventional and bizarre practices— whether by forbidding all sexual activities in the temple or by dictating precisely what kinds of sexual activities members were to have with persons he chose—Jones ensured that his followers were increasingly denied the integrity, autonomy, and ownership of their own bodies and how they were to function and interact with others. These prerogatives were taken over by Jones and those he appointed until the final scene, in which he ordered his flock to commit mass suicide and dictated the manner and the sentiments they were to experience in their demise.

Sexual politics is most common in societies in times of social unrest and uncertainty of values. For many individuals, joining a cult is a means of avoiding issues of intimacy and sexuality. In a study of the members of the Unification Church, Galanter and his associates found that 86 percent of those studied felt that people who were not members of the sect should "avoid thinking about sex," just as they did.[75] A church leader commented, "Romantic love is a recent innovation and it's a failure."[76]

Whether or not a particular cult encourages sexual promiscuity (as did the Church of God), discourages it (like the Unification Church), or manipulates sexual relationships (People's Temple), the lack of freedom in allowing their followers to function according to their own preferences is a manifestation of sexual politics. In sexual political regimes, followers are relieved of the burden of choice and need not address their fears about their own capacities for caring and intimacy. In these regimes, cult leaders become heir to sources of tremendous energy and power. However, in order to create a bond and an emotional valence with his followers, as LaBarre has indicated, a charismatic leader must have common ground with them. Both Jones and his disciples seem to have been unable to acknowledge their fears of intimacy. A self-liberated leader may have freed his followers up to examine those fears. Tragically, despite Jim Jones's doctrine of sexual liberation, he did—apparently to a massive degree—deny his own fear of intimacy. In other words, while he demanded bizarre sexual experimentation, at the same time, Jones forbade the demonstration and expression of genuine caring and intimacy among members of the People's Temple. He became obsessed by what psychoanalyst Michael Eigen has called "demonized anality," which leads to ubiquitous spoiling of everything within and around himself. It may lead to murder, rape, pillage, and violation of one's own and others' self-respect and integrity.[77]

Authoritarian personalities, defensive and cognitively closed-minded, are largely inflexible in trying to make sense of their lives. That is, they seem incapable or unwilling to withstand high degrees of anxiety in situations that are cognitively complex, ambiguous or fraught with considerable uncertainty of outcome. Rather, they seek to stifle this easily aroused anxiety with quick, easy and absolutely "correct" solutions. Such people, happy only when able to hold unswaying convictions in their belief systems, are ripe for charismatic leaders like Jim Jones.[78]

It follows, then, that members of most, if not all, cults are indoctrinated to believe that they are superior to everyone else—i.e., they alone possess the truth.

By the same token, officially sanctioned psychological monitoring is integral to the regimentation of cult life, recruitment, and indoctrination.

To ensure obedience to doctrine, critical thinking is strongly discouraged by practices that suppress negative thoughts about the cult and replace them with emotional dependence on the leader.

SUFFERING AND FANATICISM

One characteristic of the People's Temple that contrasted strikingly with other contemporary cults was the wide cross-section of socio-economic and age groups, including an unusually large population of elderly people and married couples with children. Apparently, Jones's remarkable ability to look into the hearts of others, combined with his slick rhetorical skills, enabled him to appeal with equal magnetism to many different kinds of people. In a Judeo-Christian society, moreover, his teachings had a familiar ring: as he reproached his followers for their materialism, he also asserted that endurance of suffering is a sign of human courage. One thinks of traditional martyrologies, with their descriptions of early Christians impatiently awaiting their torture as "they joyously sang hymns to their last breath."[79]

The Roman poet Virgil's depiction of bedevilment sounds eerily like the inner voice of Jim Jones: "If I am unable to move the gods above, then I shall stir up those in the nether world."[80]

Jones manipulated the fears and guilts of his followers in order to convince them that they would not be morally respectable unless they suffered deeply. Since his poor and minority parishioners were already apprenticed in toil, frustration, and limitation, such moral respectability was near at hand.

Middle-class and professional members, however, were continually forced to go in search of suffering in order to justify themselves for being "haves" rather than "have-nots." In his book on authority, sociologist Richard Sennett contends that this endeavor can gradually take complete control of a person's intentionality: "The need to legitimate one's beliefs in terms of an injury or suffering to which one has been subjected attaches people more and more to the injuries themselves."[81] As a result, they conspire at their own suffering.

By sowing mistrust and fear regularly among them, Jones turned his followers against each other, but of course they came to him for redress.

He also manipulated their delusional systems in regard to outside forces surrounding the People's Temple, warning that their loyalty to him made them the targets of conspirators. The precise identity of these conspirators, thanks to his erratic worldview, changed from day to day. To the suggestible minds of his flock, there were a myriad of possibilities, including organizations, like the FBI and the CIA, that are actually involved in surreptitious activities. And in the background of any delusional prophecies, we must remember, is a sobering truth: for the first time in history, we have the means to annihilate the world. Under these conditions, it is understandable that Jones would be at least half believed and that his frightened followers would turn to him for divine revelation and deliverance.

His prophetic visions were typically apocalyptic: "All black people in America are going into concentration camps or be hung—except those who stay here with me. I will protect you when the time comes."[82]

Slowly but irreversibly, then, the People's Temple developed into a fanatic cult whose members lost touch with what they intended for themselves as purposive beings.

Fanatical acts are generated from profound despair, but also from the desire to achieve deeds not deemed possible through ordinary efforts in the normal course of events. The consciousness of the fanatic has been accentuated or manipulated so that he comes to identify with a group whose ideology and values and, frequently, political causes and physical actions are in conflict with, or imagined to be, with the outside world. Membership in fanatical groups, therefore, integrally involves risk to the lives and beliefs of other people.

Does fanaticism involve courage, as some believe, or is it nothing more than flight to avoid inner psychological turmoil? On April 15, in the year 73 C.E., nearly a thousand Jewish Zealots, besieged by Roman legions at the fortress of Masada, killed themselves rather than be taken prisoner. Were they courageous, or fanatic? The distinction comes, I believe, in the source of the action taken. In courage, there is an accentuated sense of self, indeed a love of self, and when others are involved, love of them is motivation for an act of bravery. By that definition, the Zealots were courageous.

But fanatic identification contributes to a loss of self. A follower who identifies with a charismatic leader and despises his identification with others has an aching need to forgive himself for shameful weaknesses he cannot condone in anyone else, so he tries to distance himself from his self-hatred by burying it in others, and despising others for what he has projected onto them.

There was nothing heroic about Jones's followers. Timid, devoid of passion and purpose, they came alive only when their leader granted them permission. Experiencing the self as weak and uncertain, his followers psychologically split off the positive, desirable aspects of their personalities and perceived them as virtues of the leader, his cause, or his ideology. Left with nothing but their sense of "badness," they were prepared to sacrifice themselves so that the psychically disowned, separated "good" self could survive and reign.

The kind of individuals who find their way into religious cults generally lack the courage to break away from this self-destructive process. In the cruel and exacting mentality of those reared to believe they lack human goodness, an implacable conscience claims that if the self cannot be all-powerful and all-knowing, then it does not deserve to endure. Only the omniscient, omnipotent leader is worthy of survival. What shame vulnerable cultists cannot achieve in reality they magically try to achieve in their identification with their leader.

The history of malevolence is a long tale of those who avoided acting according to the dictates of conscience; indeed, they feared responsibility and looking inside themselves for guidance. Unable to tolerate their private shame at their incompetence as individuals, they magically assumed that their hurt selves could overcome shame without exposing their psychic vulnerability. Lacking a source of inner inspiration, they looked to strong forces outside themselves, as we have seen, and put themselves at the mercy of powerful others.

In this way, paranoid prophets and tyrants through the ages replaced the bicameral mind. Their vatic voices became ever more sinister and destructive in their demands. Hitler's rise to power, as Ernest Becker pointed out,[83] built upon his intuitive ability to act on his followers' yearnings, promised a heroic victory over shame, weakness, limitation, and death. He convinced them that he could deliver on that promise and expunge the humiliations of the Treaty of Versailles by restoring Germany's cultural and military superiority. In that pursuit, the misery of their individual lives would become irrelevant.

THE TRUE PROPHET

How do today's destructive cult leaders like Jones and Koresh compare with the inspired prophets of antiquity? The sages of ancient times— Buddha and Jesus, Socrates and Confucius—were deeply concerned about the welfare of their disciples. In addition, as the German philosopher and psychiatrist Karl Jaspers writes, their basic masculine characters were natural and striking.[84] (In contrast, one can never be sure who the mercurial, pretentious Jones and Koresh really were.)

Each of the ancient prophets presented himself as an ordinary being engaged in the constructive development of selfhood. Rather than tell others how to live or lead them into social action, these sages demonstrated patiently by personal example. They also created a climate in which their disciples could question how best to conduct life and reach their own conclusions. While Jesus believed in the paramount value of life in the hereafter, he apparently did not minimize the importance of the present world or ask his followers to sacrifice their mortal existence.

Above all, the true prophets did not teach their disciples to hate or flee those who opposed them, for, as Jaspers notes, they all proclaimed that human love should be universal and unlimited. Nor did any of them need the dubious proof of having others validate their beliefs or demand others to die for them; Socrates resolutely chose his own death, and Jesus braved fear and doubt alone on the cross.

By not presenting himself as omniscient or omnipotent, the true prophet allows his people to transform themselves by choosing their own ordeals, rather than suffer trials he imposes upon them. They then have the possibility of becoming as capable as he.

The obvious contrast, of course, is that destructive charismatic leaders demand that their adherents blindly follow the leader's doctrines in order to validate his stature as god, prophet, and man of worth. Not surprisingly, therefore, Jones rationalized and excused himself from even the token ordeals that he imposed upon his compliant parishioners, including children.

Hitler, Jim Jones, and others of their ilk are representative of the bicameral mind for those who feel lost and abandoned—especially those who fear self-examination because they are convinced that they lack human goodness. These followers are susceptible to fanatic acts in the context of the authoritarian regime's ruthless disregard for life and death in promising immortalization through the glory of the regime. Hitler and Jones, though for somewhat different reasons and to different proportions, *used* and were *used by* their followers to commit atrocities. For that reason, the unidimensional explanation that a powerful leader coerces his followers into bizarre, tragic behaviors is, as I have tried to show throughout this chapter, dangerously simplistic and erroneous.

We must understand that these leaders, far from having demonic powers or ruling entirely by the force of their paranoid psychoses, are hoisted aloft by followers who are unwilling to examine their own personal duplicity and malevolent urges. If we do not all gain the courage to live as we intend and restrain others from committing acts contrary to their own consciences, then such terrible sagas as the Holocaust, the Jonestown massacre, and the Serbian holocaust will not be historical anomalies; they will be just three among many chapters in an unending volume of atrocities.

In the next chapter, I will show how some of the social and political factors discussed in this chapter played upon the shame-vulnerable personality of a young man and contributed to his malevolent role in the atrocities of his nation.

CHAPTER TWELVE

The Forging of the Malevolent Personality

*The first evil choice or act is linked
to the second; and each one to the one
that follows, both by the tendency of our
evil nature and by the power of habit,
which holds us as by a destiny.*

— TRYON EDWARDS

P ERHAPS THE LAST PLACE I WOULD HAVE EXPECTED TO ENCOUNTER
someone involved in serious crimes against humankind was the night-
time college course I teach in understanding human behavior. Physically
unprepossessing Emil, tall, lanky, in his early twenties, typically wore faded
jeans and a blue bandana as head-gear to class, he stood out instantly
from the other students because of the long, jagged scar down his right
cheek. Usually, he was accompanied by his wife, Alicia, older than he,
who was also taking the course.

Halfway through the fall semester, Alicia, a prosecutor in the U.S.
District Attorney's office, approached me guardedly in the hallway after
class and asked to speak privately for a moment. Drawing me into an al-
cove, she asked if I really believed the views that I had presented in class
or was just expressing the "politically correct" attitudes of my profession.

I had been drawing upon my experiences with patients who have
"grandiose egos," to argue that such deeply hurt people should be understood, not condemned. In my opinion, I explained, the immense humiliations they have suffered in the past compel their seeming indifference

and lack of empathy for other people's misfortunes. Although they often may seem to be "romanticizing their own egos," they are actually involved in desperate efforts to create a fictional self, thus enabling themselves to survive psychically and perhaps physically as well.[1]

Alicia, after staring at me indecisively for some time, said quite simply and without discernible emotion, "My husband is completely indifferent to the pain of other people."

I asked whose pain she meant, guessing that she was the victim of his abuse, but she ignored the question. Eyes downcast, her arms tense, with palms extended, she asked if I would talk with Emil. I explained that he would have to contact me himself if he wanted me to see him for a psychological consultation.

He called me the morning after our final class meeting. Explaining in heavily-accented English that it was not safe for him to say much on the telephone, he asked me if I could be trusted. When I asked him to be more specific, he was scarcely less mysterious.

"Personal tragedy," he said. "As a victim of the cruelties of the Serbian civil war and other matters, I am depressed and quiet. But I suppose it looks different to other people. I can say no more."

Briefly, I explained the rules of confidentiality that govern all information he might report to me during consultation.

During our first session, Emil asserted that he wanted to stop abusing Alicia and sketched his background in a rapid-fire staccato that was not fully comprehensible. Born in a small mountain town in what was then Yugoslavia, he could not remember his biological father, whom his mother described as a talented musician too poor to marry her. Leaving his violin as a pledge to return, he set off to find work with a wealthy relative in Belgrade, but he never returned. Emil's mother never learned what had happened to him.

In Emil's account, his stepfather, Pertof, was a rough, impulsive old man, a highly skilled mechanic given to instant but stubbornly held opinions. A semipro boxer in his youth, he had thrown over his career to join his relatives and townsfolk in the mountains to fight with Marshal Tito against the invading Nazis. Throughout Emil's upbringing, Pertof retained his prizefighter's physique and aggressive attitude.

Emil was convinced that Pertof strongly preferred his own two sons, from a previous marriage, to his stepson. Handy like their father, these stepbrothers, Pavlos and Stavos, spent most of their time cleaning, repairing, and trading or purchasing knives and guns, treating these destructive weapons with the admiration and respect they did not seem to accord human beings. On numerous occasions, they had menaced and driven away the relatives of young women who accused one or the other of them of seducing and impregnating her.

In Emil's recollections, his mother, regarded as unquestionably the most beautiful woman in town, was moody, flirtatious, and uneducated. Even men who had known her all their lives turned their heads to watch her as she walked by, and she took great pride in being the object of their desire. She admired beauty wherever she found it, especially wildflowers and romantic music, and she encouraged her son to play his father's violin. He never found out how she came by the money to pay for his private lessons.

She earnestly supported Emil in most matters, but she rarely sided with him in his frequent arguments with his stepfather. Instead, she rebuked him for being selfish and not appreciating what Pertof had done for them. At those moments, Emil said, he hated his mother, feeling uncared for and all alone in the world.

When I asked Emil for his "personal story," he became visibly restless, squirming in his chair and occasionally biting his nails.

"I have an early memory," he said, "when I was a boy of, perhaps, seven years of age. I was walking to the house in town where my music teacher lived. My dog, Überhound, came as usual from my home two miles through the woods to greet me at school and carry my books for me. As we passed through the streets, I began to feel nervous. I had no idea why. I felt like running home, but if I did, I'd have no good reason to explain to my mother why I missed my lesson.

"After walking a few more blocks, I saw a crowd of men in the street. I see them clearly to this day. Their backs are to me. There are sounds of heckling and laughter from the crowd. Their laughter resounds with challenges and taunts. I hear words like 'intellectual' and 'Jew banker.'

"The crowd partially separates. Men move to the right and left of the road. A couple of them are leaning on metal trolleys used to transport heavy merchandise among the shops in town. As the crowd separates again, I see them as individuals in profile. Most appear to be coarse workingmen, and my stepbrother Pavlos is among them. There are a few shopkeepers as well, who have left their stores to investigate the commotion. To my left I see some glass object glistening on the street in the gloomy late day—it's autumn—giving off prisms of silvery light. The crowd separates once again.

"A man lies sprawled in the gutter. With considerable effort, he is trying to sit upright. He manages to partially erect his torso after a few minutes. He is over fifty, small, frail, with thinning gray curly hair and a thick, short beard. The crowd backs further away from this fallen man. There is a bicycle on the pavement nearby. It is dented, out of shape. I see that the glass object is a pair of broken eyeglasses, lying in the gutter. The bearded man on the ground is finally able to sit upright weakly. His pants legs are ripped. Blood oozes from cuts below each knee.

"He is begging someone, anyone, who saw what happened to come forth. People answer him with taunts like, 'I didn't see anything, unless you are a rich Jew and can pay me.' Then a short, stocky youth races out of the crowd, yelling, 'Hey, Jew, maybe you see better with four eyes!' He kicks the eyeglasses toward the slight, bearded man with a strong soccer kick. The man tries to put on his broken glasses, but the wire frames are hopelessly bent. The crowd roars with laughter. The man pounds his small fists impotently on the ground. After a few minutes, he just lies there and sobs."

Bewildered and upset, Emil ran home, crying. Pertof, who was home working on the engine of a truck, grabbed him forcefully by the arm as he tried to enter the house and demanded to know what was wrong. The boy reluctantly told him the whole story, including Pavlos's presence on the scene.

The old man looked him in the face, with what seemed for a moment as an expression of concern. Then he struggled to speak, but managed only a kind of gurgling sound. Finally, he just slapped Emil hard across the face. The boy reeled, stumbled, and fell against the side of the truck, but he quickly picked himself up. His cheek and lower lip stung. He felt liquid creeping down his face, wiped his mouth, and saw blood.

"Why did you hit me?" he demanded.

"You are a Christian," his stepfather snapped. "What the hell does it matter what happens to a Jew? Wise up, kid, if you want to survive in this world!"

As Emil entered the house, his mother was standing by the parlor window, evidently having witnessed this scene. She beckoned him to come in and sit down.

"I am going to tell you a story," she said, "that your stepfather told me years ago. It is something he saw during the war, when he had been captured by the Germans."

Under guard himself at a railroad station, the young Serbian/Yugoslav soldier watches as men, women, children, and infants emerge slowly from the boxcars of a long train. At the head of a ramp, a commanding figure in the black uniform of the Nazi SS Medical Corps stands silhouetted against the cloudy dark sky. He is about thirty-five years old, his uniform ironed to knife-edge perfection. Below him, the civilians mill about in confusion, searching for loved ones, trying to orient themselves in this desolate place. Some run back and forth; others crawl in the mud.

As the emptied train begins to pull away, billowing large puffs of gray smoke, the German officer shouts in a firm baritone voice:

"Attention! Stop moving around! Listen carefully to what I tell you!"

The crowd freezes in place. One white-bearded man, perhaps eighty years old, is floundering about on the ground. His black clothes are caked with mud, his eyeglasses bent and hanging askew. A woman crawls next to him, a babushka covering most of her face. The old man turns to her, as if they are related.

"That imposing man standing there on the ramp," he says. "Maybe they've sent him to save us!"

The officer is singing loudly, passages from *Die Meistersinger,* while gracefully swinging his riding crop from left to right, right to left, as the prisoners are herded toward the gates of a concentration camp. Intermittently, he interrupts his aria to indicate which prisoners should go *links,* which *rechts.* The camp is set in a large muddy field without any vegetation, surrounded by a thirty-foot-high barbed-wire fence. Guard towers rise up from this barrier at fifty-yard intervals.

With his rifle, a sergeant jabs people lying on the ground, prodding them to stand up and move quickly into the camp. Some are struggling with their belongings. The sergeant catches the eye of his superior.

"Carry only what you are wearing!" the officer shouts. "Leave everything where you are! Do what I say!"

As the young Yugoslav watched, he learned an unforgettable lesson. What did these people do? They were doing exactly as they had been told, as if things might turn out all right in the end. They were making haste to enter the death camp.

Emil's mother told him about other horrifying experiences that his stepfather had witnessed or endured during the Nazi occupation. Then, looking him straight in the eye and speaking in the harshest voice he had ever heard her use, she repeated the lesson her husband had learned:

"It is better to be a Nazi and survive than to be one of those people who are so helpless and naive that they have no choice but to pray to God that the Nazis are there in order to deliver them from harm!"

Emil had been named by his half-German biological father for his German grandfather. Inevitably, the very name Emil reminded the Serbian Pertof of both his wartime ordeals and his wife's sexual relationship with someone of German blood.

But if he hated Germans, he despised their cowed, unprotesting victims, whose helplessness at the train station he had watched with a shame he did not understand. He had held on as much as possible over the years to the strength and mental fitness of his robust youth so that he would never be so pitifully dependent on the mercy of devils like the Nazis.

Emil's mother explained to her son that Pertof was incapable of clearly expressing either his self-pride or his loathing of weakness. Nevertheless, by sternly demanding that Emil root out all vulnerable sensibilities, he was earnestly trying to help his stepson prepare for life. This was the core problem between them: Emil's refusal to become as hardened emotionally as Pertof.

Emil's first reaction to his mother's story was relief. Not only did his stepfather not hate him, it seemed; he might even, for some inexplicable reason, care about him a little. Slowly, however, the boy began to recognize that Pertof's caring was conditional. It required more physical vigor and mental hygiene than Emil felt he possessed. Emil decided he never wanted to earn Pertof's wrath again. No, never again! It was too unbearably painful.

From then on, he determined, he must try to behave like his two stepbrothers, who seemed to please the old man by meeting his expectations. The idea made him shudder involuntarily. Surely, he did not have to become completely like Stavos and Pavlos, with their coarse, offensive manners toward people and their brutality toward animals. Still, if he forced himself to spend more time with them, perhaps he could learn to imitate only their strengths of character, such as their fearlessness and directness, and avoid picking up their odious habits. He was not optimistic about the prospect.

Not long afterward, Pertof developed lung cancer. A lifelong heavy smoker, he had repeatedly promised his wife to quit but started up again whenever he became angry, which was often. He rationalized his behavior by boasting that he came from a long line of smokers who all lived to very old age. In Emil's eyes, this excuse subverted the old man's image. What had appeared to be courage and resoluteness was largely, it turned out, a matter of physical forcefulness.

Pertof died, and his widow was soon involved in a relationship with a wealthy older man, a wine merchant who owned a fine home on a lake. He was so brutal that Emil's mother often complained to her son. During wild drinking parties at his house, he liked to do such things as lift her skirt and show off her private parts to his rich friends, and he was no less cruel when sober. Nevertheless, as she explained to Emil, she stayed with this boor because he was a good lover. Some younger men might be good lovers too, she admitted, but they were inconveniently poor. She told Emil that as soon as he graduated from school and she no longer needed the extra money, she would look for a decent man. But even after the boy quit school to find work, she remained with the wine merchant.

At this point, Emil paused and looked searchingly at me, as if trying to read my soul.

"Are you wondering if what you've told me is important?" I ventured. "Or are you wondering what I might do with information that you haven't mentioned yet?"

"You might be right about both matters, Doctor," he answered. "What concerns me most immediately is that I am considered by some people—who they are doesn't really matter now—to be a criminal. If I am a criminal, then I am a most-wanted criminal. The one matter I know for certain is that there are people who are looking for me. They're after me with guns, knives, or anything else they can get their hands on."

"If that's true, they must believe you've done something terrible."

"Oh, yes. And consequently, I fear for my safety here with you."

"Okay, I hear you." I let him decide for a moment whether or not to believe me. "On the other hand, I cannot help you unless you speak more directly about what is going on with you."

With an impatient shrug, Emil shot back, "And I can say no more until I am far more assured than I am feeling right now that it is safe to tell you more information about myself."

I leaned forward. "What is said here remains here, as I've already told you. I'm pledged to secrecy. Why can't you believe that?"

"Under normal circumstances, I might. But I am not a normal man, and what I need to speak to you about is so . . . well, let's call it 'extreme.' So extreme that I cannot rely upon your customary assurances about following the ethical considerations of your profession."

"And again I ask you why."

He sighed. "Listen, I don't really know how to express what I fear, so I'll say it this way: You tell me you'll keep your mouth shut because of your ethics, but ethics are really baloney! You doctors *say* you have ethics, and lawyers *say* they have ethics, and businessmen *say* they have ethics." He laughed bitterly. "What good, really, are all these ethics? If I kept on talking with you, I would have to . . . what is the word you use?"

"Broach?"

"Yes, I would have to broach some things . . . such events . . . Nowhere in the annals of human history have there been concerns, so-called ethical concerns, with more moral depth."

"Come on! You make it sound as if you have information about the most terrible thing that has ever happened in the history of the world."

Emil shuddered visibly. "Don't doubt it for a minute!" he exclaimed. "And because of how it would affect you personally, all of your famous ethical considerations might become, as my wife the attorney would say, 'null and void.' "

"And then what would happen, if that's the case?" I asked.

"Then your professional responsibilities toward me would be canceled or ignored."

I took us back to the main point.

"Just what circumstances are we talking about?"

"Evil," he replied, his face suddenly distorted with a hideous sneer.

"Evil? What kind of evil?"

"The worst kind." His face went blank, impassive. "How can you help me with evil? Psychoanalysis and psychiatry are no better than theology, or what Alicia calls 'jurisprudence,' in dealing with evil. None of these professions have found a way to understand evil or a way of fighting it. Evil gets its way. It endures where virtue pales and withers. None of us knows for sure if evil is ever overthrown. In the real world, whatever your psychoanalytic theories say, evil outlives us all."

I was finding this difficult to follow.

"What does that mean?"

Emil snorted. "What I'm asking is: What actually happens to evil people, or what you doctors refer to as 'evil objects'?"

Still unsure what he meant, I asked, "Well, what does?"

"No one can say!" he shouted triumphantly.

"No one?"

"I can tell you," Emil continued excitedly, "about evil criminals I have known, who've come out of their hiding places and stand bare of their disguises. These former monsters are now enfeebled, empty cartons of their previous selves. We might even mistake them for any other old creeps, except for one enduring quality: they refuse to feel any guilt, any remorse for their crimes. In fact, most of the time, they don't even remember them. So where has their evil gone? Does it have a life of its own? If it doesn't, then why does it seem that their evil has vanished into history, just as their dreadful secrets are hidden away forever?"

I could see that Emil's intellectual questioning was a means of circling around some great hurt that he was not willing to speak about personally and directly. At the beginning of the session, I had assumed that he was cautious with me because of possible legal implications, but I had been wrong. Rather, it was I whom he feared, not the police, for to him I represented moral authority. I sensed that he feared he had done something for which I would not forgive him.

Long before meeting Emil, I had pondered another factor in the problem of confession, which was also playing a part here.[1] Ironically, no mat-

ter how urgently a person wants to rid himself of a painful burden by con-
fessing, he just as urgently needs to withhold the shameful secret. Inordinately powerful agents require his silence. They are the painful loyalties
he feels toward others, loyalties that demand that he protect people in his
past from disclosure of their shameful, perhaps incriminating, or even
malevolent involvement in his life.

Of course, even though I work under the same requirements of confidentiality as does a priest, I cannot grant absolution. Instead, I must work
to enable the victim of a painful secret to question his loyalties to the
people who, he fears, demand that he suffer his mystery alone. In other
words, the patient's narrative, with its hidden shames and guilts, is an unfinished story. As I've noted before, we are meaning-oriented beings; we
typically regard the events of our lives evaluatively. Consequently, I must
help my patient rewrite his narrative, with the hope that in the process he
will find a more viable, more hopeful way to live.

In light of this aim, despite Emil's evident fear of me as a moral authority, I suggested that he stop his philosophizing for the time being and
continue his narrative.

Emil's two stepbrothers contributed heavily to his erratic upbringing.
When not fashioning or repairing their weaponry, Stavos and Pavlos
spent their time seducing women. Over time, they brought the boy into
their escapades, which both frightened and stimulated him. Never before
had they sought out his company.

Late one afternoon, when Emil was playing in the woods with his dog,
the brothers approached in the dwindling daylight, all smiles. This took
him off guard, since they were usually gruff with him.

"What a great dog Überhound is!" Pavlos said. "So big and strong."

"And lusty," Stavos echoed. "We ought to get your dog a girlfriend."

"Come on, let's get the dog a girl!" Pavlos grabbed the dog's collar and
started pulling him toward the barn, while Stavos restrained Emil in his
huge arms.

"Oh, let him come and watch," Pavlos shouted over his shoulder. "It's
time for him to be a man."

By the time Emil could catch up, Pavlos and Überhound were already
inside the barn, which was dimly lit with a kerosene lamp. Several of his

stepbrothers' hunting and drinking buddies were crowded together in the back. As the last arrows of late-afternoon sunlight flashed into the barn, Emil made out a strange scene: a woman was tied to a low wooden beam, surrounded by the men, who were listening intently. Someone was interrogating her about her sex life, but she was not cooperating. Finally getting fed up, Pavlos called her a "drunken whore" and tore off her dress. The men laughed crudely at the sight of her pink undergarments.

Emil felt a strong impulse to run away, to get out of that horrible place and never see his evil stepbrothers again. But at the same time, he felt a tingling sensation running up and down his back, then hot and cold shivers crisscrossed his stomach, flushing his groin and sliding down his legs into his boots. He wanted to see what was going to happen to the woman, even as he knew he should flee from what was obviously a cruel and indecent act. To escape this moral bind, he leaped into the air. When he landed, he spun around, rushed past Stavos, and dashed out the door.

But he did not go deep into the woods. Pulled back by some unfathomable, compelling urge, he crept through the growing dusk toward an opening in the back wall of the barn. To overcome his characteristic sensitivity, squeamishness, and aversion to rough play, he told himself that it was indeed high time he became a man. As he found an unobstructed view, he became excited.

The woman was now completely naked and trussed up tightly. One of the men handed a small brown pot to the interrogator, who dipped his hand in it and rapidly applied a frothy solution to the woman's groin and up her back. When he was finished, Pavlos released Überhound's collar, and the dog raced toward the woman. Knowing well his stepbrothers' escapades with animals, Emil assumed that the frothy solution was made from the juices of bitches in heat.

That night, Emil had a disturbing dream. Wearing the starched black dress uniform of the Nazi SS Medical Corps, he enters an enormous ballroom with a German inscription above the door: "Wansee."[2] Below two fifteen-foot-wide flags—one for Germany, the other for the Third Reich— are the traditional indications of a black mass.[3] The cross on the altar is grotesquely twisted, the altar itself covered with a black mattress, and the censers filled with burning opium. The acolytes are sinister-looking youths, their sneers implying that they were indoctrinated as children to virtually every sin and vice. They breathe in the smoke billowing from the unholy censers, swaying with intoxication. The members of the congregation are nude under loose animal skins and beastly masks.

The celebrant of the black mass wears black leather boots and a black cape emblazoned with frightful dragons and other satanic symbols. The cape is open at the front to expose his genitals. As he recites the Roman Catholic litany and prayers backward, the communicants respond with loud animal howls and grunts. A nude young woman, moving in a trance as if drugged or hypnotized, is firmly led to the altar by the debauched acolytes. The priest waves them away and effortlessly lifts the woman onto the mattress on the altar, placing her head on a pillow below the twisted cross. He forces her to spread her arms outward and places a black candle made from human fat in each outstretched palm.

"I greet thee in the name and love of Our Lord," he gleefully intones.

A young blond woman, dressed in sheepskin, slowly approaches the altar in a state of ecstasy mixed with disdain. She suckles an infant. Startled, Emil recognizes her as the woman in the barn. Suddenly, she wrenches the baby from her breast and thrusts it at the priest. Emil recoils in horror at the infant's face, which is half human, half canine.

In a monotone, the blonde declares, "I offer my flesh to our patron."

By this time, the congregation has been incited to a frenzy by the opium smoke and the goings-on. Shrieking blasphemies and cursing the saints, they dance around furiously. When several tear off their masks, they are recognizable as Adolf Hitler, Joseph Goebbels, Heinrich Himmler, Hermann Göring, Joseph Mengele . . . and Emil.

The dreaming Emil sees himself run up the aisle, push aside the priest, leap upon the altar, and copulate with the woman lying there. Simultaneously, all of the other celebrants, as if possessed by demons, carry out their lusts on one other.

In late adolescence, Emil had a job that involved weapons. In order to keep the price of farm produce artificially high, some of the wealthier growers in the area hired him and a group of his friends to prevent other farmers from getting their goods to market. Emil and his band of enforcers, led by Stavos, were often involved in shoot-outs and brutal beatings. In the beginning, this violence upset him, but after a few months, during which some of his friends were beaten or shot by thugs hired by the other side, he was able to dismiss the brutality as just part of the job. Its only meaning for him was as a warning to stay alert and always be on the winning side.

Various ethnic groups in the Serbian areas of Yugoslavia have been suspicious and resentful of each other for centuries. When the death of the centralized Communist state collapsed the nation of Yugoslavia into opposing ethnic enclaves, Stavos's rough-and-ready band was quickly pressed into paramilitary service in the ensuing civil war. Frequently, Emil told me, they were involved in the rape and murder of noncombatant citizens.

In one incident, Stavos and his cohorts captured a village after a week of exhausting fighting. They found only a few old men, some women and children, because all the able-bodied men had been conscripted or had fled. As the victors filed down the street, a child's ball rolled into the dust near Emil. Smiling, he scooped it up, walked over to the little boy, returned the ball, and tousled the kid's auburn hair. The thought crossed his mind that it would be nice to have a wife and child someday.

Just then, a regular army officer passed by in a jeep. He stopped, studied the situation, and then called Stavos over. He whispered something to the gang leader, who began to protest.

"Shut up and follow orders," the officer snapped, "or you'll be shot!"

Stavos nodded, then assembled his men. He announced that the army was not equipped to handle prisoners, but neither could the townspeople be trusted not to resupply their soldiers, who would then be better able to recapture the area. In short, the villagers had to be killed.

Emil's story raises the question: Does anyone have a moral justification to participate in an atrocity, even if to refuse would result in his death or that of someone dear to him? While recognizing that the decision to refuse to kill *would be an excruciatingly difficult one,* justifying killing under almost any circumstances seems far more unacceptable. Yet many of the World War II military trials seem to have held that those soldiers whose lives would have been lost if they did not kill prisoners were not responsible for murder.

Emil claimed that he cannot remember the actual shootings, only the aftermath. Feeling detached, as if looking from the vantage point of another person, he took in the sight of the bloody bodies of women and children and the old men scattered up and down the street. He asked himself, more out of simple curiosity than from moral indignation, what had happened to these people: Who had committed this act?

Gradually, heat flooded into his gut, turning unexpectedly to searing pain that surged throughout his body. These sensations were followed by the distant thought that he was somehow implicated in the bloody scene, but he could not at the moment figure out how.

Apparently, Emil was experiencing the *psychic numbing* that Robert Lifton believes is the necessary accompaniment to brutal, extreme behavior. He seems to have been in the process of shifting blame for his behavior to his doppelgänger, or "second self."

The increasing viciousness of the doubling process can be seen in the shooting event. By shifting blame to his doppelgänger, Emil did not need to take cognizance of the gradual transformation of his personal morality—from a sensitive, decent young man to a member of a murderous gang. In Rank's classic *The Double*, the second self is shown to increasingly replace the original self as the doubling process continues, in matters large and small, until it finally takes over, represents the personality in its entirety.[4]

For months afterward, Emil remained disturbed by his involvement. But after a while, his concerns took on a defensive quality. Whatever he had done, he rationalized, could not be avoided. He was a soldier in a war and had done what he was told.

Nevertheless, he feared discovery and arrest as long as he stayed in the Balkans, because he believed that war crime trials would take place in Serbia in the near future. So he escaped to the United States and found refuge with some of his mother's relatives.

In the few sessions we had together, I found Emil to be heavily addicted to rationalizations by which he justified his heinous crimes.

"I am a human being," he said one day, "so anything I've done is part of the human repertory. Nothing is right or wrong in itself, including the shootings in that town. All our lives, we search for a fine distinction between right and wrong, but we find in the end that there is no such thing. Instead, the boundary is jagged, not firm, because life is mysterious and uncertain."

I asked him to explain further.

"There are things that we are not destined to know in this lifetime. They beg our moral limitations."

I have learned through the years that it is usually deleterious to confront a patient baldly with his tenuous psychological reality; however, given the seriousness of the situation at hand, I was unable to remain professionally neutral.

"Your fears compel you to believe that there are limits to what we should examine about human life," I argued. "My own curiosity refuses restriction. We have a duty, as well as a right, to question everything. All your life you have wanted to avoid colliding with the obstacles confronting you. But you seem unwilling to find out why you're unable to avoid them."

From my point of view, Emil's involvement in malevolent acts was the predictable continuation of his earlier decisions and actions. As a sensitive child frequently exposed to the cruelty of others, he was repeatedly misguided about how to understand and respond to his feelings. But at the same time, it is important to recognize that Emil had also come into contact with people who were kind and caringly responsive, including his wife, Alicia.

The turning point in the development of his malevolent personality was the decision to return to the barn. From then on, he worked at patterning his behavior after the actions of his stepfather and stepbrothers. By the time he met Alicia, his character was too well forged in malevolence for him to inhibit his insensitivity and abusive behavior toward her, much as he claimed he wanted to.

He explained this inability in coolly rational language: "Once you are able to convince yourself that most of the human race are nothing more than insects, then all the crimes you commit against people are tolerable. You're even proud of yourself."

I asked him why he felt the need to justify his cruelty, whether toward Alicia or anyone else. He responded with a storehouse of anecdotes showing how other people had been undependable and treacherous to him throughout his life. When I asked him to be more specific, he became enraged. Shooting his fist in my direction to underscore his point, he shouted that anyone who had ever participated in, witnessed, or simply did nothing to protect him from his own brutal life deserved to be treated with contempt. Because he was a man who paid his debts, his cruel actions were justifiable revenge.

In contrast, he had an almost loving regard for weapons. He told story after story, beginning with events in childhood, in which his skills with guns and knives had saved him from being killed by other people.

Unfortunately, I was not able to complete my course of treatment with Emil. During our sixth session, I asked him to examine closely the reasoning he was using to justify his abusiveness toward Alicia: for example, his threatening her with weapons when she made him angry or slapping her around to excite his sexual appetites. He smiled and said with obvious pride that she had never been attracted to passive men, as if this observation were sufficient justification. When I responded by looking askance, he jumped out of his chair.

"All right," he barked, "I'm cruel and insensitive toward people, even people I should care for. But it's a tough world out there. Little people don't have a snowball's chance in hell. Besides, it's too late to turn back now!"

I countered that it is never too late to try to make amends. I was thinking of Martin Buber's writings, explaining what I believe to be bedrock moral wisdom.[5] His ideas reveal an important distinction between Jewish and Christian notions of sin and redemption. Christian theology emphasizes redemption through confession to God of wrongdoing; Judaism, by acting to correct the wrong. Christian theology holds that individuals can have direct contact with God and on this basis personally reestablish a proper moral relationship with Him. Judaism maintains that human beings cannot know God directly; therefore, they show their godliness through their behavior with other people. Accordingly, preoccupation with one's wrongful behavior leads to a shameful avoidance of others. Consequently, Buber stresses that the violation of a moral law is a lesser sin than the more serious one of recognizing that one has done wrong and yet not trying to do anything to right that wrong with the people harmed by one's behavior.

By seizing upon Buber's concept of good and evil, I was trying to provide Emil with an opportunity to reexperience a sense of moral choice that he had gradually lost and finally relinquished through the development of his malevolent character. Evil is generally regarded as a force that opposes the healthy life forces. Interestingly, the word "evil" is the obverse of the word "live." The reason evil opposes life, Buber tells us, is that it is ignorant of the cravings of the individual's whole soul:

Evil cannot be done with the whole soul. . . . Evil is lack of direction and that which is done in it and out of it as the grasping, seizing, devouring, compelling, seducing, exploiting, humiliating, torturing and destroying of what offers itself. Good is direction and what is done in it; that which is done in it is done with the whole soul, so that in fact all the vigour and passion with which evil might have been done is included in it.[6]

Based upon my understanding of Buber's ideas, I told Emil that he had the opportunity to hold his malevolent acts up metaphorically as a mirror to try to understand and appreciate the joys and satisfactions of living that had eluded him because he lost his sense of choice over how he was living his life. In other words, his malevolent acts were inferior compromises because he had not given himself the opportunity to recognize all of his needs consciously; in fear and shame, he had given attention to his immediate defensive and creature needs rather than to his deeper spiritual and humane concerns.

I pointed out to Emil that both the perpetrators and the victims of malevolence, such as those who have participated in the horrors of the Holocaust, become possessed and overwhelmed by what they have done or experienced. As a result, they become emotionally blunted to their own feelings—and to the sensibilities of those who care for them—in a desperate attempt to block self-hatred and recrimination. Those who reach out to them, as Emil's wife did, are contaminated with contempt for caring for them—people unworthy of care and love.

Unfortunately, Emil was not ready to hear me. He bolted out of my office, but only after shouting one last defense:

"It's easy for you to talk! You speak facile words while sitting comfortably in the seat of moral righteousness. But you are not superior to me. You just haven't been tested. I've been alone and terribly afraid all my life. I've been to hell and forced to follow the orders of devils. What would you have done in my place? No better than me, I'll bet!"

I never saw him again.

I am exploring the serious issue of malevolence in this book in order to provide a better response to its dilemma than did Emil. Having demonstrated the problems of malevolence, I shall examine constructive solutions in the concluding chapters. Among the ashes of human tragedy, we must plant the generative seeds that will nurture the phoenix of productive purpose and creative power.

Because of space considerations, I have provided only a limited amount of information about my therapeutic practice in the preceding chapters. For the reader to understand better the therapeutic context in which the patients revealed their secrets to me, I offer in the next chapter an overview of my therapeutic attitudes and practices.

CHAPTER THIRTEEN

Friendship as the Basis of Psychological Healing

Whoever is in possession of a true friend sees
the exact counterpart of his own soul.

— CICERO

TRADITIONALLY, TRANSFERENCE ANALYSIS — THAT IS TO SAY, MAK-ing assumptions about a patient's earlier experiences on the basis of his contemporary interactions with people—has been regarded as the most powerful tool available for personality modification. The transference model, however, enjoins the psychotherapy practitioner from demonstrating certain essential psychosocial behaviors that would allow the patient to realize the skills required for satisfying interpersonal activity. In other words, transference analysis can indicate why a patient lacks warmth, optimism, and caring for other people, but it doesn't show him the steps needed to develop these attributes.

Consequently, for the patient to acquire interpersonal competence, once everything that should be analyzed is examined, therapist and patient need to assume a Socratic dialogue—in which both evince a progressive willingness to share reciprocal reactions to the other.[1]

In search of a model to implement the Socratic dialogue, psychologists have turned from examining psychopathology to the study of normal and creative lives. In recent years, they have rediscovered that the social and emotional basis of a life lived well is *friendship*.[2] Since we live in the community of others and generally achieve our greatest satisfactions in other people's company, the highest aim of humanity, as Aristotle long ago indicated, is found in genuine companionship. The phenomenology of friendship has been stated simply and well in Ralph Waldo Emerson's "Essay on Friendship."[3] Emerson tells us: "A Friend is a person with whom I may be sincere. Before him I may think aloud." This apt description will constitute my operational definition of friendship in this chapter.

PROBLEMATIC NATURE OF FRIENDSHIP IN PSYCHOTHERAPY

All doctors soon learn that patients consult them far less often for specific illnesses than because they are unhappy and seek relief from their loneliness and despair. Countless numbers of people find themselves entrenched in lives that are barren of intimate, trusting companionship. Psychotherapy patients bear witness to the consequences of the absence of satisfying friendship in marriage and family, collegial and peer relationships, in the contemporary world. For many, the search for a wise, caring friend to inspire and support them has been long and futile. They suffer from an inability to secure intimate fulfillment well. Self-esteem and a sense of living well are dependent upon being desired, understood, and appreciated by others. Moreover, a sense of security is bolstered by the awareness that one can turn toward people who care. Conversely, repeated rejection and failure to foster caring from others lead directly to feelings of inadequacy, depression, and intense loneliness.

Fortunately, psychotherapists not only are listeners to their patients' tales of despair; they also live in the same world as do their clients. It is the practitioner's enlightened presence in their shared world that gives hope for a more optimistic life for the patient. I believe that genuine healing requires more than the wisdom of understanding. It also demands that the practitioner extend to patients the goodwill and friendship that are derived from the practitioner's firm place in the world outside the consulting room.[4]

Yet just as there are societal and subjective factors in the world at large that militate against friendship, so are there professional and personal factors in the practitioner that hold him back from genuine friendship with patients. I believe that the five most basic reasons for the lack of genuine friendship in psychotherapy are the following:

1. Practitioners have indicated that when real relationships are encouraged, the therapist's countertransferential impulses more easily get out of hand than when the practitioner is a nonactive participant. Moreover, it is difficult to define what is technically and ethically proper in a real relationship between a patient and a therapist.

2. Many practitioners would also contend that they have something far more profound to offer than friendship. They would further indicate that special training as a psychotherapist is not required to be a friend. Almost anyone can offer companionship.

3. Many therapists would be embarrassed to be paid for friendship. This would be especially true if friendship implied mutual, although not necessarily equal, benefits to each of the people involved.

4. Most psychotherapeutic theories teach that patients learn best psychologically if their impulses are frustrated rather than gratified.

5. The problem with calling for friendship in psychotherapeutic practice is that many practitioners have considerable difficulty with making friends themselves. Many people who are drawn toward practicing psychotherapy struggle conflictually with issues concerned with relatedness. A wise practitioner, Alan Wheelis, wrote thirty years ago that the problem of intimacy is for many analysts the principal determinant of their careers. The problem, he indicated, is "the conflict between the tendencies that lead to closeness and the fear that is evoked by closeness." Becoming a psychoanalyst, he wrote, is a compromise between these vacillating needs:

[The analyst achieves intimacy] by hearing secrets none other can hear, not even a priest; for a priest cannot take so much time. He [the analyst] will enter hidden recesses of another life none other can enter: for no one else is possessed of such sensitive technique. At the same time he will maintain the isolation he requires. Indeed, it seems that psychoanalysis not only permits, but demands isolation.[5]

GENUINE FRIENDSHIP IN PSYCHOTHERAPY

Many psychotherapists would react to what I have stated above by indicating that competent practitioners are by definition friends to their patients. In other words, they demonstrate their friendship by their expression of caring and concern about the conditions of the patient's well-being. These concerns are generally felt personally, exceeding that of simply doing professionally responsible clinical work. In Emerson's words, these practitioners are people with whom the patient may speak sincerely and openly without fear of condemnation.

I would respond that the practitioner's friendship *toward* his client is a necessary, but not sufficient, condition of *genuine* friendship. Genuine friendship cannot be one-sided. Friendship without *reciprocity* is inconceivable.[6] Without the experience of being of assistance to others and being recognized and appreciated for these efforts, interpersonal relations remain sterile and ungratifying.

In arguing for a friendship basis for practice, I am not suggesting that it is normally advisable for practitioners to share with their patients the contents of their personal lives. Nonetheless, there are some vital responsibilities, I believe, that practitioners must always keep in mind. They should never distort or deny reality. Their patients have sufficient problems finding confidence in their own judgments, without additional confusion brought on by their therapist's misleading them, no matter how benevolent their intent.

Of course, no matter how well intended therapists are toward their patients, they cannot ensure that a genuine friendship will develop. On the other hand, they can allow themselves to be open to the possibility. Therefore, I strongly believe that therapists cannot allow their theory or their character to preclude the possibility of friendship. We are never someone's friend in spite of ourselves.[7] Consequently, the practitioner must acknowledge all concerns that affect the therapeutic relationship. If a patient says, for example, "You look terrible. I am concerned about you," the practitioner needs to inform the client that there is a conflictual issue in his life and he is (hopefully) dealing with it. Moreover, the practitioner should also express a tacit appreciation, at least, for the patient's concern and then explore how the client's perception might affect their working and being together. I believe that expressions of caring and compassion should not be discouraged in patients, although, obviously, there are limitations on how these feelings may be appropriately acted upon in the therapeutic situation. Beyond these limits are areas of exploitation. Can these limits be specified beforehand? That is to say, can the proper parameters of therapeutic friendship be prescribed, as the various disciplines that constitute the profession of psychotherapy have prescribed proper, ethical behavior in the therapeutic situation? Since I prefer to emphasize Socratic dialogue rather than prescribed procedures of psychotherapy, . . . I believe that the boundaries of friendship are best explored and negotiated in sincere emotional interchange during the course of psychotherapy. Yet whatever parameters are drawn, I would assume that they should include such qualities as honesty, trust, respect, safety, support, generosity, acceptance, understanding, commitment, and mutuality.

In short, goodwill and exchange of friendship play a crucial role in healing loneliness, suffering, and despair. They also contribute to our understanding and enhancement of who we are, as well as provide the vehicle for our caring and support of others. Consequently, unless a genuine friendship is allowed to develop in the therapeutic situation, real healing and personal growth for the client are mitigated. It has been pointed out that we come to know another person meaningfully only through friendship.[8] It seems to me that impressive discoveries of psychological insights in psychotherapy need to be matched by warm and moving responses of friendship. This is hardly strange! Most traditions of healing through the ages have been based upon friendship's tutelage.

Psychological healing rarely occurs in one decisive, broad leap. Instead, it usually requires many small steps along the way. Certainly, there are no shortcuts for overthrowing the deadly despair and self-contempt of malevolence, a debilitating condition that evolves over a lifetime. Effective treatment is an intuitive, compassionate art.

Although we have learned from empirical studies some of the factors that influence malevolence, we can also miss the essential determinants of any therapeutic effort—by definition, an encounter between two people involved in a deeply emotional endeavor—to the extent that we prematurely regard psychotherapy as a science.

Nothing so complex and richly human as the meeting between patient and practitioner can be relegated to a formula. Each person who becomes a healer has his or her own raison d'être for pursuing psychological understanding. This concern influences how the practitioner listens to the clinical material.

THE SHARED PERSONAL JOURNEY

If those called to the profession of healing have a keen interest in learning about themselves, as indeed they should, they will find that a psychotherapeutic career can provide a fairly comfortable living while also allowing them the opportunity to better the lives of others.

No less important, it gives them a means of continually examining their own lives. Practitioners who think they already know themselves well enough from their own personal therapy and self-exploration and have no interest in further self-examination will find their work dull and mechanical. If they are unable to recognize the nature of their own pain, they cannot be responsive to the suffering of others.

On the other hand, practitioners eager for further personal growth will be continually curious about the inner lives of their patients in terms of what they can learn about themselves. Consideration of the interpenetration of the two separate experiences, patient's and practitioner's, will lead to conscious examination of the complexity of the human condition, especially when it regards the meaning of suffering. In other words, the creative energy that is required to respond to another person arises out of the maelstrom of continual self-discovery. In contrast, scientific knowledge never provides immediate insight into ourselves or others; at best, it offers a vicarious approximation of inner life as viewed from the role of an objective, risk-free observer.

During one Thursday session, a client of my own age whom I treated twice a week during the early years of my practice brought up her visit home the following weekend to see her parents. She launched into a litany of conflictual issues that she had not successfully broached with her family. The reluctance to deal directly with issues was symptomatic of her superficial relations with other people—a defense to prevent others from expressing displeasure with her. I decided that if I systematically returned the patient to her conflictual family issues, she and I would have a frame of reference for exploring the basis of her avoided issues with other people. As I began to discuss the strategy with her, I realized that if I were to bring up her avoidance issues with her family on a regular basis I would be espousing a hypocrisy. I was involved in some of the same issues with my own family. I felt uncomfortable with asking her to attend to something that I myself needed to do. She seemed pleased to hear that I personally shared her dilemma. She was not put off by having a therapist who was "all too human"; instead, whenever she was aware I had traveled home to New York, she faithfully brought up whether or not I had dealt with my own family. This alliance seemed to foster a climate of joint journey, although I was relieved that she didn't try to play therapist to me. This therapeutic experience early in my career enabled me to recognize vividly that therapeutic work is an illusory palliative of superficial discourse unless the practitioner's unfinished journey is vivified in the process.

Rather, the use of the healer's insight into his own pain is a basic tenet of healing others. Practitioners consciously aware of their own journeys involve themselves with their patients as companion travelers. Put another way, one guides another best over terrain that is similar to one's native land, because only the tested can inspire the fearful. Those practitioners who have been sheltered from a need to express their desires openly or have cowered in the underbrush of their own personal journeys have neither a compass to offer the brave nor a sturdy walking staff to bolster the unsteady gait of the fearful.

This personal journey aptly symbolizes shamanic wisdom and the essential developmental process of contemporary psychotherapy, in which the most effective practitioners utilize their own life experiences as the major source of their expertise. Ideally, such therapists realize that a deeply subjective understanding of themselves is the most potent human instrument available for responding to the hurt and suffering of their fellow humans.

This belief, I feel sure, is not contested; at issue is the degree of vulnerability the therapist can be expected to experience. Hour after hour, day after day, it is undeniably difficult to face certain aspects of oneself. It is much easier to distance or deny these aspects as reflected by a patient, especially one who has committed heinous crimes. Nevertheless, the startling truth is that during any given session, psychotherapists may be touching on some of their own deepest vulnerabilities.

Sheldon Kopp, a well-known and seasoned practitioner, has stated this position forcefully: "I am no longer willing to accept anyone as my patient to whose pain I do not feel vulnerable."[9]

From this point of view, we can readily recognize why psychotherapy is such a demanding profession; we can even wonder whether practitioners are not actually trapped masochists. But I believe another interpretation is more valid: while treating their patients, they are courageously coming to terms with their own demons and the unintegrated aspects of their inner selves.

THE CORE RELATIONSHIP IN PSYCHOLOGICAL HEALING

Long-term studies of mother-child relationships indicate that the genuineness of the mother's compassion plays a crucial role in determining the extent of her child's optimism in dealing with other people. To me, the implication is that the psychotherapist's "real person" is the source of effective responsiveness in treating the malevolent personality.

To undo the feelings of shame and abandonment that fuel malevolence, the patient has to replace the compassionate attachments he once enjoyed, or even experience such an attachment for the first time. In other words, sophisticated theoretical speculation does not heal the shame, madness, or despair—the treatable ingredients of malevolence. The healing springs from the therapist's own attitudes and personality. These qualities separate those who promote healing from those who exacerbate suffering.

I have increasingly recognized that I must be emotionally engaged and psychologically responsive in order to reach patients who have been painfully shamed by emotionally unavailable caretakers in their tender, developmental years.

For me personally, I've discovered, the best approach is not to cloak who I am behind the anonymous persona of impersonality I was taught to assume during training. The willingness of a patient to face shameful, fearful aspects of the self is closely tied to my own *transparency* in our sessions.

By openly identifying with the hopes, fears, ambitions, and travail of my patients, I am able to learn from their experiences. Indeed, this *en-*

lightened mutuality and genuine reciprocity is essential to healing. The exchange of money for services does not in itself promote healing; rather, each participant in a healing relationship has to feel that something of psychological value is being exchanged.

In the earliest years of my practice, my patients gifted me with a variety of perspectives on many life experiences that I had not yet encountered for myself, such as the phases of development and impediments to growth that inevitably visit relationships in the long term. In later years, I have profited from my encounters with those whose experiences I can never directly enter, such as the inner lives of women and the experiences of people from unfamiliar cultures.

In return, I have often enabled patients to derive meaning from their struggles by offering them the courage and values I've earned through my own. If therapists free themselves to discover the caring in their own despair, they can enable their patients to discover value and meaning in the midst of suffering.

Nietzsche said much the same thing: "Physician heal thyself! Then wilt thou also help thy patient. Let this be his best cure to see with his eyes him who maketh himself whole."[10]

By acknowledging his feelings toward his patients, the therapist offers his passion—not its specifics, but its validity, its legitimate entitlement for its own sake. For without passion, there is no life. Only by speaking from his own passion can the therapist truthfully claim that he is able to create *consensus reality* with his patient—that is, negotiate and make contracts so that each can meaningfully experience the assumptions the other holds about the world. This consensus reality is necessary in order to expunge the mystique from psychotherapy, allowing both participants to admit their own struggles and humanity and deal equitably with each other.

In effect, as the American philosopher Robert Solomon suggests, the therapist can no longer speak of emotions as belonging to other people: "A description of someone else's emotion is one thing; understanding one's own is something else. And our problem is to understand *for me (us)*, subjectively what it is *to have* an emotion."[11]

Consequently, clients need *courage* from their therapists as well as ideas. Courage—that is, moral courage—is the only answer to life, in the face of what is.

The therapist's *personal concern*—his faith that his patients' examination of their assumptions about being-in-the-world will be worthy of them—will in fact enable them to be as they intend rather than fulfill some psychological theory of the therapist's.

OBSTACLES IMPEDING EMOTIONAL RECIPROCITY

One of the most serious problems in the training of psychotherapists is the mistaken stress upon finding out what is *wrong* with patients. In my analytic training, in particular, I was taught to look for deficiencies or the aberrant in patients. In effect, a prevailing academic lack of interest in the constructive aspects of human development is an unfortunate legacy of classical psychoanalytic theory. My training focused too exclusively on what is hidden, denied, or disturbed in patients' lives.

Once in the world of actual practice, however, I became increasingly impressed with the human ability to triumph over adversity[12] and how such positive attributes as courage, daring, decency, and wisdom can develop under even the most unlikely conditions. Now I strongly believe that therapists need to balance the deficiencies in patients' lives with what is hopeful and healthy about them. Otherwise the consulting room becomes a negatively charged examination room rather than a sanctuary and a place for constructive growth.

The clinical language used to describe and explain patient behaviors to colleagues and to oneself tends to reinforce the traditional emphasis on the pathological. If the therapist conceptualizes his patients in dehumanized cant or jargon, he is apt to treat them accordingly. Indeed, clinical language seems more accurately descriptive of physical objects than expressive of human problems and motivations. For this reason, I assume, theologians like Jeffrey Russell believe that psychology is actually an extension of physics, unable to address and describe intelligently the moral and the spiritual needs of humankind.

Using the *language of health* rather than of pathology is important, because the patient's overriding need is to find positive qualities about himself and his life in order to establish his personal identity in a self-enhancing way. The most difficult goal, indeed the turning point on the road to healing, is enabling him to trust in *his own goodness*. If my patient cannot secure the recognition of his own worth from his actions and his impact on me, from where else will it initially come?

I don't believe that human behavior is directed by negative or pathological motivation and causation. To restate: the recurring theme of human existence is our striving for personal identity, significance, and unification. As a psychoanalyst, I may not always be able to identify the cause of someone's behavior, but once I do, it invariably turns out that the patient has been acting in a way that makes sense to her in terms of her choices. She takes the action that is most preferable; of course, for her, as for all of us, the problem is that she too often finds herself in situations where every choice she perceives as available is less preferable than she would like.

As a psychotherapist and social theorist, I have searched for the foundations of a psychological theory of human behavior that is not reductionistic. That is to say, I have not been satisfied with theoretical positions that attempt to explain human endeavors in terms of one or two determinants, especially if, in doing so, they do not convincingly explain both the ills that befall humans and their highest, most notable achievements. Something important is absent when we account for human behavior in terms of drives, as I was taught in my psychoanalytic training, rather than human purpose, as I was informed by my undergraduate training in philosophy.

Unfortunately, far too few studies of human behavior provide insights into how positive human attributes develop. Current theories of human development reflect, of course, the mainstream psychological bias, which has emphasized loss and psychopathology in how people live their lives, while at the same time paying relatively little attention to the positive and creative mainsprings of human development.

A lack of interest and responsiveness to the constructive aspects of human development by psychological theorists is a second unfortunate legacy of the parochial influence of classical psychoanalytic theory, which reduces all human strivings to conflictual drives. It employs clinical evidence to try to demonstrate that adulthood, with rare exceptions, is the re-creation of childhood issues. Maturation in adulthood, analytic theory contends, is made possible by successful resolution of the psychosexual issues of pre-Oedipal and Oedipal periods of life. Therefore, all of the important aspects of personal character are inexorably cast within the early years of life.

Fortunately, while classical psychoanalytic theory dominated psychology for the first half of this century, three major psychological theorists who have gained prominence in the second half have helped me to recognize the sources of constructive growth.

The first is the Swiss psychologist Carl Jung, who contended that the ultimate goal of personality is *to achieve a state of selfhood and self-realization.*[13] From his perspective, for self-realization to occur, we must requestion and recast our core beliefs; in so doing, we should ask such existential questions as: Where have I been? Where am I now? and Where can I reach in the time I have remaining in life?

The second important contributor to contemporary theories of human development is Erik Erikson.[14] Following Jung's path but with a Freudian map to describe the terrain, Erikson formulated a psychological theory to describe personality development from the cradle to senior maturity. Like Jung, he believed that personality development is a lifetime assignment, one that does not cease with an Oedipal resolution in childhood.

Erikson's work is based on the principle that anything that grows has a floor-plan. The parts arising from this development have their own particular time of ascendancy, until all the parts function as a whole. More specifically, he contended that there are eight psychosocial stages in the human life cycle. Each has a specific growth requirement, informed by a particular conflict and generated from the contention of instinctual and social demands on the person. Because of the urgency for successful handling of these developmental tasks for healthy maturity, each of the stages is a potential arena for crisis. If the specific developmental task that dominates that period of the life cycle is not successfully addressed, the person's capacity to adapt will be adversely compromised by increased vulnerability to instinctual and social demands.

The third important psychological theorist is George Kelly,[15] who believed that an individual creates his own way of perceiving the world by formulating his experience in terms of *constructs* that have varying degrees of predictive efficiency. The operative principle that guides the use of one construct rather than another is that the need to make sense of one's being-in-the-world organizes all our other needs and motives.

The ideas of Jung, Erikson, and Kelly have suggested to me theoretically sensible ways of organizing my patients' experiences constructively. Consequently, in my initial contact with a patient, I accentuate what is hopeful and positive in her attitudes, behaviors, and intentions. I conceptualize and express my responses to her revelations in *positive connotations*. I try to avoid attributing any negative or pathological causes to her behavior. I assume on principle that which she strives to accomplish, although perhaps misdirected in execution, has a legitimate, healthy goal.

Mr. Jones had been charged with sexually molesting his stepson on two occasions and would shortly be brought to court on criminal charges. His attorney having advised him that the court would look more favorably upon him if he voluntarily sought psychiatric help and entered into a treatment program, he reluctantly consulted me as a private practitioner. Inarticulate and uneducated, Mr. Jones, mustached, with thick eyeglasses, was a passive-dependent person of around fifty years of age who had a chronic alcoholic pattern. Both incidents occurred while he was intoxicated. He saw no need for psychological treatment, claiming that stopping his drinking would guarantee nonoccurrence. But he did agree to go along with my recommendations.

A few months after I began seeing him, he was given a five-year suspended sentence. His probation was based upon continuing to be "under a doctor's care" for the entire period of probation, or, at least, until the doctor believed that he was cured. The terms of "doctor's care" were left vague. I did not feel entirely comfortable continuing to work with Mr. Jones once he had been sentenced, because I was certain he would have discontinued psychotherapy if he could. In other words, he had not freely contracted to work with me. Upon reflection, however, I decided my reasoning was overly idealistic if not inane. Freedom and choice cannot realistically be conceptualized as absolutes; they are possible only with a defined situation. Although there were serious consequences for our actions, Mr. Jones and I both had the freedom to discontinue working with each other. He did not have to accept me as a therapist; the locale in which I practice is saturated with psychotherapists. I chose to work with Mr. Jones because he was paying me a reasonable fee and because I felt that I might be of help to him. Despite his inarticulateness and stubbornness, I found him likable. His freedom from a prison sentence was dependent upon his continued psychotherapy, I agreed therefore only to report his attendance at sessions to his probation officer, if this information was requested of me (it never was).

Given psychotherapy as an alternative to prison, Mr. Jones had more of a choice in how he would use the sessions than in whether he would attend them. Since he was paying for the sessions, it was his prerogative to use them as he wished. It was my responsibility to explore with him in language he could relate to my notions as to what psychotherapy was about and what it could and could not reasonably accomplish for him. Mr. Jones had grown up in a rural mountain area. I made frequent analogies to raising crops and animals and educating young children for responsibility, relating my notions about psychotherapeutic work to experiences with which Mr. Jones could identify. I made specific recommendations about how he might use the sessions in terms of the difficulties he was experiencing in his marriage.

Mr. Jones expressed more annoyance than guilt about the events that had engendered his legal difficulties. He blamed them on the abuse he received from his wife and stepchildren. Given his minimal insight and even less concern about his behavior, a scrutiny of Mr. Jones's developmental history could well have taken up the five years of probation without necessarily modifying his character structure or leading to mastery over his marital situation, so I suggested that the focus during the sessions be contemporary. Because he was a very withdrawn person whose only significant, albeit conflictive, relationships were with his wife and stepchildren, I recommended that his family join him in his sessions. He readily agreed, on the basis that it was his wife's neglect of him that forced him to commit the acts that caused his troubles. She should therefore have to share his punishment by attending his sessions.

He spent most of the sessions complaining about his wife's mistreatment of him. In reaction, Mrs. Jones expressed frustration and resentment that he was not willing to articulate or demonstrate any caring for her. Ironically, despite the legal and moral difficulties he found himself in, Mr. Jones was a person with a strong sense of justice. Indeed, his morality conflicted with his wife's childish, impulsive, and irresponsible system for relating with others. It was at those times when his wife treated him unfairly, depriving him of sexual satisfaction and affection, that he became intoxicated and used his lack of emotional expression to punish her. He refused to express caring for her because, he claimed, "It ain't do any good!" She retaliated by impulsively spending money on commodities he regarded as "junk." Mr. Jones became more resentful and withdrawn. Mrs. Jones, in reaction, refused to attend any more therapy sessions. Their respective systems of fairness came into volatile conflict in her justifying her withdrawal from therapy by saying, "The court told you that you have to go to treatment. I don't have to go to the doctor. Only you do!"

Their marital relationship was based on a revenge contract. They were implicitly saying to each other:

MRS. JONES: If you don't express caring for me, then I won't give you any emotional support. I will not only withhold sexual relations, I will also make you suffer your psychotherapy treatment as punishment rather than attend sessions so that we can work as partners in a relationship.

MR. JONES: If you don't treat me fairly, I'll withdraw from you, get drunk, and withhold money, since that is all you seem to want from me.

The revenge contract in their relationship resulted in a "Mexican standoff." Since each basically mistrusted other people, neither would retract sufficiently his or her wont to hurt so that the other could take a psychological risk and express caring. Both of the Joneses lacked sufficient experience in a trusting relationship in their personal development. Each required immediate reward in order to give to another person.

To resolve this difficult impasse, several contractual issues had to be dealt with. For Mr. Jones, money had a punitive value within the therapeutic situation. Paying me and attending sessions was punishment for his having committed a socially unacceptable act. The reader may regard Mr. Jones's situation as atypical—a resistive client forced to pay for treatment he prefers not to receive. If the reader looks more closely at the function of money in psychotherapy, he will realize that payment is frequently an unintended but quite real punishment, even for clients who pursue treatment willingly and enthusiastically. In short, meaningful and productive psychotherapy is less expensive than incompetent and unproductive work. In productive psychotherapy, client and practitioner arrive together at goals and pursue them in a mutually agreed upon fashion. Their work is efficient because they have agreed on what they are seeking and how to evaluate what they achieve together. In unproductive and uncontractual therapy, the therapist is rewarded for his inefficiency until such time as the client finally has enough sense to terminate the relationship.

Mr. Jones had less freedom to terminate therapy than do most clients, who are not having their attendance monitored by a law enforcement agency. If he dropped out of treatment, his behavior would more likely be regarded as his unwillingness to be helped, rather than as a result of my lack of skill. Moreover, because he appeared to trust me more than he did most other people, he was unlikely to seek another practitioner, regardless of how ineffectual I might be in handling his situation. Thus, I could continue to see him and have him pay me every week regardless of his progress. Indeed, I could reap more financial rewards for his lack of progress than from having him improve sufficiently so that the requirement of psychotherapy could be removed from his probation. Consequently, to restore power to Mr. Jones, I had to transform money from a vehicle of punishment to a source of reward. Mr. Jones regarded his psychological treatment as a five-year sentence, regardless of his progress; therefore, he had little external incentive to take his efforts in therapy seriously. If, however, he could pay increasingly less money for therapy based on his taking psychological risks, he would then have a clear and meaningful incentive for taking a risk.

I felt that it was also crucial to bring Mrs. Jones back into the sessions. She would not return unless he articulated caring for her, so I said to Mr. Jones in a session, "It seems to me that you care for your wife but that you refuse to give her the satisfaction of letting her know that you do." He replied that while this might be true, he would not tell her that he cared, because it wouldn't do him any good. She would continue to treat him unfairly.

I offered Mr. Jones what I referred to as a "no-financial-risk gamble." I told him, "You say that if you told your wife that you cared for her, she would ignore your statement and just treat you as badly as before you made the statement. What if you could gamble on your point of view, and if you were wrong, you would win some money? I say this because you have expressed to me the concern that coming to these sessions week after week is expensive. Therefore, I will charge you one dollar less on your next session, provided you tell your wife that after a discussion with me you realize that you care for her, and provided she responds favorably to your statement, contrary to how you believe she will respond. On the other hand, if she responds as you claim she will, the bill will stay the same for the next session, but you will have lost nothing." I planned to use other financial incentives in the future to encourage more psychological risks on his part.

The approach I was using has an absurd aspect. Mr. Jones would reap a financial reward by demonstrating that his limited but entrenched view of his wife was invalid. In the past, his anger and withdrawal evoked a predictably unfavorable response from her. As a person with a strongly moralistic orientation, Mr. Jones was rewarded only with moral indignation. The situation that I presented him with, on the other hand, provided him with an incentive for proving himself "wrong" for his lack of demonstrative caring. If Mr. Jones deviated from his characteristic withdrawal and his wife reciprocated with affection, *uncertainty* would be evoked in their relational system. If this uncertainty persisted for any period of time, each would be compelled to reexamine expectations of and from the other.

I was aware, nonetheless, that there were strong forces in their relationship for avoiding a reexamination. Mr. Jones's willingness to take psychological risks would not happen based only on my rewarding him. Mrs. Jones was simply too much more significant to him than I was. Her power to punish him was considerably greater than my capacity to reward him. To establish fairness and balance in their relationship, it was necessary that Mrs. Jones return to the sessions. This was easier said than done.

Mrs. Jones was caught up in a struggle between strong impulsive urges and cruel internal authority figures. She experienced most demands upon her as unfair. She attempted to free herself of these demands by dysfunctionally childish mechanisms, saying in effect, "If my husband expects me to be at the sessions, then I won't attend even though I actually enjoy them!" In other words, Mrs. Jones avoided facing her internal conflicts and contradictions by externalizing them. She skillfully but unwittingly "encouraged" her husband's angry reactions. His reactions "justified" Mrs. Jones's not meeting her promises to him to attend sessions or to meet his emotional needs. As long as I or any other authority surrogate insisted that she must do something, she would rebel. She would be able to get in touch with her internal contradictions only at such time as she was confronted by the realization that rebellion against other people did not rid her of her internal turmoil. Consequently, in a session that Mr. Jones attended alone, I told him that I would like him to tell his wife that she didn't have to attend sessions, and she would understand why I said this. As soon as Mr. Jones gave my message to his wife, she was on the phone, yelling at me: "I know I don't have to attend sessions. You bastard! You don't have to tell me that!" I pointed out that that was why I had said to her husband that she would understand. I had, with my provocative statement, made explicit the conflictive contractual relationship between Mrs. Jones and me. I had indicated that she didn't need to rebel against her husband and me to prove that she was a voluntary participant and an adult. I went on to indicate the time of Mr. Jones's next session, adding that if she cared to, we would be glad to have her attend. She attended the sessions from then on.

In the next chapter, I return to the story of Richard and Jennifer, discussing the required steps for healing shame and despair.

CHAPTER FOURTEEN

Healing Shame and Despair

Shame opens a path
to ourselves.
— MAX SCHELER

P SYCHOLOGICAL TREATMENT WITH A PROFESSIONAL PRACTITIONER is advisable for seriously shamed people. However, the person himself can do much to heal his shame and despair, as suggested in this chapter.

Following the traumatic encounter with Richard, Jennifer retreated to her secluded studio apartment. She stayed home from work. She could not face her coworkers. She was certain that the humiliation that she had incurred could be read on her face. She also shut off her telephone so that she wouldn't have to speak with anyone.

Susan, a concerned close friend and colleague, tried for several days to reach her. Knowing that Jennifer didn't answer her phone when she was despondent and unable to ask for help, Susan went to her friend's apartment. Jennifer reluctantly opened the door and, after some gentle but probing questions, plaintively told Susan:

"My life isn't working for me. I seem to be losing everything—including me." Jennifer then reported what had happened at Richard's door.

Susan looked straight at Jennifer. Gently placing her hand on her friend's shoulder, she said:

"Jennifer, you may feel at this moment that you are the only person in the world who gets treated badly. But believe me, many of us have gone through the same awful experience as you. I certainly have! Let me tell you what happened to me. But remind me before I leave to recommend a book that I think can help you."

The volume Susan spoke of, a popular book on the problem of shame, quickly captured Jennifer's curiosity. The stories seemed rather familiar. She wondered if she had seen them in manuscript at the publishing house where she worked.

As she read the stories more carefully, she became increasingly aware of a burning sensation in the pit of her abdomen. The descriptions, which seemed to leap off the page and lunge at her, frightfully captured many of her own life experiences.

In less than an hour, Jennifer understood for the first time that the horrible feelings she harbored about herself had to do with her sensitivity to shame and humiliation. Feeling ashamed, Jennifer learned, is a powerful, but unquestioned, conviction that in important ways one is flawed and incompetent as a human being.

She thought back over the innumerable times she had felt taken advantage of but powerless to change the situation because she feared that protesting would cause other people to get angry and abandon her. Nothing frightened Jennifer as much as the prospect of being alone for the rest of her life. She had been willing to tolerate almost anything, including being treated badly, to avoid being abandoned.

As Jennifer delved into the stories, she was heartened to learn that many people like herself, who had experienced the unfathomable misery of shame, had overcome their excessive sensitivity to being shamed and had gone on to lead lives informed with pride, competence, and feelings of self-worth. By giving her helpless feelings a name, Jennifer was for the first time in a position to do something about her troublesome emotions.

Shame, she read, is a normal part of life. As a complex emotion, it comes in a variety of shapes and has a multitude of different functions. Not all experiences of shame are deleterious. Quite to the contrary! In small doses, shame is a prod to self-improvement. In digestible amounts, shame spurs personal freedom by providing a means for penetrating self-discovery. Positive shame comes from the recognition that we do not know ourselves and the significant people in our life sufficiently well in order to live fully and with pride. Healthy responses to feeling shame derive from our willingness to openly examine and do something constructive about aspects of ourselves that cause us to feel bad and that we can reasonably change.

Jennifer chose to believe that discovering the book about shame was a propitious opportunity. If she was to overthrow her intense unhappiness, she must learn specifically how other people have done so. From studying the cases of those in the book who had recovered from shame, Jennifer extracted the basic steps in overcoming debilitating shame and humiliation:

First, you must learn to recognize the presence of shame in the ways you become unhappy and distressed.

Second, you need to learn the language of articulate emotion in order to give hurt and shame a clear voice.

Third, it is necessary to share your intimate feelings with a concerned and caring person.

Fourth, you must halt the vicious cycle of being humiliated, feeling ashamed, hiding and not correcting the situation, then feeling weak and cowardly for tolerating it, which results in additional feelings of shame. To stop this destructive pattern, you must learn skills in defining yourself positively and seeing to it that other people behave toward you in decent and nonhostile ways: and finally, you need to use the self-awareness and the skills newly acquired from following the preceding steps to repair existing relationships and to explore challenging new ones.

Jennifer spent the weekend in her apartment carefully canvassing the specific ways that she related to people. In every interaction she considered, with the notable exception of activities in which she excelled, she was embarrassed to recognize that if she was not inwardly calling herself harsh and terrible names for being unsure of herself, then she was allowing others to discredit her by treating her indecently.

She traced her current traumatic patterns of relating with people to how family members had interacted with her when she was growing up. Their profusion of negative criticism and harsh judgments had evolved into a *punitive inner voice* that rarely afforded Jennifer the acknowledgment that she had done something praiseworthy. Indeed, her reproachful inner voice hurled the very same accusations at her adult behavior as her parents expressed to her as a child.

She also discovered that her inability to feel legitimate entitlement depended on the denial of her hurt and other negative emotions. Her inner voice magnified the anger she harbored toward herself and, occasionally, others. At the same time, this voice ignored her feelings of sadness and loneliness from the failure to achieve the intimacy and closeness with others that she craved.

The book recommended the recitation of provocative emotional passages from poetry, literature, and drama as facilitating an articulate vocabulary to represent states of feeling. Jennifer went over to her bookcase and drew out her favorite books.

She came across a passage in a novel by Somerset Maugham that conveyed sentiments about herself that she had been struggling to express with Richard. In Maugham's *Of Human Bondage*, Philip, a young boy with a clubfoot, has been ridiculed by his classmates for his awkward limp. The school bully has twisted Philip's arm so painfully that Philip puts his foot out of the corner of the bedsheets, enabling the other boys to see his deformed foot.

> Philip had got his teeth in the pillow so that his sobbing should be inaudible. He was not crying for the pain they had caused him, nor for the humiliation he had suffered when they looked at his foot, but with rage at himself because, unable to stand the torture, he had put out his foot of his own accord.

Jennifer intuitively sensed that she had made a major breakthrough in understanding her hurtful feelings. She was more afraid of self-criticism than she was of others' judgments about her.

Telling herself that she was a shy and easily embarrassed person had been just an excuse for not sharing with Richard and other people, whom she wished to get closer to, unpleasant qualities in herself that she did not wish to face. She now recognized that in the cleansing openness of speaking about her suppressed feelings with people who cared about her, she would be able to root out and repudiate feelings about herself that were untrue, unreasonable, and unfair.

Jennifer's task now was clear to her. With considerable trepidation, yet no less firm resolve, she turned on her phone and dialed a familiar number.

"Richard, you didn't think that you would hear from me again, did you?"

"I *am* surprised. Why are you calling?"

"I'm not going to plead tearfully about getting together again. I don't even know if I want to."

"Then I'm really puzzled why you're calling."

"Richard, you've been the person with whom I've been closest. I've made an important discovery about myself—and about you too, for that matter. Are you interested in finding out what it is?"

"Sure—fine! If you think you know something about me that I don't, why shouldn't I listen to you! By the way, there's something different in your voice, Jennifer. I think I like it."

Over the phone, Jennifer gave Richard a cogent synopsis of what she had learned about shame and its consequences. Then her voice softened. She told him that she was no longer angry at him. She understood now that his distancing behavior toward her was probably indicative of his vulnerability to her pain and misery. She carefully discussed the concept of borrowed shame, giving a few examples from what she had read.

Jennifer's words struck a chilling chord in Richard's emotional memory. A vivid image of his father's eyes flashed before him. He felt the cold compress of what he associated as loneliness and sadness creep over him— feelings Richard had never before consciously attributed to his father.

They arranged to meet at Richard's apartment the next evening. Jennifer brought over a simple dinner. They had no cocktails or wine. They agreed to set aside the entire evening, without any unnecessary distractions.

The discussion continued in subsequent evenings. Richard began to feel impatient. Having discussed at length how hurt and humiliation had influenced their relationship, he felt that they now should be able to reveal what they needed from each other.

"Jennifer, okay! Okay! I already understand the theory. Now what about the practice? What can I do to help you feel better about yourself?"

"That, dear Richard, is precisely my problem. If I am going to grow up emotionally, I'll have to learn to take care of myself. I can't allow you or anyone else—as much as I may want to be taken care of—to continue to protect me from life's unpleasantness."

"Do you think there's any hope for us as a couple, Jennifer?"

"I don't know that. But I'll tell you what I would like. In following the suggestions in the book on shame, I've read something by the German writer Rainer Maria Rilke that I'd like you to think about. He says that love is the binding of two strangers who step forth to disclose themselves, withholding nothing and risking all. If we're ever to get together again, you are going to have to trust me. It's really all right with me if you're not always able to care for me the way I'd like. That is, as long as you talk to me about your feelings, without anger or distancing yourself from me."

"You sound different from the Jennifer I used to know. There've been some real changes in you in the last couple of weeks."

"Maybe. But I can't celebrate yet. It's going to take some time to heal wounds I acquired over a lifetime. It's just that I realize that hiding from my shame has deprived me of being merely human. What you and I have going for us is that we can care about each other because we are human—all too human!"

When Jennifer left Richard's apartment that evening, she had a vibrant sense of having crossed the line from being an avoidant person to being one who was more willing to explore life's opportunities and deal with whatever would be cast her way. Jennifer also sensed that, having gained a considerable amount of insight into herself in negotiating a more shame-free relationship with Richard, she needed to get involved in activities that would increase her sense of competence and self-worth.

Two afternoons a week, Jennifer left the safe and familiar literary world she had lived in for so long to be a volunteer in an after-school program for children with learning disabilities. It gave her considerable satisfaction to see how well the children responded to her.

She realized that being of assistance to others and being recognized and appreciated for these efforts went a long way toward reversing the destructive messages her inner voice had been broadcasting to her psyche about how incompetent, unworthy, and unwanted a person she was.

An inherent problem with most psychotherapy and psychoanalysis is that the extraordinary emphasis given to the patient's concerns frequently results in the magnification of self-importance. To finally heal shame, the ashamed must learn that the world does not begin and end with him. By realizing that he can do much to help other people with their feelings of shame and sense of incompetence, he learns the ways that he can help himself and also earn the right, in his sense of equity, to ask others to assist him. In my clinical work, I encourage people who suffer from toxic shame to involve themselves in some social project that both is beneficial to others and enables the patient to participate in some area of the world that he avoided in the past because of a sense of incompetence.

Having considered the treatment of individuals dealing with shame and despair in this chapter, we need to find ways of dealing with an even more complex problem—how to improve our society so that fewer people develop into malevolent personalities. I discuss my proposal for this project in the next chapter.

CHAPTER FIFTEEN

Constructive Responses
to Malevolence

The only necessary thing for
the triumph of evil is for
good men to do nothing.
— EDMUND BURKE

IN 1992, A TWO-YEAR-OLD BOY WAS ABDUCTED AND BRUTALLY MUR-
dered by two preadolescent boys in Merseyside, England. Responding
to worldwide revulsion and disbelief that children could be so cruel and
destructive, Prime Minister John Major advanced a remedy: "Society
needs to condemn a little more and understand a little less."[1]

Even many social critics offended by this kind of political reactionism
contend that it is counterproductive to try to understand criminal malevolence. In their view, most people involved in socially aberrant behavior are
reacting to their enforced, dead-end circumstances—that is, they have
been rendered powerless to compete fairly with others by the regulating institutions of society. Such critics would therefore argue that the answers to
malevolence lie in studying the steps by which society creates unfair advantages for some socioeconomic and ethnic groups while discriminating
against others. In a sense, they are suggesting that poverty, ill health, and
scarcity of educational and vocational opportunities are wicked, not the
people who commit malevolent acts. Individuals are portrayed as impotent
in the face of massive corporate and governmental institutions.

For example, the influential psychologist and social philosopher David Bakan asks rhetorically, "Should the analysis of evil focus primarily on the individual or an organization of individuals?" His answer:

> The major evils of the modern world, such as poverty, unemployment, terror, torture, malnutrition, pollution, industrial accidents and war, result from systems and organizations rather than individuals. . . . What psychologists see so often today are the frustrations of individuals who are victimized in direct and indirect ways by the systematic factors in society, by the systems in which the major actors are government and corporations. Often it is the very impotence of the individual with respect to these systemic actors that is a major cause of psychological suffering. . . . These system-problems . . . [often are] motivated by a kind of Dr. Strangelove rationality, characterized by exaggerated rationality in connection with means and a dwarfed rationality in connection with values. . . . Large evils are just the magnification and cumulation of small individual evils. The evils of systems and institutions may be quite independent of the vices and virtues of the persons who compose them."[2]

As can be inferred from my arguments so far, I do not agree with either the political reactionism of Major and his fellow conservatives or the casual explanations of the crime apologists.

In regard to the first camp, we have hardly expended too much effort in trying to understand malevolence. Quite to the contrary! Crime would not be so rampant in the United States if we had. Actually, we generally avoid trying to understand the precise reasons behind cruel, destructive acts, because the acts themselves are so frightening to us. And isn't it only through enlightened understanding of malevolent individuals that we can hope to redirect human personality and personal identity toward compassion, decency, and constructive caring for others?

In response to the crime apologists, I would agree that one has to be naive or insensitive to institutional abuses in our society to deny the role played in criminality by important sociopolitical factors. At the same time, I would counter the general argument by pointing out that media accounts of crimes in the business and government sectors as well as crimes of passion and violence among the citizenry prove conclusively that criminality is no less normative among the privileged than among the disadvantaged. Indeed, the old adage "Behind all great wealth lies a great crime" is perhaps as accurate as it is cynical.

Besides, blaming society for malevolence is a dysfunctional "cop-out." To argue that society is malevolent is to use what psychologists call a "hypothetical construct,"[3] an abstraction of the concept of a social institution. But social institutions are in fact composed of people like you and me. Whether or not we identify with those who oversee our social institutions, they are in fact influenced and supported by our actions—and perhaps even more so by our inaction, ignorance, and indifference.[4] Therefore, I suggest we explore our own fears and insensitivities in order to learn what role social institutions play in fostering malevolence. As we do so, we must consider malevolence as a serious moral problem, not just the result of inexplicable psychological causes.

Do we, as a society, have the methodology and knowledge necessary, first, for understanding malevolence and, second, for dealing constructively with the problem?

On both points, I believe that we do, even though the problem of malevolence, being multicausal, is enormously difficult and complex. Most important, I suggest we use an interdisciplinary approach based upon cooperation among the professions, for the past shows emphatically that no one profession can successfully tackle the issue alone. Consequently, I don't believe it is useful, or even meaningful, to *reduce* the problem of malevolence to the language, explanatory concepts, and solutions of any one discipline.

Freud and others who identified a universal human tendency to destructiveness notwithstanding, malevolence is not our inevitable fate. I prefer the analysis of the Trappist writer Thomas Merton: "In actual fact, we are suffering more from the distortion and underdevelopment of our deepest human tendencies than from a superabundance of animal instincts."[5]

Malevolence, generally regarded as a crime against other people, can also be responsible for the violation of one's human potential. Each of us has the right to an enlightened, cohesive sense of personal identity, but this self is not provided for us ready-made, is it?[6] It is forged by our willingness to enter the shadow of our personalities and struggle with the kinds of moral questions raised by malevolence in our society.

Perhaps one of the most significant of human characteristics is that we are more clearly defined by what we do not know about ourselves than by what we do understand. Our fears decisively shape our personal identities, feeding our desire to find simple answers to the problems of living.

Colin Wilson, whose work I mentioned earlier, claims that criminals want to simplify life, because they are ashamed of their difficulties with caring and compassion.[7] Similarly, each of the patients I've discussed in the five stages of malevolence believed that he lacked the emotional skills to respond competently to other people's needs. To defend against their shame, those in stages III through IV acted as if other people didn't deserve to be treated decently, because they were so contemptible. But what about people in the first two stages?

In a potentially dangerous misinterpretation of my five-stage theory, some readers may see Julius and Chris as victims only, not potential evildoers, and focus on the Roys, Jasons, and Emils. But as a society, we can no longer afford to regard malevolence as a problem caused by aberrant other people. We all have the potential for destructive actions if we are alienated from ourselves.

Daniel Boorstin, the historian of ideas, points to an underlying dynamic in U.S. society, which shows that the wish to simplify life is not confined to criminals: "Today people want to arrive there, without going through the process of getting there."[8]

Boorstin's insight relates to our study of malevolence in the following way: what is considered "good" in a society is based on the common interest of its members, which entails consideration of the future; by contrast, the malevolence that denies the common interest and the well-being of others also denies the future.

Georges Bataille, in his incisive analysis of the subject of evil in literature, supports a belief similar to mine—that malevolence is allowed to grow because it is fostered in a condition of intoxication or madness in which the selfish instincts of childhood predominate and are acted upon with no concern for their consequences to the self or others.[9] Selfish childhood instincts, ultimately unsatisfiable, are always present-oriented. They prepare the ground for malevolence by causing alienation and despair.

This is clearly evident in the progression of the American dream over the past century. In rural frontier society, we took pride in our achievements and those of our community. There were abuses toward certain strangers, of course—native Americans and African Americans, for example—yet for the most part, we felt a moral obligation to assist neighbors and strangers alike: indeed, anyone less fortunate. Most important, we believed that the capacity to work and participate fully in our daily world is the essence of a life lived well.

Gradually, however, we have become an affluent society in which capital and possessions rather than our labor and generosity are regarded as reflections of the good life. For most of us, I believe, working hard and becoming involved in the problems of the less fortunate are no longer seen as the fulfillment of a well-developed lifestyle but as time-consuming servitude that interferes with enjoying the benefits money can buy. According to the new American ethos, then, the rewards of the good life are to indulge ourselves and be indulged by others. Therefore, the less one is involved in the lives of others, the more one is seen as an achiever rather than a person of servitude.

This new materialistic ethos has another invidious consequence: when money is prized above all else, one generally doesn't know or even care where those who pay have derived their money. In the past, when we put greater value on someone's efforts than on his wealth, we were better able to appreciate how his efforts touched and lent value to our own lives.

Since a number of my patients accepted the new American ethos early in life and made their fortunes quickly, I believe I have some evidence that such materialistic achievements soon pall. The vices of cynicism and apathy—alcoholism, drug abuse, gambling, cynical manipulation of others, broken relationships—still plague them.

There are many such people in a society as affluent as ours, and they are dangerously prone to violent behavior that feeds on frustration and rage. Ironically, though they tend to be well educated, it is ignorance that prevents them from recognizing the long-term consequences of their behavior. Socrates was right: People do not willingly choose malevolence; ignorance leads them into vice.

Today, ignorance prevents many of our most talented but alienated citizens from recognizing that one of the most enduring of human satisfactions is derived from cooperative involvement in a caring, compassionate community. Let us consider how such a community—indeed, a just society—could be created now by using the principles of the American dream we have lost to materialism.

Much like individuals, societies can gradually forge a malevolent personality over time through acts of insensitivity and indifference. I live in New York, a city where lawlessness is running amok. Newsmagazines, editorials, and letters to the editor suggest that much the same thing is true in cities across the nation. Of course, this surge in civil disobedience didn't happen overnight; it reflects the intensifying erosion of the quality of life in our society. It began when our social institutions showed themselves incapable of coping with violations of a less serious nature,[10] and we allowed the erosion of societal expectations to continue.

I estimate that a pedestrian crossing a Manhattan street with a green light has about a fifty-fifty chance of not having to dodge an irate driver who doesn't want to be restricted by traffic regulations. Such blatant violation of statutes by some, which adds to the prevailing climate of insensitivity and indifference, makes it easier for others to justify their own violations. Eventually, they cross the line from discourtesies and minor legal infractions to more extreme acts.

When I was growing up in New York, drunks in the hallway, aggressive in-your-face panhandlers, homeless legions on the street, and the blasting of portable stereo equipment were not familiar strands in the tapestry of daily life. The community did not allow them. In recent years, however, onlooker indifference to acts of victimization has led to a level of noninvolvement previously thought impossible.

On the other hand, as Elie Wiesel reports in his book *Night*, about his concentration camp experiences as a child, onlooker apathy was influential in past malevolence too. He recalls that the most terrible part of his suffering was not Nazi cruelty but the indifference of bystanders. To avoid this deadly apathy, we must always ask: What is my moral obligation in this matter? What am I doing about it now?

These two questions, I submit, need to be understood in the context of the golden rule common to all conventional ethical systems—that is, we should not allow anything to happen to others that we would not wish to happen to us. Albert Camus, Nobelist and veteran of the French resistance, warned us that we should be neither victims nor executioners and should avoid social institutions that allow this victimization.[11]

To create a just society, I suggest that we must first place greater emphasis on people than on property or policies. For example, how can we afford to tolerate recent Supreme Court decisions that allow states to disregard newly discovered evidence of a convicted killer's possible innocence in order to proceed promptly with his execution?

Since malevolence is caused by the lack of fulfillment of some profound human need, should we not establish a legal system and regulatory agencies that will effectively handle such basic concerns as justice, health, nourishment, and the environment in light of egalitarian principles? Malevolence is less likely to occur when people aren't beleaguered with unmet fundamental and acquired needs.[12] According to psychologists Nevitt Sanford and Craig Comstock, most acts of extreme destructiveness have been committed by people who believe they have been given prior permission.[13]

What is most frightening about these people is that in justifying their behavior, they don't recognize their malevolence. (In contrast, in Milton's *Paradise Lost*, Satan was well aware of his wickedness; Iago in Shakespeare's *Othello* saw his malignity.) Their denial of their dangerousness makes it crucial to keep lethal objects away from them.

It is obvious that we must seriously and vigorously implement programs to quash the deadly force of drugs and street weapons. Yet, as the last few years have clearly shown, achieving this goal is exceedingly difficult, in large part because economics plays a more significant role in malevolence than we might suspect.[14] Because drugs and weapons are lucrative commodities, corruption has become widespread in law enforcement and pro-gun lobbies have developed enormous political clout. The well-funded obstacles to the passage of rational gun-control leglislation are in effect, to quote former New Jersey Governor James Florio, "a sneak attack against sanity."

Of course, even the most determined enforcement of drug- and gun-control laws can never be sufficient in the real world. This suggests that we must find ways of teaching alternatives to violence in handling frustration and resentment; this theme needs to be stressed in the family, in schools, and in other places where values should be taught.[15] For example, schools could devote less time to the recitation of facts and computer instruction and more time to exploring students' values and inner experiences.

We also need to bring victims and perpetrators together in professionally led encounters, so that the perpetrators of violence can experience the victims as real people, not simply as displacements for their impacted humiliation and hurt. The victims, on the other hand, need the opportunity to express constructively their rage at people who represent those who have hurt them. Obviously, there are potential dangers involved, yet pioneering programs, such as one at Rikers Island correctional institution in New York City, show that an understanding and undoing of shaming involved in the intersubjectivity of crime can come out of these encounters.

Certainly, far more concern needs to be given to how we speak with one another in our everyday interactions, for our humanity is forged by our words as well as our actions. Whenever we express ourselves freely and articulately, we can reach others and sensitize them to our true sentiments and desires.

Unfortunately, contemporary everyday language typically fails to convey personal import and intimate revelation. It is replete with profanity, anger, and threat. People from all walks of life, and all levels of education, in our "in-your-face" society, use profanity quite regularly in public conversation. To be sure, profane words can dynamically express emotions in emotionally trying or highly charged sexual situations. But as a basic part of everyday speech, profanity reveals the speaker's inability to articulately express personal concerns and intentions. In so doing, our bonds with others fall away, and we are compelled to express ourselves by physical means, ignoring human considerations.[16] Such physical expression includes rage and violence.[17]

Articulate language, by contrast, builds constructive bridges with other people, without which the problem of malevolence cannot be completely broached. Regardless of the accumulation of information we acquire about the nature of malevolence, we will be unable to successfully utilize this knowledge until we regain a trust in the inherent goodness of ourselves and our fellow humans.

Notes

ONE The Problem of Malevolence

1. Samuel Yochelson and Stanton E. Samenow, *The Criminal Personality* (Northvale, N.J.: Jason Aronson, 1993).

2. In 1969, the eminent sociologist Kurt Wolff came to a conclusion about behavioral scientists' attitudes toward evil that still holds true today: "To my knowledge, no social scientist, as a social scientist, has asked what evil is. 'What is evil?' is a question that rather has been raised (both in the West and in the East) by philosophers and theologians, as well as by . . . unrecorded people since time immemorial." "For a Sociology of Evil," *Journal of Social Issues* 25, no. 1 (1969), pp. 111–25.

3. Quoted in Reuven Kimmelman, "Judging Man by the Standards of God," *The Jewish Monthly*, May 1983, pp. 12–18.

4. The notion of "diminished capacity" in English common law is an example of the attempt to reconcile jurisprudence with advanced thinking among philosophers and psychologists. The McNaghton Rule (1843) was the first legal recognition by statute that responsibility for a crime is somewhat mitigated by the mental condition of the perpetrator. Enlightened British psychiatrists regarded the concept as humane protection for defendants who

otherwise would be executed for actions that they had an impaired capacity to understand and control. Though considerably revised by British and American legislation over the years, McNaghton has remained the medico-legal basis for the insanity plea, the insanity defense, and the insanity verdict in English-speaking countries. It is important to recognize that insanity and mental illness are not equivalent. In modern psychiatric texts, the insanity defense is invariably attributed to discoveries of scientific medical psychology; actually, however, the concept of insanity clashes with contemporary psychiatric understanding of mental illness. That is, jurisprudence views possible guilt in a dichotomous way: one either is or is not responsible for a criminal act. By contrast, psychiatry and the behavioral sciences hold that human behavior is rarely completely black or white; there are degrees to the capacity for knowingly and willingly behaving in a certain way. This crucial difference in defining responsibility lies at the heart of the conflict between the legal profession and the behavioral sciences.

5. Jeffrey B. Russell, *Mephistopheles: The Devil in the Modern World*. (Ithaca, N.Y.: Cornell University Press, 1986), p. 21.

6. Robert Nozick, *The Examined Life* (New York: Simon & Schuster, 1989).

7. Robert J. Lifton, *The Broken Connection: On Death and the Continuity of Life* (New York: Basic Books, 1979).

8. Otto Rank, *Beyond Psychology* (New York: Dover, 1958).

9. See Erich Fromm, *The Heart of Man* (New York: Harper & Row, 1964).

10. *Manchester Guardian Weekly*, November 8, 1992.

11. See Georges Bataille, *Literature and Evil* (New York: Urizen Books, 1973).

12. The causes and clinical implications of shame are still a fairly neglected area of psychological inquiry. Usually, the most complex, difficult cases of despair have been attributed to the agent of guilt rather than the steward of shame. *The Psychological Abstracts*, a subject index of all psychological publications, lacks a separate category for the elusive effect of shame, which is subheaded under "guilt." In short, shame and its emotional variants remain among the most seriously misunderstood emotions in contemporary behavioral science literature. See Carl Goldberg, *Understanding Shame* (Northvale, N.J.: Jason Aronson, 1991).

13. Charles Darwin, *The Expressions of the Emotions in Man and Animals* (New York: Philosophical Library, 1955).

TWO The History of Evil and Its Psychological Theories

1. Richard Cavendish, *The Powers of Evil* (London: Routledge & Kegan Paul, 1975).

2. Sigmund Freud, "Totem and Taboo," *The Basic Writings of Sigmund Freud*. New York: Random House, 1938, p. 848.

3. Paul Ricoeur, *The Symbolism of Evil* (Boston: Beacon Press, 1967).

4. See Rollo May, "Creativity and Evil," in *Facing Evil*, ed. Paul Woodruff and Harry Wilmer (La Salle, Ill.: Open Court Press, 1988), pp. 71–81.

5. See Dennis Wheatley, *The Devil and All His Works* (New York: American Heritage Press, 1971).

6. Ibid.

7. Ibid.

8. Quoted in *Psychology Today* 22, no. 12 (December 1988), p. 8.

9. Max Scheler, *The Nature of Sympathy* (London: Routledge & Kegan Paul, 1954).

10. See Ernest Becker, *The Denial of Death* (New York: Free Press, 1973).

11. Many theologians, even those sympathetic to Jung's other ideas, take strong exception to his notion of God as an evolving deity. One of them, Professor Maurice Friedman, reviewed an early draft of this book and asked to be disassociated from my discussion of Jung's theory. Others, including Samuel Klagsbrun, M.D., who has been trained as rabbi, psychiatrist, and psychoanalyst, favor the Jungian view. Dr. Klagsbrun writes: "I frequently thought that God's relationship to Adam, Noah, and Abraham indicates a growth on God's part as well as on man's part. It is God who is absolute with Adam, whereas he behaves almost as an equal negotiator at a corporate table with Abraham. The respect for man and the relationship of man as a partner in the world is an enormous change." Excerpted from personal correspondence.

12. Carl G. Jung, "Answer to Job," in *The Portable Jung*, ed. Joseph Campbell (New York: Penguin Books, 1976).

13. Ibid.

14. David Parkin, Introduction, *The Anthropology of Evil*, ed. D. Parkin (London: Basil Blackwell, 1985).

15. See Colin Wilson, *A Criminal History of Mankind* (New York: Carroll & Graf, 1984).

16. Sigmund Freud, *Civilization and Its Discontents* (New York: W.W. Norton, 1930).

17. Ibid., pp. 65–66.

18. Ibid. Einstein had written to a number of the world's great thinkers during the 1930s requesting that they put their mental energies toward ways of averting what appeared to him to be the vast destructiveness of a pending world war.

19. Carl Rogers, Reply to Rollo May's letter to Carl Rogers, *Journal of Humanistic Psychology* 22, no. 4 (1982), pp. 85–92.

20. Rollo May, "The Problem of Evil," *Journal of Humanistic Psychology* 22, no. 3 (1982), pp. 10–21.

21. Michael Eigen, *The Electrified Tightrope* (Northvale, N.J.: Jason Aronson, 1993), p. 181.

22. Alice Miller, *Prisoners of Childhood* (New York: Basic Books, 1981).

23. Melanie Klein, *Contributions to Psycho-analysis* (London: Hogarth Press, 1974).

24. Carl Jung, *The Collected Works of C. G. Jung* (Princeton, N.J.: Princeton University Press, 1960).

25. Robert J. Lifton, *The Nazi Doctors* (New York: Basic Books, 1986), pp. 418, 442.

26. Joel Norris, *Serial Killers* (New York: Doubleday, 1988).

27. M. Scott Peck, *People of the Lie* (New York: Simon & Schuster, 1983), p. 69.

28. Erich Fromm, *The Anatomy of Human Destructiveness* (New York: Holt, Rinehart & Winston, 1973).

29. Ervin Staub, *The Roots of Evil* (Cambridge, Eng.: Cambridge University Press, 1989).

30. Fromm, *Anatomy of Human Destructiveness*.

31. Fromm, *Heart of Man*.

32. Hannah Arendt, *Eichmann in Jerusalem* (New York: Viking Press, 1963).

33. Ernest Becker, *Escape from Evil* (New York: Free Press, 1975), p. 122.

34. Ibid.

35. Fromm, *Heart of Man*, p. 117.

36. Ibid., p. 128.

37. Ibid., p. 131.

38. Ibid., p. 135.

THREE Shame and Malevolence

1. Uriah Heep, a character in *David Copperfield*, is a famous example of the passive-aggressive personality. He pretends to be humble, meek, and benevolent but is actually scheming, hateful, and resentful. His strategy is based upon the

assumption that most people, preferring to believe the best of others, are easily deceived. He gains the advantage by telling people what they want to hear.

2. See Helen Bloch Lewis, *Shame and Guilt* (New York: International Universities Press, 1971).

3. Robert W. White, "Sense of Interpersonal Competence," in *The Study of Lives*, ed. R.W. White (New York: Prentice-Hall, 1963), pp. 73–93.

4. See Murray Blimes, "Shame and Delinquency," *Contemporary Psychoanalysis* 3 (1967), pp. 113–33.

5. See Ronald Potter-Efron and Patricia Potter-Efron, *Letting Go of Shame* (New York: Harper & Row, 1989).

6. See Jane Middleton-Moz. *Shame and Guilt* (Deerfield Beach, Fla.: Health Communications, 1990).

7. Erik Erikson, *Childhood and Society* (New York: W. W. Norton, 1950).

8. See Brian Masters, "Evil Is as Does Jeffrey Dahmer," British *GQ Magazine* 45 (March 1993), pp. 79–92.

9. June P. Tangney, Susan A. Burggraf, and Patricia E. Wagner, "Shame-proneness, guilt-proneness and psychological symptoms," in *Self-Conscious Emotions: Shame, Guilt, Embarrassment and Pride*, ed. K. S. Fischer and J. P. Tangney (New York: Guilford Press, 1995).

10. Georg Hegel, "The Logic of Hegel," in *The Encyclopedia of the Philosophical Sciences*, trans. William Wallace (Oxford, Eng., 1892).

FOUR Child of Scorn

1. H. H. Hart, "The Eye in Symbol and Symptom," *Psychoanalytic Review* 36, no. 1 (1949), pp. 1–21.

2. M. Ponzo, "Puede tener el mal de ojo una explicación científica?" *Revista Psicología General Aplicado* (Madrid) 4 (1963), pp. 747–52.

3. Otto Fenichel, "The Scopophile Instinct and Identification," *International Journal of Psychoanalysis* 18 (1937), pp. 6–34.

4. Because of my keen interest in group psychotherapy, I was assigned eleven patients diagnosed as "paranoid schizophrenic" for my first group at the hospital. Julius was a participant for about six months.

FIVE The Role of the Double in Malevolence

1. *The Portable Plato*, ed. Scott Buchanan (New York: Viking Press, 1963), pp. 146–47.

2. Ibid., p. 147.

3. Doris Eder, "The Idea of the Double," *Psychoanalytic Review* 65, no. 4 (1978), pp. 579–614.

4. David Winter, Introduction to Otto Rank, *The Don Juan Legend* (Princeton, N.J.: Princeton University Press, 1975).

5. See C. Rosenfeld, "The Shadow Within: The Conscious and Unconscious Use of the Double," *Daedalus* 92 (1963), pp. 326–44.

6. Hermann Hesse, *Steppenwolf* (New York: Frederick Ungar, 1928), pp. 77–79.

7. S. M. Coleman, "The Phantom Double: Its Psychological Significance," *British Journal of Medical Psychology* 14 (1934), pp. 254–73.

8. Otto Rank, *The Double* (New York: New American Library, 1971).

9. In the novel, Dorian Gray, a handsome, talented young man in Victorian England, falls under the influence of a cynical aristocrat who encourages him to indulge his lusts to the utmost. Early on, Gray's portrait is painted by a well-known society painter. As he commits ever more heinous acts, his outward appearance remains fresh and youthful over the decades, but the painting is gradually disfigured and blotched.

Oscar Wilde, "The Picture of Dorian Gray," in *The Portable Oscar Wilde* (New York: Penguin, 1982).

10. Julian Jaynes, *The Origins of Consciousness in the Breakdown of the Bicameral Mind* (Boston: Houghton Mifflin, 1976), p. 75.

11. Wilson, *Criminal History*, p. 130.

12. R. Joseph, *The Right Brain and the Unconscious* (New York: Plenum, 1993), p. 22.

13. Ibid.

14. Ibid.

15. Ibid., p. 97.

16. Ibid., p. 47.

17. Ibid.

18. Wilson, *Criminal History*.

19. Frank W. Putnam, "The Physiological Investigation of Multiple Personality Disorder: A Review," *Psychiatric Clinics of America* 17, no. 1 (1984).

20. R. C. Hall, A. F. LeCann, and J. C. Schodar, "Amobarbital Treatment of Multiple Personality," *Journal of Nervous and Mental Disease* 166 (1978), pp. 666–70.

21. M. M. Mesalem, "Dissociative States with Abnormal Temporal Lobe EEG: Multiple Personality and the Illusion of Possession," *Archives of Neurology* 38 (1981), pp. 176–81.

22. W. Taylor and M. M. Martin, "Multiple Personality," *Journal of Abnormal Psychology* 39 (1944), pp. 281–300.

23. F. W. Putnam et al., "Evoked Potentials in Multiple Personality Disorder." Presented at the American Psychiatric Association Annual Meeting, New Research Abstract No. 137, 1982.

24. Noting that most of the control subjects had no acting training, the authors suggest the possibility that experienced professional character actors might be capable of producing differences in EEG-evoked potential.

25. Gustave Gilbert, *Nuremberg Diary* (New York: New American Library, 1961).

26. It is easy to see a facsimile of the doppelgänger. Take a photo of a person's face, cut it down the center, and note the differences between the two halves. Better yet, get a photographer to synthesize a full-face photo from one of the halves. The face made from two left sides will be very different from the synthesis of two right sides.

27. *Doppelgänger* is German for "second self." I use this term to refer to the second self because of the venerable German tradition of portraying the double in fiction. Moreover, the first psychological study of the double was originally written in German: Otto Rank, "Der Doppelgänger," in *Imago* 3 (1914), pp. 97–164.

28. Lifton, *Nazi Doctors*.

29. I have explored the subject of the doppelgänger more extensively in the following articles: Carl Goldberg, "What Ails Antonio? The Nature of Evil," *Journal of Psychology and Judaism* 9, no. 2 (1985), pp. 68–85; Carl Goldberg and Jane Simon, "Towards a Psychology of Courage: Implications for the Healing Process," *Journal of Contemporary Psychotherapy* 13, no. 2 (1982), pp. 107–28; Carl Goldberg and Jane Simon, "The Role of the Double in the Creative Process and Psychoanalysis," *Journal of the American Academy of Psychoanalysis* 12, no. 3 (1984), pp. 341–61.

six Child of the Devil

1. I have written about this experience in my book *Understanding Shame*, pp. 163–84.

2. Michel Foucault, *Madness and Civilization* (New York: New American Library, 1965).

3. Leslie H. Farber, *The Ways of the Will* (New York: Harper & Row, 1968).

4. Taken from Dylan Thomas's poem "Do Not Go Gentle into That Good Night."

5. I was taken aback and embarrassed by what Chris told me. Apparently, Belphegor was an astute listener, for he had caught several analytic errors on

my part. More important than questions of correct technique, however, is the integrity of the analyst's attitudes. To the extent that therapist behavior violates common sense, decency, and compassion for patients, it is misdirected and even dangerous.

6. In Greek mythology, Prometheus was a god who was severely punished by Zeus, king of the gods, for teaching humankind the secrets of fire and many arts.

SEVEN The Role of the Mirror in Human Suffering

1. These implicit powers are associated with numerous superstitions about mirrors. In one virtually universal myth, cracking or destroying a mirror will bring bad luck. Others warn that powerful spirits residing in mirrors are able to take possession of the vulnerable human soul. For example, in traditional Jewish custom, mirrors and other highly polished surfaces are draped during ritual mourning, because the deceased can linger in the glass during this period, seize those foolish enough to gaze into the undraped reflection, and carry them off to the dark other world.

2. Jeff Greenberg et al., "Evidence for Terror Management Theory II," *Journal of Personality and Social Psychology* 58, no. 2 (1990), pp. 308–18.

3. See Carl Schneider, *Shame, Exposure and Privacy* (Boston: Beacon Press, 1977).

4. Ovid, *Metamorphoses* (New York: New American Library, 1958).

5. Carl Goldberg, *The Seasoned Psychotherapist* (New York: W. W. Norton, 1992).

6. Harold Searles, "Schizophrenia and the Inevitability of Death," *Psychiatric Quarterly* 35 (1961), pp. 631–65.

7. Yochelson and Samenow, *Criminal Personality*.

8. See Bataille, *Literature and Evil*.

9. See Wilson, *Criminal History*.

10. Becker, *Denial of Death*, p. 63.

11. Shame has the capacity to spur our greatest human achievements by making us conscious of the conditions necessary for feeling self-worth and for developing a sense of purpose. The desire to know begins with the recognition of what one does not know. Constructively, shame can produce that recognition and further suggest that what one does not know is knowable, should be known, and can lead to further understanding of what is not yet known. Shame provides a mirror to reflect parts of the self that are typically hidden. Experiences of shame are so vivid and painful because they foster an

accentuated, disturbing sense of self-consciousness. In these moments, we become aware, albeit fleetingly, of aspects of ourselves—such as our ambitions, longings, sentiments—that are both valuable to who we are and open to misunderstanding and derision.

12. Actualized people develop a noble vision, a code of conduct, and a worldview that transcend those of their fellow beings. Shakespeare's Hamlet is a man physically capable of action, but he does not act to avenge his father's murder because, like Oedipus, he has a more scrupulous conscience than those around him. He is caught between filial duty and his moral and spiritual abhorrence of taking revenge. See Carl Goldberg, "The Shame of Hamlet and Oedipus," *Psychoanalytic Review* 76, no. 4 (1989), pp. 581–603.

13. For more information on Gina's story, see Carl Goldberg, "Mirror of Your Eyes," *The Psychotherapy Patient*, 5 no. 3/4 (1989), pp. 197–205.

EIGHT Transition from Victim to Perpetrator of Malevolence

1. In 1864, Cesare Lombroso, a young Jewish physician in the Italian army, conducted informal studies during his leisure in order to compare "honest" with "vicious companion" soldiers. When he returned to civilian life, he studied criminals in the general population, eventually concluding that he had discovered the origins of criminality. In his book *L'Uomo Delinquente*, published in 1899, Lombroso claimed that he had identified the "born criminal," recognizable by such characteristics as "enormous jaws, high cheekbones, prominent superciliary arches, solitary lines in the palms, extreme size of the orbits, handle-shaped or sessile ears," as well as by "insensitivity to pain, irresistible craving for evil for its own sake, the desire not only to extinguish life in the victim, but to mutilate." Quoted in Christopher Hibbert, *The Roots of Evil* (Boston: Little, Brown, Company, 1963), p. 186.

2. Harold Searles. "Schizophrenia and the Inevitability of Death," *Psychiatric Quarterly* 35 (1961), pp. 631–65.

3. Erikson, *Childhood and Society*.

4. See Helen M. Lynd. *Shame and the Search for Identity* (New York: Harcourt, Brace, 1958).

5. Ibid.

6. See Allen Wheelis, *The Seeker* (New York: New American Library, 1960).

7. See Rollo May, Ernest Angel, and Henri F. Ellenberger, eds., *Existence* (New York: Simon & Schuster, 1959), p. 68.

8. Carl Goldberg, *Therapeutic Partnership* (New York: Springer, 1977).

NINE Madness and Malevolence

1. Niccolò Machiavelli, *Discourses*, ed. and trans. Peter Bondenella and Mark Muse (New York: Penguin Books, 1979), Chapter 3.

2. Buchanan, *The Portable Plato*.

3. Wilson, *Criminal History*.

4. Yochelson and Samenow, *Criminal Personality*.

5. Gilbert, *Nuremberg Diary*.

6. Lifton, *Nazi Doctors*.

7. Lewis Coser, "The Visibility of Evil," *Journal of Social Issues* 25, no. 1 (1969), pp. 101–9.

8. Professor Thomas Robischon of Antioch College, Los Angeles, has been very helpful to me in elucidating the philosophical issues involved in making moral choices.

9. Hannah Arendt, *Eichmann in Jerusalem: A Report on the Banality of Evil* (New York: Viking Books, 1963).

10. B. Clarke, "Beyond 'The Banality of Evil,'" *British Journal of Political Science* 10, 1980, pp. 417–39.

11. Gerald L. Borofsky and Don J. Brand, "Personality and Psychological Functioning of the Nuremberg War Criminals: The Rorschach Data," in *Survivors, Victims and Perpetrators: Essays on the Nazi Holocaust*, ed. J. E. Dimsdale (Washington, D.C.: Hemisphere, 1980), pp. 359–403. The authors note: "At the present time we as psychologists have been unable to satisfactorily 'explain' the motivations and personality organization that prompted the NWCs to such grotesque and inhuman acts."

12. Ibid.

13. See Roy Porter, *A Social History of Madness* (New York: E. P. Dutton, 1989).

14. R. Walter Heinrichs, "Schizophrenia and the Brain: Conditions for a Neuropsychology of Madness," *American Psychologist* 48 no. 3 (1993), pp. 221–33.

15. Morton Schatzman, "Madness and Morals," in *The Radical Therapists*, ed. Jerome Angel (New York: Ballantine, 1971), pp. 65–96.

16. Porter, *Social History*.

17. See Prescott Lecky, *Self-Consistency: A Theory of Personality* (Garden City, N.Y.: Doubleday, 1961).

18. C. M. Rosenquist, "Differential Responses of Texas Convicts," *American Journal of Sociology* 38 (1932), pp. 10–21.

19. Quoted in Leonard W. Doob, *Panorama of Evil: Insights from the Behavioral Sciences* (Westport, Ct.: Greenwood Press, 1978).

20. Ronald Markman and Dominick Bosco, *Alone with the Devil: Famous Cases of a Courtroom Psychiatrist* (New York: Bantam Books, 1990), p. 69.

21. Lionel Dahmer, *A Father's Story* (New York: Morrow, 1994).

TEN Experimental Malevolence

1. Eric Bentley, ed., *Naked Masks: Five Plays by Luigi Pirandello* (New York: E. P. Dutton, 1952).

2. Yochelson and Samenow, *Criminal Personality*, p. 40.

3. Wilson, *Criminal History,* p. 59.

4. Carl Goldberg, "The Role of Passion in the Transformation of Anti-Heroes," *Journal of Evolutionary Psychology* IX, nos. 1–2 (1989), pp. 2–16.

5. "Psychopath" is a clinical term generally applied to criminals and others who seem unwilling to sincerely examine their own motivations. Many behavioral scientists believe that clinicians tend to apply this label to patients they don't like and/or find they cannot help. In the latter case, the label in effect absolves the clinician of any responsibility for not being able to help the patient.

6. Anna Freud, *The Writings of Anna Freud*, vol. II (New York: International Universities Press, 1966).

ELEVEN Courage and Fanaticism

1. P. Cushman and L. S. Moses, "Cults, Religious Needs and Mind Control," *National Jewish Monthly*, May 1980.

2. Ibid.

3. J. Castelli, *Washington Star*, July 16, 1980.

4. Richard Sennett, *Authority* (New York: Knopf, 1980).

5. See Carl Goldberg, *In Defense of Narcissism* (New York: Gardner Press, 1980).

6. M. Galanter et al. "The Moonies: A Psychological Study of Conversion and Membership in a Contemporary Religious Sect," *American Journal of Psychiatry* 136, No. 2 (1979), pp. 165–70.

7. M. Galanter and P. Buckley, "Evangelical Religion and Meditation: Psychological Effects," *Journal of Nervous and Mental Disease* 166, no. 10 (1978), pp. 685–91.

8. Carroll Stoner and Jo Anne Parke, *All God's Children: The Cult of Experience—Salvation or Slavery?* (New York: Penguin Books, 1979).

9. William James. *The Varieties of Religious Experience* (New York: Modern Library, 1929), p. 196.

10. To my knowledge, no study of female cult leadership has been made by behavioral scientists.

11. Flo Conway and Jim Siegelman, *Snapping: America's Epidemic of Sudden Personality Change* (New York: Dell, 1979). The reader is referred to this book for a vivid description of what happened at Jonestown. See also L. Wright, "Orphans of Jonestown," *The New Yorker*, November 22, 1993, pp. 66–89.

12. "CBS's report on Jonestown: Making of a 'Savior,'" *Newsweek*, April 21, 1980.

13. The Branch Davidians and the Order of the Solar Temple are two recent examples.

14. C. A. Krause, *Guyana Massacre: The Eyewitness Report* (New York: Berkley Books, 1978).

15. Jeannie Mills, *Six Years with God: Life Inside Reverend Jim Jones's People's Temple* (New York: A and W Publications, 1979).

16. *Newsweek*, April 21, 1980.

17. Krause, *Guyana Massacre*, p. 198.

18. Carl Goldberg, unpublished manuscript.

19. Mills, *Six Years*.

20. Galanter et al., "The Moonies."

21. Krause, *Guyana Massacre*, p. 37.

22. Robert Lindsey, "Can California Control 'Sham' Religious Sects? And Should It?" *New York Times*, July 20, 1980.

23. *Newsweek*, April 28, 1980.

24. Mills, *Six Years*.

25. Ibid.

26. J. P. Nugent, *White Night: The Story of What Happened Before and Beyond Jonestown* (New York: Rawson, Wade, 1979).

27. Krause, *Guyana Massacre*.

28. *Newsweek*, April 28, 1980.

29. Ibid.

30. J. Swartz, "Another Sort of Terrorism," *American Psychological Association Monitor* 11, no. 6 (1980), p. 2.

31. Conway and Siegelman, *Snapping*.

32. J. T. Ungerleider and D. K. Wellisch, "Coercive Persuasion (Brainwash-

ing), Religious Cults, and Deprogramming," *American Journal of Psychiatry* 136, no. 3 (1979), pp. 279–82.

33. Philip Slater, *The Pursuit of Loneliness* (Boston: Beacon, 1970).

34. Stoner and Parke, *All God's Children*.

35. Hadley Cantril, *The Psychology of Social Movements* (New York: Wiley, 1941).

36. N. R. Maier, "The Role of Frustration in Social Movements," *Psychological Review* no. 49 (1942), pp. 586–99.

37. A. L. Edwards, "The Sign of Incipient Fascism," *Journal of Abnormal and Social Psychology* no. 39 (1944), pp. 301–16.

38. C. W. King, *Social Movements in the United States* (New York: Random House, 1956).

39. Herburt Blumer, "Collective Behavior," in *New Outline of the Principles of Sociology*, ed. A. M. Lee (New York: Barnes & Noble, 1951).

40. S. Elridge, *Fundamentals of Sociology* (New York: Crowell, 1950).

41. Stoner and Parke, *All God's Children*, p. 28.

42. Ibid.

43. Ungerleider and Wellisch, "Coercive Persuasion."

44. E. M. Pattison, N. A. Lapins, and H. A. Doerr, "Faith Healing: A Study of Personality and Function," *Journal of Nervous and Mental Disease* 156, no. 6 (1973), pp. 397–409.

45. Robert J. Lifton, *Thought Reform and the Psychology of Totalism* (New York: Norton, 1963). Lifton studied the effects of "brainwashing" of prisoners of war by North Koreans during the Korean War.

46. Ibid., pp. 429–30.

47. Conway and Siegelman, *Snapping*.

48. Mills, *Six Years*.

49. The adroit use of psychological techniques is confirmed by W. Hill, "Some Aspects of Group Psychotherapy and Psychodrama Used in a Modern Cult," *Group Psychotherapy* 21, no. 4 (1968), pp. 214–21. Hill, a psychiatrist, examines several group psychotherapy and psychodrama principles and techniques in a cult he investigated.

50. Mills, *Six Years*, p. 158.

51. A. Deutsch, "Tenacity of Attachment to a Cult Leader: A Psychiatric Perspective," *American Journal of Psychiatry* 137, no. 12 (1980), pp. 1569–73. Deutsch reveals that profound submission of cult members can occur even in the absence of enforced threats from outside influences, elaborate strategies of persuasion, or threats against those who wish to leave.

52. Krause, *Guyana Massacre*.

53. Lifton, *Thought Reform*.

54. Ungerleider and Wellisch, "Coercive Persuasion."

55. Stoner and Parke, *All God's Children*, p. 238.

56. Nugent, *White Night*, p. 8.

57. *Newsweek*, April 28, 1980.

58. Krause, *Guyana Massacre*, p. 48.

59. Eric Hoffer, *The True Believer: Thoughts on the Nature of Mass Movements* (New York: New American Library, 1951), p. 103.

60. Weston LaBarre, *Culture in Context* (Durham, N.C.: Duke University Press, 1980), p. 52.

61. L. Festinger, H. W. Riecker, and S. Schacter, *When Prophecy Fails* (Minneapolis: University of Minnesota Press, 1956).

62. Mills, *Six Years*, p. 51.

63. Krause, *Guyana Massacre*, p. 34.

64. Ibid.

65. Stanley Milgram, *Obedience to Authority* (New York: Harper & Row, 1974).

66. Nugent, *White Night*, p. 26.

67. Hoffer, *True Believer*, p. 106.

68. Nugent, *White Night*, p. 17.

69. "Shaman" is the term used to describe people of wisdom who possess healing powers and have since preliterate times been assigned the role of tribal healer and spiritual guide in many non-Western societies.

70. LaBarre, *Culture*, p. 52.

71. Mills, *Six Years*, p. 147.

72. Mills, *Six Years*.

73. Nugent, *White Night*.

74. Mills, *Six Years*.

75. Galanter et al., "The Moonies."

76. Castelli, *Washington Star*, July 16, 1980.

77. Michael Eigen, "One Demonized Aspect of the Self," in *Evil: Self and Culture*, ed. M. C. and M. Eigen (New York: Human Sciences Press, 1984).

78. Goldberg, *In Defense of Narcissism*, pp. 33–45.

79. Theodor Reik, *Masochism in Modern Man* (New York: Farrar, Straus, 1949), p. 355.

80. "Flectere si nequeo superos, Acheronta movebo." Virgil, *Aeneid*, book VII, l.312.

81. Sennett, *Authority*, p. 150.

82. Mills, *Six Years*, p. 98.

83. Becker, *Escape from Evil*.

84. Karl Jaspers. *Socrates, Buddha, Confucius and Jesus: The Paradigmatic Individuals* (New York: Harcourt, Brace, 1957).

TWELVE The Forging of the Malevolent Personality

1. See Goldberg, *Understanding Shame*.

2. The Wannsee Villa in Berlin is the house where Nazi bureaucrats met on January 20, 1942, to plan the "Final Solution," the destruction of Europe's Jews. With a slight change of spelling to the German *Wahnesse,* the name would mean "sea of insanity, frenzy, and delusion."

3. For some of the details of the black mass, I have consulted Dennis Wheatley's *The Devil and All of His Works* (New York: American Heritage Press, 1971).

4. Otto Rank, *The Double: A Psychoanalytic Study* (New York: New American Library, 1979).

5. Martin Buber, *Good and Evil* (New York: Scribner, 1953).

6. Ibid., pp. 130–131.

THIRTEEN Friendship as the Basis of Psychological Healing

1. Arthur Burton, "The Mentoring Dynamic in a Therapeutic Transformation," *American Journal of Psychoanalysis* 37 (1977), pp. 115–22.

2. Daniel J. Levinson, *The Seasons of a Man's Life* (New York: Ballantine, 1978).

3. Ralph W. Emerson, *Essays* (New York: Harper, 1951).

4. Carl Goldberg, *On Being a Psychotherapist* (Northvale, N.J.: Jason Aronson, 1991).

5. Allen Wheelis, "The Vocational Hazards of Psychoanalysis," *International Journal of Psychoanalysis* 37 (1957), pp. 171–84.

6. Ignace Lepp, *The Ways of Friendship* (New York: Macmillan, 1971).

7. Ibid.

8. Ibid.

9. Sheldon Kopp, *If You Meet the Buddha on the Road, Kill Him!* (New York: Bantam, 1971), p. 23.

10. Friedrich Nietzsche, *The Philosophy of Nietzche* (*Thus Spake Zarathustra*), New York: The Modern Library, Random House, 1954.

11. Robert C. Solomon, *The Passions* (Garden City, N.Y.: Doubleday, 1976), p. 171.

12. In my book *The Seasoned Psychotherapist*, I discuss the first empirical study of the lives and practices of experienced psychotherapists, with particular emphasis on what they have learned through extensive clinical careers about triumphing over adversity.

13. Carl Jung. *The Basic Writings of C. G. Jung* (New York: Modern Library, 1951).

14. Erikson, *Childhood and Society*.

15. George Kelly, *A Theory of Personality* (New York: W.W. Norton, 1963).

FIFTEEN Constructive Responses to Malevolence

1. *New York Times*, February 18, 1993.

2. David Bakan, "Response to Rollo May," *Journal of Humanistic Psychology* 22, no. 3 (1982), pp. 91–92.

3. "Hypothetical construct" is the scientific term for the inferred operative force that is compelling the behavior of people and/or inanimate objects under investigation. This force cannot be directly observed. For example, if nine baseball players are wearing the same uniform, we call them a "team." When the unselfish individual efforts of the players seem to further the cause of the team as a whole, we infer that "team spirit" is operating. This team spirit is a hypothetical construct, having no meaning apart from the actions of the individual baseball players.

4. Because we dislike anything that disturbs our tranquillity, we gladly cede authority to those who seem willing to sacrifice their own tranquillity to take care of us in times of crisis. What we may fail to recognize is that many such people actually thrive on conflict and chaos. They wait impatiently for crisis like vultures, unable to tolerate a placid external world because of torments within themselves. We have given such people power in crucial positions in our social institutions, and the cost is enormous: the immoral secret operations of our government, the patent physical abuse of citizens by police, the corruption of those hired to enforce drug laws, and the disregard in our highest courts for humanity and human rights.

5. Thomas Merton, *Life and Holiness* (New York: Herder and Herder, 1963), p. 22.

6. See Paul Stern, *In Praise of Madness* (New York: Delta Books, 1972).

7. Wilson, *Criminal History*.

8. Daniel J. Boorstin, *The Image: A Guide to Pseudo-Events in America* (New York: Macmillan, 1992).

9. Bataille, *Literature and Evil.*

10. This point of view was expressed by Chief of Detectives Aaron Rosenthal of New York City Police Department, quoted in "For a Gentle City" by Bette Dewing in *Our Town*, a community newspaper on Manhattan's East Side, 1993.

11. Albert Camus, *Notebooks* (New York: Harcourt, Brace, 1961).

12. See Doob, *Panorama of Evil.*

13. Nevitt Sanford and Craig Comstock, eds., *Sanctions for Evil* (San Francisco: Jossey-Bass, 1971).

14. In Hans Askenasy, *Are We All Nazis?* (Secaucus, N.J.: Lyle Stuart, 1978), the author points out that economics rather than sadism decided which extermination methods the Nazis used in the camps. Lethal gas and furnaces were simply cheaper than more "humane" methods.

15. It is advantageous to society to bring together a large cross-section of people to discuss and participate in social and civil concerns. Typically useful formats include town meetings, roundtable discussions, and community at-large approaches.

16. In two passages in previous works, I discuss methods for learning to speak with emotional articulateness: *Understanding Shame*, pp. 281–83, and *On Being a Psychotherapist*, pp. 238–47.

17. In an innovative program in Los Angeles, some younger members of the Fourth Reich Skinheads of nearby Orange County were given the opportunity to have a three-day-long dialogue with a group of Jews, including several Holocaust survivors, and African-Americans. The program's organizers claimed it was successful. *The New York Times*, January 1, 1994.

Index